THE NEW COMPLETE

Ch. Monadnock's King, Ch. Monadnock's Pando, and Mulpus Brooks the Roadmaster—a classic study.

THE NEW COMPLETE

SIBERIAN HUSKY

*Based on the Original Masterwork
by Lorna B. Demidoff and Michael Jennings*

Michael Jennings

SECOND EDITION

HOWELL BOOK HOUSE

New York

Maxwell Macmillan Canada
Toronto

Maxwell Macmillan International
New York   Oxford   Singapore   Sydney

Howell Book House   Maxwell Macmillan Canada, Inc.
Macmillan Publishing Company   1200 Eglinton Avenue East
866 Third Avenue   Suite 200
New York, NY 10022   Don Mills, Ontario M3C 3N1

Macmillan Publishing Company is part of the Maxwell Communication Group of Companies.

Library of Congress Cataloging-in-Publication Data

Jennings, Michael, 1948–
    The new complete Siberian Husky / Michael Jennings. —2nd ed.
        p.   cm.
    "Based on the original masterwork by Lorna B. Demidoff and Michael Jennings".
    ISBN 0-87605-339-8
    1. Siberian huskies. I. Title.
    SF429.S65J46   1992
    636.7′3—dc20   92-2665
                                                                        CIP

Macmillan books are available at special discounts for bulk purchases for sales promotions, premiums, fund-raising, or educational use. For details, contact:

Special Sales Director
Macmillan Publishing Company
866 Third Avenue
New York, NY 10022

10 9 8 7 6 5 4 3 2 1

Printed in the United States of America

Lorna B. Demidoff (1950).

To the Memory of Lorna Demidoff

"My greatest weakness has always been a kid
looking for a sled dog"
—*Lorna Demidoff*

Pando, King, Roadmaster, Otchki, Vanya, Belka and Akela were just some the famous names Lorna Demidoff gave the Siberian world as she gave herself to a lifetime's dedication to the breed. By now her name is virtually synonymous with the breed throughout the world, and the animals she bred decades ago are still referred to, quite universally, by their familiar "call names." They are in the trees of life, what we call pedigrees, of almost all Siberians alive today.

This edition of the book, which she coauthored in the original, is dedicated to her memory. She was a great dog driver, breeder, exhibitor, judge and teacher. She was a founder of the Siberian Husky Club of America, many times its president, its Honorary Chairman of the Board, the Fancy's most cherished breeder-judge, and many, many other things. She was also a charming lady and a good friend.

Above all, she never forgot that "kid looking for a sled dog" who will keep the breed strong by loving and nurturing it for what it is: an eager, working sled dog with a centuries-old tradition.

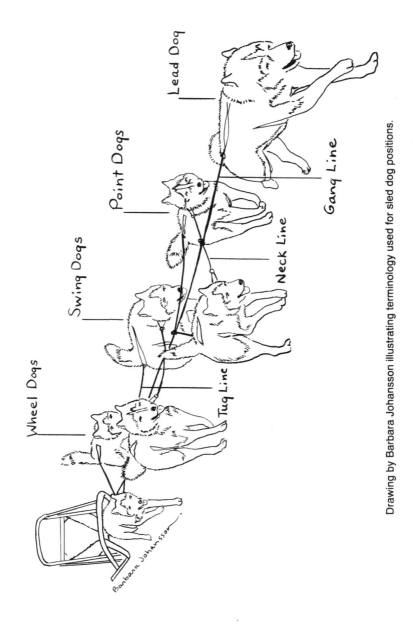

Lead Dog

Point Dogs

Swing Dogs

Wheel Dogs

Gang Line

Neck Line

Tug Line

Barbara Johansson

Drawing by Barbara Johansson illustrating terminology used for sled dog positions.

Contents

Kreevanka.

A trio of historically significant Siberians in the North American
development of the breed.

Ch. Vanka of Seppala II.

Valuiki of Cold River.

About The Author

$\mathbf{M}$ICHAEL JENNINGS was born in New Orleans, Louisiana, and grew up in southwestern Iran where he broke and trained race horses. His interest in the Siberian Husky goes back to 1966 when, as a student in high school, he saw his first Husky. For the last twenty years he has been an ardent student of the history, form and function of the breed, while his line of Demavand Siberians has gained an international reputation for classic beauty and athletic prowess. A poet, Mr. Jennings lives on Otisco Lake in upstate New York with his wife, son, dogs and cats. He served for several years on the Board of Directors of the Siberian Husky Club of America, and is, at this writing, its First Vice President.

Michael Jennings.

Mrs. Jean Fournier with 16-year-old CH.Toko's Mr. Chip of Yago CD (CH. Marlytuk's Ahkee of Huskywood x Toko's Sweet Charity of Yago). Bred by Jean, "Chip" is the only Siberian Husky to win Best in Show, High Scoring Novice Obedience and Top Stud Dog Awards from the Siberian Husky Club of America.

Foreword to the Second Edition

It is a tremendous compliment to this book to include in it this Foreword by one of of the Siberian Husky's most distinguished friends. Jean Fournier, current delegate to the American Kennel Club from the Siberian Husky Club of America, has served as SHCA President, Director, Corresponding Secretary and presently is the Judges' Education Chairperson. In 1974, she founded the Connecticut Valley Siberian Husky Club, is past president of the Dog Judges' Association of America, past president and Bench Show Chairman of the Farmington Valley Kennel Club and editor of its Bulletin, a multiple award winner from the Dog Writers' Association of America. As an AKC-approved judge of all Working breeds as well as a portion of the Sporting and Herding breeds, her travels have taken her to judging engagements all over the continental United States, Alaska, Hawaii, the Netherlands, Japan, Canada and Italy. She has had the honor to judge at the Westminster KC, the Centennial show of the AKC and twice at the SHCA national Specialty.

ONE OF the happiest repercussions of the Siberian Husky's ongoing popularity is the demand by its admirers for education and information. To help satisfy this demand there now comes an articulate, contemporary account of the state of the breed in this second edition of its universally recognized masterwork—THE NEW COMPLETE SIBERIAN HUSKY.

For the first edition, the collaboration of Lorna Demidoff and Michael Jennings resulted in a truly peerless reference. This new edition continues to fulfill the need of today's Siberian fanciers to become more familiar with the true nature of this engaging Arctic dog and to better understand its many sides.

Even though Lorna's passing came much too soon, her influence can be felt through the work of Michael Jennings, who shared her great adventure and individual passion for the Siberian Husky. The adventure and passion is here for all in the second edition of the breed's literary masterpiece.

True purists are in total agreement that specific understanding of the Siberian's natural, yet primitive, virtues is essential to the collective appreciation by its legion of friends. I can almost visualize the fresh, new thoughts and words on the pages that follow first inspired in Michael through Lorna as they shared the same sensitivity and respect for the independent soul of the Siberian Husky.

Together with the marvelous chapters that helped the first edition become Best Breed Book of 1978, we can now relish a host of new delights—Ann Cook's History of the Racing Siberian, Michael Jennings' timeless, aesthetic tributes—Dialectics of the Breed, Breeding is an Art and more—all executed with mastery, scholarship and love for the breed.

THE NEW COMPLETE SIBERIAN HUSKY likewise spotlights many Siberians of the past decade with enlightening, often exciting photographs, accounts of currently active kennels and fanciers who have shaped contemporary history.

Whether the reader is a newly-charmed admirer or a shameless slave to long-term, contagious "Siberianism," this wonderful text will surely enhance every reader's admiration for and knowledge of the breed. THE NEW COMPLETE SIBERIAN HUSKY is a *must* for the library of *every* owner, breeder, exhibitor, judge, obedience enthusiast and racer—everyone who cares about Siberian Huskies.

We are grateful and indebted to Michael Jennings for providing a second look at the Siberian Husky and lasting memories of Lorna Demidoff—the Mistress of Monadnock—who, if she were still living, would surely proclaim this edition as "the ultimate frosting on a one-of-a-kind cake!"

It's definitive . . . it's historical . . . it's ALL Siberian.

—JEAN FOURNIER

Preface to the Second Edition

In THE FIRST EDITION of this book, we claimed history as our prime concern: the breed's evolution from a Paleolithic tool of remarkable ingenuity to a highly prized, strikingly beautiful purebred dog in the American Kennel Club tradition whose popularity is now truly international.

We claimed that after 1960 the proliferation of kennels and fanciers made it impossible even to list every significant dog or kennel after that period, and this is truer today than ever.

So we have used this update opportunity simply to try to improve or clarify our original story: with additional photos, a more Siberian-focused racing history chapter by Ann Cook, a breeding essay, and a chapter on the dialectics of form and function as they have shaped the breed over the last several decades.

Leonhard Seppala and his Siberians, winners of the All Alaska Sweepstakes in 1915 and 1916, pictured at the "Ruby Derby" in 1916. Note the length of leg on these dogs.

1

The Siberian in Alaska

GOLD WAS FIRST DISCOVERED IN ALASKA IN 1880 near the present site of Juneau. But it was not until 1896, when prospectors from the Juneau area struck gold in the Klondike region of the neighboring Yukon Territory, that the gold rush, as such, really began. With this strike, thousands from all over the world poured into the Yukon and Alaskan territories. Some found gold, but most didn't. The rush did not last long and the last major strike was made in Fairbanks in 1902. During the peak of the rush luckier prospectors might dig or pan as much as $5000 worth of gold dust in just a few days. But with eggs selling at a dollar apiece, few kept their hard-earned diggings long. Often the richest man in town was the "swamper," whose duty, or privilege, it was to sweep the sawdust, rich with gold dust from carelessly handled pokes, from the barroom floor.

But if few of the thousands of new inhabitants shared in the newly found wealth, all shared in the hardships. And foremost among these, probably greater than the problems of simple cohabitation, or crossing the Rockies, or a run of bad luck, was the severe, treacherous and almost constant cold. Many died from it and more left because of it. But as the fervor of the rush subsided and life in the mining towns took on the almost-staid qualities of well-regulated businesses, those who stayed came to depend, like their Indian and Eskimo predecessors, upon the sled dog for survival.

Nowhere was this more the case than in a small settlement on a spit of land jutting into Norton Sound. By an odd quirk of fate appropriate to a boomtown, the words "No Name," scrawled on a map by a clerk in the Territorial Land Office, had been misread and the town came to be called Nome. Nome entered the ranks of boomtowns when, in 1899, gold was discovered in nearby Daniels Creek. Situated as it was on a narrow peninsula with room for only a single main street along its length, the sudden explosion in population in 1900 created a "tent city" all along the frozen beach. With ice shutting off all communication by sea for the greater part of the year, Nome residents became completely dependent upon the only other means of transportation to the outside world—dog team. Consequently, it has been estimated that at the turn of the century there were probably more dogs per capita in the town of Nome than anywhere else in the world.

Like the inhabitants themselves, these dogs were a varied lot. Some were native dogs—thick-coated, erect-eared, arctic types; others showed their more southern heritage—flat-coated, lop-eared dogs who had either migrated north with their owners or, as was probably more commonly the case, had been shanghaied and shipped north for profit. Generally they were large, brawny, fierce dogs, and, like the inhabitants themselves, the ones who survived were accustomed to hard work, severe cold and relatively little food.

Since life virtually depended upon these dogs, a good one was not only a possession of great value but an object of immense pride and prestige as well. It is not surprising, then, that at night—when the men gathered around the potbellied stove of a local saloon—the topic of conversation was often dogs. And as the night progressed and the tales grew taller, the feats of this leader or that leader, or the speed of one or another team took on marvelous proportions. And with each man extolling the virtues of his team while pointing out the weaknesses of his neighbor's, the debates grew increasingly heated. Some teams were fast for short distances, while others had more stamina; some could nose into a blizzard, while others could run well with a tail wind; some hated breaking trail in deep snow; others couldn't take glare ice. And so the disputes continued.

Finally, Allan "Scotty" Allan, who was to become one of the most popular figures in Alaskan history, proposed that they run a race to prove once and for all just who did have the best team. Although Scotty had made a fortune in the gold fields, he had lost it all with the sinking of a steamer he had bought and was at this time employed as the bookkeeper for the Darling and Dean Hardware Merchants. While he was an excellent dog driver himself, it was, in fact, his children's habit of "racing" their dogs that inspired him to suggest this idea to the dog drivers of Nome.

It became immediately apparent, however, that this could not be just an ordinary race. In order to prove anything it would have to be a big event, have public interest and support, be well organized with machinery to make and enforce rules, and be a fair test of the capabilities of dogs and drivers alike. After months of discussion, the Nome Kennel Club was

"Scotty" Allan, veteran of Alaskan dog racing, with famous leader, "Baldy of Nome."

Trophy cup of the All Alaska Sweepstakes.

John Johnson, the "Iron Man," with two of his lead dogs. Kolma, the most notable, is at left.

3

formed in 1907 in order to organize and sponsor the event. Albert Fink, a lawyer, was its first president and helped in the drafting of the rules. Basically they were as follows:

—All drivers had to be members of the Nome Kennel Club.

—All dogs had to be registered with the club.

—A driver could have as many dogs on a team as he wanted, but all who started had to be brought back, either in harness or on the sled, and all dogs would be specially marked at the start of the race to prevent substitutions along the trail.

—There could be no "pacing" or teamwork of any kind. When two teams traveling in the same direction came in close proximity, the one behind would be given the right to pass and should be given any assistance necessary in passing by the forward driver. This rule, however, would not be considered in effect during the last leg of the homeward stretch.

In addition to these rules, there was a long list of technicalities.

But it was the laying out of the course itself that was the prime consideration. For if the race was indeed to prove which was the best team, the course would have to test every aspect of the dogs' and drivers' capabilities. Finally a course from Nome to Candle and return was decided upon, a distance of 408 miles that included extremely varied driving conditions. There was sea ice, tundra, mountains, timber, glaciers and even one valley that was almost always engulfed in a blizzard, no matter how fair the weather elsewhere.

It was decided that the race should be held in April when climatic conditions were most ideal. In order to get dogs and drivers in proper condition, preliminary races were held all winter, starting in October with a seven-mile race and working up to seventy-five miles just prior to the proposed date. Such intensity of focus naturally resulted in a reevaluation of the entire sled dog scene. Special enriched diets were fed and dogs were weighed daily. Drivers gave considerable attention to the condition of their dogs' feet, toughening pads against sharp ice. Innovations, like flank protectors for short-coated dogs and green netting or goggles for protection against snow blindness, were tried. Sleds were made lighter, and lines and harnesses were improved. Thus the lot of sled dogs in general was vastly improved, and the rate of progress in driving techniques accelerated greatly.

THE ALL ALASKA SWEEPSTAKES

The first All Alaska Sweepstakes was held in 1908 and was more or less in the nature of an experiment. In this race and in the 1909 race, the usual heavy basket sled was still used. Subsequently a lighter racing sled was developed and used. Starting procedures also underwent some refinement in these early years of the race. In the 1908 race, starts were spaced at two-hour intervals and each team's time was calculated from the time it started. But with weather and trail conditions changing quickly along the course, it was found that such long intervals between starts could unduly influence the outcome of the race. Some teams might have fair weather for the major part of their run while others might run into nothing but blizzard conditions. Gradually, then, the interval between starts was decreased until 1913, from which time teams were started at one-minute intervals and all were considered to have started at the same time.

The 1908 All Alaska Sweepstakes was won by the team owned by the club's president, Albert Fink, and driven by John Hegness. The event itself turned out to be more successful than its organizers could possibly have hoped. It was THE event of the year as far as Nome residents were concerned, and public opinion demanded that it become an annual affair. Not only did the race provide an excuse for a four-day holiday, with schools closing, businesses all but shutting down and even the election of a "Queen of the Sweepstakes," it also provided an opportunity for that favorite of frontier pastimes—gambling.

In fact, it was this last nerve-racking aspect of the race that probably accounts for its immense popularity. The course ran along a telephone line which allowed constant reports on the progress of the teams to be sent back to bettors in Nome. There, assembled in the Board of Trade Saloon on Front Street, the gamblers watched progress reports on each team as they were put up on a large board. The unique aspect of the betting was that the books remained open until the first team crossed the finish line. This meant that the odds were perpetually changing; as one or another favorite fell behind, hedging bets could be placed, and consequently fortunes could be won or lost in just a few days. In addition, weather and trail conditions could change so rapidly that even the fastest, most experienced teams could be beaten by slower ones if luck was against them. Consequently few of the gamblers dared leave the saloon during the entire four days of the race. Food was brought in to them and, at the end of the race, many of the bleary-eyed men emerging from the saloon seemed considerably worse for wear than the drivers themselves. So popular, in fact, was this form of entertainment that before the start of the second All Alaska Sweepstakes in 1909, there was already more than $100,000 on the books.

This race also saw the entrance of an unknown quantity. During the preceding summer of 1908, a Russian fur trader named William Goosak had arrived in Nome with a team of dogs from Siberia that were substantially different in size, disposition and appearance from the local dogs. Whereas the native dogs were large, rangy, fierce, often wolflike dogs, prone to fighting and giving the impression of great strength, these Siberian dogs were compact, small, docile and rather more foxlike than wolflike in appearance. Although the dog fanciers of Nome found the attractiveness and amiable dispositions of these dogs appealing, the suggestion that they be entered in the sweepstakes to compete against the larger and apparently much tougher native dogs was not taken seriously. The odds makers, themselves, used to assessing teams largely on the basis of leg length, hardly gave the team a second thought, since the little dogs had considerably less leg than any other entry. Despite this unreceptiveness, however, Goosak did manage to persuade a man named Thurstrup to drive the team. So, on a cold, bleak morning in April 1909, the first team of Siberian Huskies to be seen on the North American Continent loped out of the town of Nome and into the annals of history.

They did not win the race, however, largely because of a poor strategical maneuver on the part of their driver, Thurstrup. Much of the success of a team in a race of this length depended not only upon the actual driving skill of the driver, but upon his ability to gauge the speed and endurance of his dogs; and each driver painstakingly worked out a prerace strategy based upon arduous practice. Would he drive his dogs eight hours and rest six? If he saw a chance to overtake an opponent, would he risk cutting short his dogs' rest period? Every driver tried to decide these questions well in advance of the race, and caches of food and supplies were hidden along the trail at the anticipated rest stations.

But even the best-laid plans were dependent upon such things as weather and injuries. As it happened, a blizzard struck Nome just as the race was starting, and of the fourteen teams that started, only three were able to keep going. These included the favorite, Scotty Allan, driving his mixed-breed team; Percy Blatchford, driving Allan's second-string team; and Thurstrup, driving Goosak's Siberians.

As the little Siberians managed to stay only slightly behind Allan on the way to Candle, and as reports of this reached Nome, those who had bet heavily on Allan began to grow anxious. Consequently, when Allan reached Candle, he received urgent calls urging him to shorten his proposed seven-hour rest stop and to start on the homestretch as quickly as possible. But Allan refused to risk the consequences of such action and stayed in Candle until he felt his team was sufficiently rested.

Arriving in Candle shortly after Allan, Thurstrup did not display the same self-control. Checking in with the officials there, he immediately started out again, and although he led the race for the next hundred miles, the lack of rest for himself and his dogs cost him the race, as both Allan and Blatchford managed to overtake him before the last quarter mark was reached.

Allan won the race with Blatchford taking second and Thurstrup third. But even a third-place finish was enough to convince the dog fanciers of Nome of the caliber of the Siberians. Not only had they shown their

Winners, first All Alaska Sweepstakes, 1908. Albert Fink, owner; John Hegness, driver.

Winners, second All Alaska Sweepstakes, 1909. J. Berger, owner; "Scotty" Allan, driver.

Winners, third All Alaska Sweepstakes, 1910. Col. Ramsay, owner; John Johnson, driver.

7

Winners, fourth All Alaska Sweepstakes, 1911. Allan and Darling, owners; "Scotty" Allan, driver.

Winners, fifth All Alaska Sweepstakes, 1912. Allan and Darling, owners; "Scotty" Allan, driver.

Winners, sixth All Alaska Sweepstakes, 1913. Bowen and Dalzene, owners; Fay Dalzene, driver.

Winners, seventh All Alaska Sweepstakes, 1914. John Johnson, owner and driver.

Winners, eighth All Alaska Sweepstakes, 1915, Leonhard Seppala, owner and drive.

Winners, ninth All Alaska Sweepstakes, 1916, Leonhard Seppala, owner and driver.

speed and endurance, but all who had seen them had been struck by their remarkable manageability.

The previous spring a young Scotsman named Fox Maule Ramsay, second son of the Earl of Dalhousie and a graduate of Oxford University, had arrived in Nome with his two uncles, Colonel Charles Ramsay and Colonel Weatherly Stuart, the family having invested money in the Nome goldfields. Being young, Ramsay quickly took to the life of the North, especially dog driving, and in 1909 he drove a team in the sweepstakes but did not place. But after seeing the Siberians in action, and at the advice of Ivor Olsen, a man familiar with Siberia, Ramsay chartered a schooner in the summer of 1909, paying what for those days was the not-inconsiderable price of $2500, and crossed the Bering Sea to Siberia. He returned with some seventy Siberian Huskies, obtained from the small settlement of Markovo on the Anadyr River.

From these dogs Ramsay entered three teams in the 1910 All Alaska Sweepstakes, one for himself and one for each of his uncles. The team entered in the name of Colonel Charles Ramsay and driven by John "Iron Man" Johnson took first place with an elapsed time of 74 hours, 14 minutes, 37 seconds, a time that in the history of the race was never equaled. Ramsay himself, driving his own team, took second, and the third team of Siberians, driven by Charles Johnson, finished fourth.

During the next few years luck seems to have been against the Siberian entries. Perhaps it was more than luck since it appears that, at least on one occasion, the dogs on John Johnson's team were doped. Apparently so much money had been bet on him that had he won, it would have broken the gambling ring. No one knew exactly what happened, but Johnson claimed that on a certain part of the trail his dogs kept picking up what appeared to be small pieces of meat. Soon afterward they became drowsy and finally could not be roused. Other people claimed that he had simply thrown the race. At any rate the races of 1911 and 1912 went to Scotty Allan's team of crossbreeds, with a Siberian entry driven by Charles Johnson taking third in both races. The race of 1913 went to Fay Delzene, who also drove dogs of mixed breeding, with John Johnson and his Siberians managing to capture second place. Finally in 1914, the "Iron Man" again brought the Siberians in first.

Johnson left Nome shortly after this race to go to California, but although his performances had been somewhat erratic, he had proven the superiority of the Siberian on at least two occasions. It now only remained for someone to take sufficient interest in the little dogs to further their cause.

10

LEONHARD SEPPALA

Arriving in Nome around 1900, Leonhard Seppala was better prepared than most to meet the hardships of this new country. Born in the fishing village of Skjervoy, Norway, some 250 miles north of the Arctic Circle, he had first faced the perils and hardships of an arctic fisherman's life at the age of eleven. During the summer months he had worked with his father as a blacksmith, and with the idea of eventually taking over his father's business, he had completed his apprenticeship in that trade in the town of Christiana. The constant hard work coupled with an avid interest in sports helped Leonhard to develop into a lean, sturdy young man, and although extremely small, he was both an expert skier and a proficient wrestler.

The idea of taking over his father's business and settling into the traditional life of Skjervoy lost its appeal, however, with the sudden death of his childhood sweetheart and fiancée. With her death, life in Norway suddenly seemed bleak and repetitive to the young man, and when an old friend, Jafet Lindeburg, returned from the Alaskan goldfields with accounts of a new life and unheard-of wealth, Seppala decided to emigrate. Once in Nome, he worked at various jobs in and around the mines. He also tried prospecting, when opportunity and funds permitted, but never struck pay dirt. But like most longtime residents of the peninsula, he acquired the art of dog driving, and, like the rest of the community, became an avid follower of the new and rapidly growing sport of sled dog racing.

Until the first All Alaska Sweepstakes in 1908, skiing had been the major sport in the area, and Seppala was among the best. But with the introduction of sled dog racing, the public's attention switched rapidly. Seppala had never considered himself a particularly expert dog driver, and when a friend suggested that he enter one of the small races that were held throughout the year in preparation for the sweepstakes, Seppala thought he was joking. At this time, Seppala owned a team of mixed-breed freighting dogs which he had never thought of as racing dogs. But his love of sporting events, along with his friend's persuasiveness, finally overcame his initial timidity, and he entered the Moose Burden Handicap race.

As it happened, it was a buzzard who decided the outcome of the race and, in doing so, probably changed the history of sled dog racing. Seppala had no real thought of winning the race, and when one of the faster teams pulled up behind him, he was about to pull over to let the other team by when his own team gave a sudden burst of speed. Looking ahead, Seppala saw a buzzard on the trail. And as his team gave chase, the buzzard flew up and settled again further along the trail. This kept up for about four miles until the buzzard grew tired of the game. But the extra speed had been enough, and when Seppala looked back, his competitor was no longer in sight. Crossing the finish line, Seppala was more surprised than anyone when he learned that he had actually won the race.

He knew the win had been a fluke, but the sensation of victory in this new sport was addictive, and so Leonhard Seppala, the skier, became Leonhard Seppala, the dog racer.

But he was not really in the big leagues yet, and in the years that followed, the teams of John Johnson, Scotty Allan and Fay Delzene were still the teams to be reckoned with in the sweepstakes.

In 1913, however, Jafet Lindeburg, having collected the best of what could be found of the first Siberian imports and their offspring, asked Seppala if he would take charge of raising and training the young dogs. There were about fifteen dogs in all, mostly puppies and bitches, and it was intended that they be presented as a gift to Captain Roald Amundsen for his proposed expedition to the North Pole the following year. Fortunately for Seppala and for the reputation of the Siberians, Amundsen had to cancel his expedition at the outbreak of World War I, and Seppala managed to keep possession of the dogs.

But the dogs were very young, the lead dog Suggen being the only experienced one on the team. So, when the Nome Kennel Club along with Scotty Allan suggested that the teams be entered in the seventh All Alaska Sweepstakes in 1914, Seppala was extremely dubious. He acquiesced at the last moment, however, and entered the race without ever having been over the course. This turned out to be a mistake, for as soon as the race began, a blizzard started and Seppala and his team took a wrong turn and became lost. After almost toppling over a cliff several hundred feet high in the blinding squall, Seppala finally managed to make it back to the trail. But the dogs' feet were badly bleeding and they were exhausted. Consequently he was forced to withdraw from the race.

Throughout the following winter, however, Seppala and his team trained as never before. In order to subsidize the training, Seppala began hauling freight and passengers all over Alaska, and by the start of the eighth All Alaska Sweepstakes in 1915, his team was in excellent condition. He had been careful to train far out of town so that no one had any idea of the speed of his team. This fact, coupled with his ignominious withdrawal the year before, made him the long shot of the race.

Nevertheless, Seppala won the race with ease. His nearest rival was Scotty Allan, and Seppala, expecting a homestretch battle with Allan, had intentionally "saved" his Siberians for just such an encounter. But by Cape Nome, thirteen miles from the finish, Seppala was a full hour ahead of Allan and managed to win "going away." Seppala's wife, Constance, had been elected Queen of the Sweepstakes that year, and as the cannon at Fort Davis boomed, and the whistles of the power station and fire stations shrieked to announce the winner, she was the first out to greet him.

Seppala won the next two sweepstakes in 1916 and 1917 with the same ease. After 1917, the lack of competition for him and the increase in the war effort caused the race to be discontinued. And so, what was perhaps the most spectacular chapter in the history of sled dog racing came to a close.

But in the years that followed, Seppala went on to prove the versatility of his little dogs, winning many of the shorter races and breaking many records in the process. In doing so he proved his contention that, with proper training, the Siberian could be as successful in races of medium distances as it had been in the grueling sweepstakes races. He won these races, not only in Alaska, but in Canada and New England as well; wherever he went, "the little man with his little dogs," as they came to be called, won the admiration and affection of all. What seemed to astound people most was the willingness of the dogs to work and Seppala's uncanny ability to instill this desire in them. One discouraged rival in New England described it this way:

> That man is superhuman. He passed me every day of the race, and I wasn't loafing any. I couldn't see that he drove his dogs. He just clucked to them every now and then, and they would lay into their collars harder than I've ever seen dogs do before. Something came out of him and went into those dogs with that clucking. You've heard of some men who hold supernatural control over others. Hypnotism, I guess you call it. I suppose it's just as likely to work on dogs. Seppala certainly has it if anyone has.

A fact in which Seppala took great pride was that in all the years he raced, he never used a whip on a dog. Only once was he ever called upon to even crack his whip, and that was simply to get the dogs up quickly after a rest stop in the 1915 All Alaska Sweepstakes.

Not all of Seppala's runs, however, were in the nature of sporting events, and often his most spectacular were not.

From an early age, Seppala seems to have been endowed with those qualities of courage and presence of mind that prove useful in times of crisis. At the age of nine, he dragged an older and much larger playmate

Times for the All Alaska Sweepstakes			
Race	*Winning Driver*	*Breed of Dog*	*Elapsed Hourly Time*
1908	John Hagness	Mixed Malemute	3.51 miles per hour
1909	A. A. Allan	Mixed Malemute	4.97
1910	John Johnson	Siberian	5.58
1911	A. A. Allan	Mixed Malemute	5.05
1912	A. A. Allan	Mixed Malemute	4.66
1913	Fay Delzene	Mixed Malemute	5.39
1914	John Johnson	Siberian	5.04
1915	Leonhard Seppala	Siberian	5.18
1916	Leonhard Seppala	Siberian	5.06
1917	Leonhard Seppala	Siberian	

		Siberian Entries	
Race	*Place*	*Driver*	*Elapsed Hourly Time*
1908	No entry		
1909	3rd	Thurstrup	4.54 miles per hour
1910	1st	John Johnson	5.58
	2nd	Fox Ramsay	5.34
1911	3rd	Charles Johnson	4.80
1912	3rd	Charles Johnson	4.59
1913	2nd	John Johnson	5.28
1914	1st	John Johnson	5.04
1915	1st	Leonhard Seppala	5.18
1916	1st	Leonhard Seppala	5.06
1917	1st	Leonhard Seppala	

from a fire. Later, during a storm, he helped his father rescue a boatload of drowning fishermen from the icy Arctic Ocean. Within his first few years in Alaska, he pursued and caught a man who was attempting to kidnap a young woman. Being a superior dog driver, he had managed to catch up with the man even though the latter had a considerable head start. Once having caught up, Seppala, although unarmed, managed to disarm the man and return the girl to Nome.

On another occasion, shortly after winning the All Alaska Sweepstakes in 1916, Seppala, arriving in Dime Creek after making a forty-mile run, learned that a friend and fellow sweepstakes racer named Bobby Brown had been badly mangled in a sawmill accident. The nearest hospital was in Candle, sixty-two miles away, and the townspeople, hearing that Seppala was in the area, rushed out to implore him to make the trip. It was already one o'clock and his dogs were tired. Besides, Seppala already had one passenger and was unfamiliar with the trail. Pointing out these facts, Seppala, although stating that he was willing to try, suggested that their best driver and a fresh team of dogs could probably make better time. The townspeople, however, were determined that Seppala was the best man to make the drive. They did agree to send along their best driver with a fresh team to act as guide and to take the other passenger. And so the two teams left for Candle.

It became immediately apparent, however, that the other team could not keep up, even when Seppala took the other passenger back onto his sled. At this point, Bobby Brown, who was still conscious, told Seppala that if he were kept informed of the passing landmarks, he could guide them to Candle. So the other team turned back and Seppala, carrying two passengers, continued on to Candle, arriving around eleven o'clock that night. His team had covered 102 miles in one day with sometimes two and sometimes three men on the sled. In all of Seppala's experience, he had never heard of a team making as long a drive with such a load in one day and in one drive. Unfortunately, Bobby Brown died three days later.

SEPPALA AND THE HISTORIC SERUM DRIVE

But it was in 1925, when diphtheria threatened to decimate the population of Nome, that Seppala and his Siberians gained international acclaim. It was in January of that year that the first child died of the disease, and soon others were affected. The existing supply of antitoxin in Nome at the time was small, and as the disease spread, it was quickly used up. The nearest available supply of the antitoxin was in Anchorage, 955 miles away. It could be transported by rail as far as Nenana, 297 miles north of Anchorage, but no further. The only two planes in Alaska were dismantled and sitting in Fairbanks with no one to fly them, since the only three pilots in the territory were away for the winter. The nearest operable plane was in Seattle and there was not time to bring it north. This meant that the only means of transporting the serum the remaining 658 miles from Nenana to Nome was by dog team. The trip was an arduous one in any season, but in the middle of winter, it was especially so. In the best weather, the U.S. mail teams took twenty-five days to cover the distance.

Seppala's plan was to drop some of the dogs off along the way at various Eskimo villages where they could be cared for and rested for the return trip. By dropping off a total of twelve along the way, he planned to reach Nulato, where he was to meet the team coming from the other direction, with eight. This would be a sufficient number, he calculated, since he had been informed that the package containing the serum was very light.

But after Seppala passed out of telephone communication with Nome, the epidemic increased so alarmingly that it was decided to speed up the transportation of the serum by running shorter relays night and day from the other direction. Thus, toward the end of the fourth day, as Seppala and his team were just coming in sight of the village of Shaktolik, they met the driver with the serum. Seppala had only traveled 170 miles since leaving Nome, while expecting to travel 300. Consequently, he had almost passed the driver with a word of greeting when he made out the words, "Serum—turn back." Although this would make his total journey shorter, Seppala had just covered the worst 43 miles over the ice of Norton Sound from Isaac's Point to Shaktolik, and now, with night approaching and a high wind in their faces, they would have to make it back over the ice. On this part of the journey there was the ever-present danger of the ice breaking off and drifting out into the Bering Sea. Many men had been lost this way, and with the high wind, the chances of such an occurrence were greater. Nevertheless Seppala reached Isaac's Point, making the team's total mileage for that day nearly 90 miles. The next day, on the advice of

During his first trip east, the redoubtable Leonhard Seppala and his celebrated serum run team posed for this photo on the roof of a department store in Providence, Rhode Island.

Togo, leader in the serum drive.

an old Eskimo, Seppala drove the team closer into shore. Even so, at one point, they passed only a few feet from open water where the trail they had traveled the day before had drifted out to sea. Nevertheless, that afternoon they reached the village of Cheenik where the next relay team took over.

The last relay team, driven by Gunnar Kasson, reached Nome at 5:30 on the morning of February 2, 1925, the entire trip of 658 miles from Nenana to Nome having been made in just five and one-half days. And of the 650 miles, Leonhard Seppala and his team had gone 340 while no other relay had done more than 53.

So impressive, in fact, had been the efforts of dogs and drivers in averting the diphtheria epidemic that Senator Dill of the state of Washington introduced a resolution in Congress that made the story of the serum part of the Congressional Record. One sentence of this account reads, "Men had thought that the limit of speed and endurance had been reached in the grueling races of Alaska, but a race for sport and money proved to have far less stimulus than this contest, in which humanity was the urge and life was the prize."

After the serum drive, Seppala traveled extensively throughout the United States and Canada, winning races wherever he went and providing the foundation stock for many of the early Siberian kennels in both countries. The record he compiled as a racer is undeniable. He was not only the winner of the All Alaska Sweepstakes in 1915, 1916 and 1917, but also won the Yukon Dog Derby twice, the Borden Marathon four times, the Ruby Derby, the New England Point to Point Race three times, the Eastern International in Quebec, the Lake Placid Race twice, the Poland Spring Race in Maine three times, and the Solomon Burden Race twice. In many of these he set records, some of which stand to this day.

But as deserving as he is of the title "the world's greatest dog driver," Seppala's primary concern was not simply that of personal glory. Settling late in his life in Seattle, Washington, where he helped in the breeding and maintenance of Earl Snodie's Bow Lake Kennels, he once remarked that his greatest accomplishments had been to have furthered the cause of the Siberian dogs he had come to know and love and which it had been his honor to drive for so many years, and to have bettered the treatment of sled dogs in general.

He died in 1967 in Seattle. In old age he remained what he had always been: a quiet, unassuming, humorous man, always somewhat surprised but shyly pleased when someone remembered him.

TOGO

Many if not most breeds have that one specimen which, for one reason or another, attains the status of legend and against which all who come after are held up for comparison. And as one rolls back the generations of Siberians, past this year's Best in Show winner and last year's top producer or top lead dog, always out of the white frozen landscape of the past there looms Togo: small, dark, compact, oblivious of the praises that have been heaped upon him, irreverent, foxy, and, except for that certain poise and the confident response to command, like a true Siberian, unabashedly disreputable.

Togo was born in Seppala's kennels in Little Creek, Alaska, probably in 1915 or 1916. Named after the famous Japanese admiral, he was sired by Seppala's lead dog Suggen, who led the Siberian team to loss and then to victory in the sweepstakes races of 1914 and 1915.* His dam was a bitch named Dolly. He was the only puppy in the litter and, according to Seppala, was lonely, sometimes sullen and often mischievous. He first belonged to a man named Victor Anderson, but when he proved to be too much of a bother, Anderson returned him to Seppala at the age of about six months. Seppala, in turn, gave the puppy to a woman who wanted a pet. But for all the lavish attention he received at this new home, Togo repeatedly broke his chain or jumped out the window and returned to Little Creek. Finally succumbing to the inevitable, Seppala took the little dog back and decided to keep him.

Thrilled to be back in the only environment that he apparently enjoyed, Togo roamed the surrounding tundra at will or ran loose beside the team during their daily run. This latter activity seemed to have special appeal to the puppy but soon became annoying to Seppala, since Togo loved nothing better than to come charging past the team and, watching his chance, take a nip at one or another of the dogs' ears and get away quickly.

Accordingly, when Seppala was planning a trip to Dime Creek in November, he left Togo in the large corral with a seven-foot wire fence with instructions to the kennel hand that the puppy was not to be released until a couple of days after the team had gone. Togo, quite untypically, showed no outward sign of disappointment at being left. That night, however, Togo made a leap for it and almost made it. A rear leg, however, caught in the wire and when the kennel boss came out to see what was causing the commotion he found the little dog hanging upside down on the outside of the fence with a severe gash in his leg. But the dog's only concern seems to have been to catch up with the team, and when he was cut down he quickly disappeared into the night.

Seppala had camped at Solomon that night. When he started out the next morning the team began pulling with unusual speed, and Seppala decided that they must have picked up the scent of reindeer. As the sun

*This is based upon Seppala's account of his dogs in the book, *Seppala, an Alaskan Dog Driver*, by Elizabeth Ricker, but there is some evidence that Seppala's lead dog in 1915 may have been a crossbreed named Russky.

rose and the wind died Seppala saw what appeared to be a fox on the trail ahead. Soon, scarcely believing his eyes, he realized that it was Togo. At this point the puppy charged the team, nipping the leader on the ear as he passed and succeeded in creating havoc for the rest of the day. Having bandaged his dog's leg as best he could, Seppala decided the next day that there was nothing to do with the eight-month-old troublemaker but to try him in harness with the rest of the dogs. As is customary with new dogs, he was hitched far back in the team so that Seppala could keep an eye on him. Once in harness, however, Togo started off like a veteran, as if this was just the chance he had been waiting for. And as the day proceeded and he continued to work harder than any of the adults, he was gradually promoted forward until, at the end of the day, he was actually sharing the lead position with Seppala's experienced lead dog.

Needless to say, Seppala could hardly believe what he was seeing. Here was an eight-month-old puppy who had never been in harness and who had an injured leg, but who, in his first day on the trail, had traveled seventy-five miles and pulled in ahead of the seasoned team. From that day on it was Togo who was the favorite and could always be depended upon.

Even in maturity Togo weighed only forty-eight pounds. But as the years rolled on, his strength, speed and endurance became legendary throughout Alaska, and his reputation as a lead dog was rivaled only by that of Kolyma, John "Iron Man" Johnson's famous lead dog who led the record-setting team of Siberians in the All Alaska Sweepstakes in 1910.

It is somewhat uncertain exactly when Togo became the full-fledged leader of Seppala's team. His first major race was probably the 1918 Borden Marathon. It is certain that he was the leader in most of the races subsequent to the sweepstakes and that during his years as leader he earned the title of the "world's most traveled dog," logging, by Seppala's estimation, approximately five thousand miles during his career.

In 1925 it was Togo whom Seppala counted on to lead the team on the Serum Drive. And during that run, according to Seppala, the famous leader worked harder and better than ever. But the miles had taken their toll, and the Serum Drive was the last long run the old dog made. Since he had logged 340 miles in the interest of the serum, and since the run had left him permanently lame, it is not surprising that many were dismayed when reporters from the States gave the greatest publicity to a dog named Balto, one of the second-string dogs that Seppala had left behind with his scrub team and whom Gunnar Kasson had used to relay the serum the last fifty miles into Nome. Impressed with the romantic ring of his name, reporters had simply given Balto Togo's record as a lead dog and thus publicized him as "the greatest racing leader in Alaska." Consequently, the statue that was erected in Central Park, New York, to commemorate the event bears the name Balto instead of Togo.

Fortunately fame is not a canine aspiration, and Togo lived out the

At left, Leonhard Seppala with Togo at Poland Spring, Maine, 1929. Below, 31 years later—Mr. Seppala with Ralph Morill visits Togo in his preserved state at Peabody Museum of Yale University.

remainder of his life with all the comforts and attention that he deserved. While traveling in the States, Seppala presented him as a gift to Mrs. Elizabeth Ricker, feeling that the easier life in her kennel was more suited to his age. It was at her kennel in Poland Spring, Maine, that he died on December 5, 1929.

Togo's body was taken to the Peabody Museum at Yale University where Ralph C. Morrill prepared him for exhibition with other famous dogs in the Whitney Collection. Subsequently he was moved to the Shelbourne Museum near Burlington, Vermont, where each summer Siberian fanciers from all over the country come to pay their respects to the dog that, more than any other, has come to symbolize the words on Balto's statue in Central Park, New York. They read:

Dedicated to the indomitable spirit of the sled dogs
that relayed antitoxin six hundred miles over rough
ice across treacherous waters through arctic
blizzards from Nenana to the relief of stricken Nome
in the Winter of 1925.

Endurance
                              Fidelity

                                                  Intelligence

Ch. Arahaz' Astrakhan, owned by Rosemary Fisher, presents a classic headstudy.

This historically significant photo, circa 1932, shows some important early Siberians. Left to right: Bonzo, Toto, Suggen, Sepp II, Kingeak, Snegruf, Tserko, Kreevanka and Smokey of Seppala. The driver is Harry Wheeler and his passenger is Charlie Belford, both famous drivers. The type and body proportion appears lovely on these animals, but especially so on Suggen, Tserko and Kreevanka.

22

2

Origin of the Siberian Husky

$\mathbf{T}$HE BREED THAT IS TODAY RECOGNIZED BY the American Kennel Club as the Siberian Husky has evolved directly from these early imports to Alaska and from one other importation directly to New England. The first of these imports was, of course, that of William Goosak, the fur trader. These dogs came from Markovo, one of several fairs along the Anadyr River where a dog-breeding people known as the Chukchi came to sell or trade their dogs. Impressed with the performance of these dogs in the 1909 All Alaska Sweepstakes, William Madsen acquired them from Goosak along with their first litter of pups whelped on November 29, 1908, and returned to buy fourteen more Chukchi dogs. In turn, all of these dogs were acquired eventually by John Johnson and combined with the dogs that Fox Maule Ramsay and Iver Olsen bought in 1909, also at the Markovo Fair.

As we have seen, many of the best of these dogs were gathered together in Nome by Jafet Lindeburg as an intended gift to Roald Amundsen for his proposed "dash to the pole." When Amundsen's expedition was canceled, these dogs went to Leonhard Seppala and, together with the direct imports to New England by Olaf Swenson in 1930, formed the foundation of what is known today as the Siberian Husky.

Therefore, in order to trace the development of this remarkable breed that almost overnight captured the interest of sled dog fanciers throughout the North American continent, it is necessary to look far back into the arctic past at a culture so ancient as to remain obscure even to the most ardent researchers and at a people so adapted to the climatic and political severity of their culture as to have earned the appellation "the Apaches of Siberia." These were the Chukchi people of northeastern Siberia.

When and where the first symbiotic relationship between men and wolves or men and jackals developed is unknown. How long this relationship lasted before the process of domestication began is also a matter of conjecture. We know that the dog has served man in a vital capacity of both hunting and herding cultures for hundreds, and in some cases thousands, of years. In no instance, however, has the dog been any more crucial to survival than in the sled dog cultures of the far north, and probably never has he held such a sustained and integral position in the entire economic, spiritual, and political structure of a culture as in the case of the Chukchi.

THE CHUKCHI SLED DOG

It is, of course, impossible to prove definitively that the Siberian Husky of today, as recognized by the American Kennel Club, has evolved in a state of absolute purity from the Chukchi sled dog, or that this strain had itself remained pure from some three thousand years prior to the time the first dogs were exported to Alaska. On the other hand, since there have been various arguments in the past disputing the relative purity of these dogs, it is necessary to note some of the causes of the confusion.

In the first place, the Chukchi culture was basically a Stone Age culture. The Chukchi kept no written records. For accounts of their dogs, then, we must rely upon the tales of early explorers and traders. These are often highly questionable, since these men were seldom particularly knowledgeable either about dogs or the Chukchi. Most failed to realize, for instance, that only a minority of the Chukchi people actually bred dogs as a way of life, and that these lived only along the Arctic and Pacific coasts in a reservation that was off-limits to all Russians from 1837 until 1917. The reindeer-herding Chukchi, who lived inland and along the rivers, sometimes had dogs, but these usually were mongrels. A dog seen in a village of mixed Russian and Chukchi inhabitants is unfortunately often described as a Chukchi dog.

The disparities in these descriptions are often used as evidence to support the contention that the Chukchi were in fact not breeding any consistent strain of dogs. The misunderstanding lies in the fact that although many of these dogs were bred and lived in bona fide Chukchi villages, they were not the Chukchi dogs of legend. In recent history, many arctic peoples have bred and sold dogs to outsiders in order to avoid starvation. The "Reindeer-Herding" Chukchi, as distinct from the "Dog-Breeding" Chukchi, resorted to this means of survival from time to time, even though they knew little or nothing about dogs, and even though keeping large numbers of dogs is basically incompatible with keeping reindeer, since the sled dogs kill the reindeer.

All the evidence indicates that the true Chukchi dog remained pure until the present century only along the Arctic coast within four hundred miles of the tip of Asia opposite Alaska and along the Pacific within three hundred miles of this tip. In much of the Chukchi homeland, both former and present, in which the majority of observations available in English were made, the purebred Chukchi dogs were replaced by those of other native peoples and those of the dominant Russian culture. This is particularly true in the Kolyma region, where there have been no dog-breeding Chukchi for centuries, but which persists in Western literature as the alleged source of the purebred Chukchi sled dog.

This brings us to a second problem in tracing the history of the Chukchi dog. The bulk of information is written in Russian, much of which is not available outside the Soviet Union. What little has found its way into English has done so more or less by chance.

The greatest obstacle in tracing the relative purity of these dogs, however, is the fact that it has been the official Soviet policy to discredit all isolated native breeds and to deny not only their purity but their functional value as well. In the 1930s, the Soviets, recognizing the impracticability of mechanized transport in the remoter areas of Siberia at the time, tried to promote the value of sled dogs by systematizing their breeding. This was done by discarding the earlier ethnic classifications of northern breeds by Shirinskiy-Shikhmatov and adopting a functional categorization in 1934 designed to maximize the value of the dog as a tool of economic production.

In 1934, the Soviets divided their northern breeds, then known collectively as Laikas, into four basic types. These were the sled dog, the big-game hunting dog, the reindeer-herding dog, and the small-game hunting dog. Standards for each were established in Leningrad over a three-year period by averaging the measurements of four hundred "representative" dogs. The standard for the sled dog was obtained by measuring thirty-three almost randomly selected sled dogs, not a single one of which came from eastern Siberia. The Chukchi dogs were specifically excluded from the sample because they were considered far too small for the expected freighting requirements of the future Soviet Arctic economy.

In 1947, the All Russian Cynological Congress disestablished both the sled dog and the reindeer-hunting dog (the AKC Samoyed), and grouped the two Arctic hunting types of dogs into four artificial breeds of "laikas": the Karelo-Finnish, Russo-European, West Siberian, and East Siberian. Each was a composite of three or more native hunting breeds indigenous to its area.

In 1967, the Soviet government embarked in earnest on a widely publicized and intensely debated campaign to forbid the breeding of any arctic dogs other than the four artificially created and officially recognized hunting breeds. By this time all the natural breeds of sled dogs in Siberia, which the native people had developed over hundreds of years, had already been replaced by the single large Northeast Siberian Draft Dog. And this standard sled dog was itself viewed as a relic of the early Soviet period with no long-range economic future. This is why no sled dogs or Samoyeds have ever been admitted to any Soviet dog shows and probably never will be.

Since the Soviets, however, had artificially created the only recognized breed of sled dog in Siberia, they could well claim that this dog is the only legitimate "Siberian Husky." And at one time the Soviets did in effect deny that the AKC Siberian Husky is a legitimate breed of Siberian sled dog. The Department of Nature Preservation of the USSR Ministry of Agriculture, through the Embassy of the USSR in Bern, Switzerland, suggested in 1971 that the AKC Siberian Husky either must be degenerated from the Northeast Siberian Draft Dog or else be descended from more southerly hunting breeds. In the Soviet Union, the Siberian Chukchi Sled Dog has joined the ranks of those who officially never existed.

Even before this systematic attempt to discredit and destroy the dogs bred by small isolated tribes in Siberia and to promote the Leningrad amalgamation, evidence indicates that there were only three kinds of sled dogs in Siberia whose breeding can be considered pure. The oldest kind, and the only true sled dog breeds, were kept by the four Paleo-Asiatic tribes located along the Pacific Ocean: from south to north, the Nivki (Gilyak), Itelmen (later crossbred to become the Kamchadal), the Koryak, and the Chukchi. The second kind of Siberian sled dog is a combined hunting-draft dog, of which there were only two breeds, both from interior Siberia. These were developed by the only other major Paleo-Asiatic tribe, the Yukagir, and by the Uralic Ostyak. The Ostyak dog looked surprisingly like a Siberian Chukchi Sled Dog and forms the base of the officially recognized hunting breed known as the East Siberian Laika. The third kind of Siberian sled dog is the combined herding-draft dog, of which only one pure breed ever existed, the Samoyed sled dog. Each of these seven breeds of dog developed in different conditions of snow cover, temperature, terrain, and hunting requirements, and each was unique in performance capabilities, except that the Koryak was almost identical to the Chukchi dog.

The conformations of these seven breeds of sled dog native to Siberia reflect their basic use. The smallest are the true sled dogs, which are distinguished by their relatively short coupling producing a length not much greater than the height. The southernmost of these, the Nivki, was developed to pull sleds fast through deep snow between the year-round villages on the Amur River and the winter sea mammal hunting grounds one hundred miles away on the island of Sakhalin. This dog had long, thin legs but maintained the "square" proportions of height to length typical of true sled dog breeds.

The largest of the purebred sled dogs are the hunting-draft dogs, because they were originally developed so that one, or at most two, could pull the hunter's game-laden sled. It was these dogs, many of which stood 33 inches at the withers, which formed the basic stock of the Russian mixed breeds. These dogs were noted for their great size, strength, and long coupling. Although they were not originally bred as a form of human transportation, these hunting-draft dogs formed the basis of the official Soviet sled dog.

Similar to the true sled dogs in size and conformation is the Samoyed sled dog, which indeed may have a Chukchi sled dog heritage resulting from a Chukchi migration almost three hundred years ago from the Kolyma region to the Taymyr tundra of the Nganasan-Samoyeds. This 22-inch combined sled dog/herding dog is to be distinguished from the probably older Samoyed herding dog, the short-haired Loparskiy dog or Finnehund, which stands only 18 inches tall and is maintained as a pure breed by the same Samoyed owners who still breed the true Samoyed recognized by the American Kennel Club.

In contrast to these sled dogs, the pure hunting dogs and combined herding-hunting dogs of the Altaic tribes that had pushed north to the Arctic by the time the Russian pioneers had penetrated Siberia were very small spitzlike dogs. These shared the fate of many of the purebred sled dogs in the Russian settlements when they were crossed with Russian mixed breeds and with southern hunting dogs from European Russia. The resulting mongrels occasioned a comedy of misinterpretations culminating finally in a conclusion that these small mixed hunting dogs formed the origin of the dog recognized by the AKC as the Siberian Husky.

CLIMATIC INFLUENCE

Regardless of the various barriers obscuring the genealogy of today's Siberian Husky, there is nevertheless sufficient data available to make it appear more than probable that this breed descends directly from the ancient Chukchi sled dog. And to appreciate the evolution of this remarkable breed, it is necessary to have a basic understanding of the forces, both climatic and political, that were involved.

It is also necessary to have some notion of the depth of arctic time. Although in the popular mode of thinking, arctic culture is only as old or slightly older than its first European explorers, this is far from factual. Recent excavations and scholarship have not only shown that man has inhabited arctic environments for at least half a million years, but have further ascertained that the Arctic has not always been as bleak an environment as it is today. In fact, while glaciers ground south as far as Kentucky and Antarctic-type blizzards swept much of the United States, an oasis remained in the Far North. The Russian Arctic in Siberia, which is the size of all North America, remained 80 percent unglaciated and provided what was probably one of the richest hunting grounds anywhere in the world, hunting grounds which were inhabited by the mutual ancestors of the Chukchi and the Eskimos.

This primal garden, known as Beringia, was a low flat plain stretching a thousand miles north to south and connecting Asia and America. It extended far out into what is now the Arctic and northern Pacific oceans and was an immense grazing ground for the Siberian mammoth and American mastodon who browsed on the lush arctic willows, immune to all attack except by man and the giant dire wolf.

Ten thousand years ago, melting ice masses caused the oceans to rise hundreds of feet and flood all except the Beringian uplands, which now remain as Alaska and the Chukchi Peninsula. But it was not until three thousand years ago that the present cold period set in, necessitating a sled dog culture as we know it. Any varieties of sled dogs that developed along the shores of Beringia in the Arctic and Pacific oceans during the Ice Age more than ten thousand years ago probably differed substantially from those that evolved during the warmer period which reached its height from 6500–2200 B.C. And these postglacial sled dogs, who probably doubled as hunting dogs, in turn undoubtedly differed greatly from the modern Chukchi sled dog that developed in response to the changed hunting conditions of the cold climate that followed.

Hunting conditions on land have probably remained substantially unchanged in the Soviet Arctic for the past twenty thousand years. On the other hand, hunting conditions in the seas along the Chukchi Peninsula have changed drastically, since the length of the ice-free season determines the migration patterns of all the animals inhabiting Arctic waters. As the present cold period set in about 1000 B.C., it was hardest on the Chukchi for they inhabited the western side of the Bering Strait, the side always poorer in food supplies because the upwelling of water toward the Alaskan coast helped maintain a rich diet for the Alaskan sea mammals even in the coldest years. Furthermore, the growing ice shelves not only put the walrus and other rookeries out of reach of the shore-bound arctic Chukchi, it also caused a mass shift of the rookeries to the Aleutians, which had no buildup of shelf ice. As so often happens in ecological crises, the process of deterioration fed on itself and the final consumer in the food chain, the Chukchi themselves, were hurt worst of all.

In response to these harsh conditions, the Eskimos on the east of the Bering Strait developed the kayak and harpoon toggle and took to the open sea to hunt a brand-new source of food, the humpback whale. Meanwhile, in the west, the Chukchi developed a culture based on a long-distance sled dog. Because a series of wars with the Eskimos over the control of

Seppala at the finish of a Laconia race. Mrs. Elizabeth Ricker (Nansen) is pictured on the runners.

Millie Turner, Lillian Bowles, Lorna Taylor (Demidoff) and Clara Read.

the Bering Strait gradually pushed the Chukchi back to poorer and poorer hunting grounds, they were forced to develop this far-ranging, low-energy-consuming breed of dog to its highest perfection in order to survive. They could not become nomadic land hunters, as some non-dog-breeding arctic tribes may have done, because the life of the nomad is totally incompatible with the breeding of sled dogs, and, by this point, the sled dog had become sufficiently entrenched in the Chukchi life-style and religion to make the tribe unwilling to give it up. In fact, the need now to store food for even longer periods of time to feed their dogs further consolidated the Chukchi in their permanent villages along the Arctic coast.

This refusal to give up a tool once it had proved useful is part of a phenomenon called "arctic lag," a peculiar characteristic of arctic cultures. New tools or animal species become permanent innovations only rarely, and once a tool, like a sled dog, is established, it tends to survive unchanged for thousands of years until a major outside force, such as a change of climate, intrudes.

The beginnings of the modern Chukchi sled dog can thus be traced back three thousand years to the beginnings of the uniquely harsh hunting conditions and climate where the Chukchi had always lived. Their sled dogs allowed them to cover the enormous distances necessary over the ice pack in order to hunt the sea mammals upon which their survival depended. To say that for this purpose they consciously evolved a pure breed of dog, in the modern sense, is of course ridiculous. However, the uniquely severe conditions no doubt hastened the process of natural selection and caused the breed to rapidly evolve to its highest perfection, a hunting tool which Soviet archeologists compare to the simultaneous invention by the Eskimos of the kayak and the harpoon toggle. And, like other forms of adaptation to the delicate balance of arctic life, the Chukchi dog remained relatively unchanged for thousands of years until some of the last purebred descendants were imported to America less than a century ago.

POLITICAL PRESSURES

The purity of the Chukchi sled dog in Siberia up until the time of the modern exports to Alaska resulted directly from the Chukchi's unique success in maintaining political and cultural independence in the face of almost constant harassment by European invaders. Alone among all the native Siberian peoples, the Chukchi survived three hundred years of alternating Russian policies of warfare and friendship.

The policies of warfare were designed to destroy and entirely eliminate the Chukchi, but their effect was merely to strengthen Chukchi society and to improve the quality of the Chukchi sled dog by placing additional demands on it as a means of achieving superior mobility in extended guerilla campaigns. The more successful policies of "friendship" were designed to assimilate the Chukchi, and their ultimate effect, particularly under the Soviets during the past half century, was to raise the Chukchi standard of living and thus destroy both their traditional independence and the harsh laws of natural selection that had originally produced and maintained the Chukchi sled dog.

Because of Russia's desire to annex Siberia in order to monopolize the fur trade in that region and get an edge on the other European powers in the conquest of Japan and America, a long series of wars ensued throughout the 1700s between the Russians and the native tribes. These wars eventually resulted in the complete subjugation of all but the Chukchi. The causes of the Chukchi victory against Tsarist Russia have long been debated in both prerevolutionary and Soviet literature, since it represents the first successful liberation war in modern times against colonial oppressors.

This victory, or more accurately this standoff, was nevertheless at incredible expense to the Chukchi. In the year 1731, the rest of the Siberian tribes having been fairly well subjugated, the Russian Nizhnegorod led an expedition of 230 Russians and 200 Koryak and Yukagir hirelings against the Chukchi who lived in the small villages along the Anadyr River and Pacific coast. Their mission was to kill all the Chukchi they could find. When 700 Chukchi finally made a stand on May 9, 450 Chukchi men were killed and 150 women and children taken prisoner. Only two Russians were killed. A month later, on June 29, the entire Chukchi nation of 10,000 men, women and children assembled to mount an attack on the Russian invaders. The results were 300 Chukchi dead and not a single Russian casualty. This was the all-time low point of the Chukchi fortunes.

Although the Chukchi were always defeated in pitched battle, these defeats merely increased their unique determination to risk their physical survival as a people in order to maintain their independence and politico-cultural integrity. They succeeded in constantly harassing the Russians in guerilla skirmishes, because both their dog teams and reindeer cavalry could easily outdistance their Russian pursuers. When pressed, the dog-breeding Chukchi would simply move the population of an entire village out over the ice to hunt seal until the Russians had gone. One village of Arctic coast Chukchi was officially destroyed when its inhabitants abandoned their winter dog food stores of frozen walrus and disappeared out over the arctic pack ice. Six months later, just before ice breakup, the entire village returned in better shape than before.

Finally, after repeated efforts to harass and punish the Chukchi into submission had failed, the Russian Senate in Moscow on February 3, 1742, declared a policy of all-out and systematic genocide against the Chukchi nation. For this purpose, the best Cossack fighters were assembled from all over Siberia. All Chukchi men were to be killed and the women and children captured and distributed throughout the Yakutsk Province around various Russian strongholds where it was believed they would forget their independence and become Christians. Accordingly, the Russian commander Pavlutskiy embarked with four hundred of the best fighters in Siberia on February 4, 1744, but succeeded only in chasing the Chukchi out into the Bering Straits where they loaded their dog teams into skin boats and disappeared, probably to their trading partners, the Alaskan Eskimos. When Pavlutskiy tried again on June 25, after the ice had broken up, the Chukchi waited on shore until he approached and then paddled safely back and forth just out of gunshot range.

The next winter, Pavlutskiy did manage to surprise the Chukchi villages of the Chuan River region on the Arctic coast and killed all the men. He failed, however, to take any women or children captive, as required by the decree of the Russian Senate, because the Chukchi women killed their most prized possessions, their dogs, then their children, and then all committed suicide, thereby gaining a high place in the Chukchi heaven.

Finally, on March 14, 1747, rather like the American General George Armstrong Custer, Pavlutskiy tried to save his waning military reputation by charging into what proved to be a cleverly concealed Chukchi trap. Until this point the Chukchi, armed only with spears, had stood little chance against the well-armed Cossacks. On this occasion, however, by luring Pavlutskiy and his men up a narrow ravine, the Chukchi warriors managed to totally overwhelm the Russian force before the Russians had time to reload. Pavlutskiy and his senior officers were killed and the remainder of his force survived only by retreating to a makeshift fortress of dog sleds. During the battle the Chukchi managed to capture sixteen guns and some sympathetic Russian serfs to give instruction on their use.

This Battle of the Orlovoy, which took place next to the mouth of the Orlovoy River near Fort Anadyrskiy (below modern-day Markovo), marked the real end of the war against the Chukchi. Although both the Chukchi and the Russians mounted occasional attacks against each other, each confrontation merely demonstrated that the Chukchi were rapidly mastering the art of modern warfare.

Accordingly, the Russians switched their policies and decided that the most effective weapon against the Chukchis would be simply to stay out of their way until they would seek peaceful trading relations of their own accord. The switch paid off. The elimination of the threat to their integrity as a people caused the rapid dissolution of the by then Spartanlike and highly unified government of the Chukchi and resulted, finally, on February 1, 1792, in a request by the peaceful reindeer Chukchi for the reestablishment of Russian trading posts within the Chukchi domain.

Although the Russian government formally annexed all of the Chukchi Peninsula in 1789, the Russians never again tried to impose direct control over the Chukchi people, and in 1837 a treaty was signed that guaranteed the Chukchi complete political independence within the Russian Empire. It furthermore exempted the Chukchi from taxation and forbade Russians from living in the Chukchi region. In return, the Chukchi agreed to give a nominal tribute to the Russian government in recognition of exclusive Russian (as distinct from any other European) sovereignty over their land.

THE LAST OF THE PUREBREDS

The political autonomy afforded by this treaty allowed the Chukchi complete cultural independence. Thus, for three hundred years the Chukchi, and to a certain extent the Samoyedic tribes, remained completely out of the reach of European influence. Throughout the eighteenth century, the Chukchi, Koryaks, and what was left of the Itelmen on the Kamchatka Peninsula hunted exactly as they always had. In this endeavor, they remained completely in the Stone Age, subject to the same harsh laws of natural selection that had formed their own society and maintained the genetic superiority of their dogs for three thousand years. As a result of the military standoff and the 1837 treaty, according to modern Soviet historians, Chukchi culture and social life, including the use and preservation of their sled dogs, remained completely unchanged from the seventeenth at least up until the middle of the nineteenth century.

This isolation also insured the preservation of the very distinct type of sled dog developed by the Chukchi. Size, for instance, was no object among the Chukchi breeders. In fact, bred to pull light loads at moderate speeds over incredible distances on relatively little food, these dogs were the smallest of all the native sled dogs. Consequently, because they lacked either the sprinting capacity or heavy freighting ability of one or another of the other native breeds, they were considered the poorest of all such breeds by the majority of Russian observers. This was largely because, unlike many of the other tribes who prided themselves on their small teams of powerful dogs, the Chukchi minimized the load per dog by using large teams. Of course, the other tribes' dogs were not well trained enough to work effectively in teams of more than six to eight dogs. In contrast, one observer noted that the Chukchi "going on a long journey borrow from their friends and relatives as many dogs as they can, and thus have teams of from sixteen to eighteen dogs. Even double teams of more than twenty dogs are used."

Even though these dogs were generally considered the poorest by Russian commentators, their superiority to all other breeds in distances exceeding one hundred miles was readily acknowledged. Some of the best Chukchi dogs were those of the dog-breeding Chukchi along the Arctic coast that made the run at the end of winter from the annual Anuy Fair near the Kolyma River to beat the oceangoing fur traders to Alaska before ice breakup. These dogs were sometimes known as Kolyma dogs, but should be distinguished from the larger, rangier sled dogs bred by the

Russians in the Kolyma Valley. The Kolyma-Chukchi dogs excelled in distance races.

The most famous race was a challenge match in 1869 between the fastest Russian sled dog team, owned by a Russian officer, Anatovskiy, and a team assembled by a native from the fastest Chukchi dogs. A local merchant, Baramagin, paid the native to assemble the team and train it for a year just for this race. Starting at the Anuy marketplace, the Chukchi team covered the 150 miles to Nizhne-Kolymsk on a good surface in fifteen hours, arriving one hour ahead of the best Russian team in all Siberia. These times, according to one commentator, Bogoraz, were the fastest "that Siberian dogs have been known to exhibit over long distances."

Unfortunately, because few of the early Russian observers were permitted in the territory of the dog-breeding Chukchi or took particular interest in these dogs, we have few descriptions. An exploration party, however, did measure ten male dogs from the Chukotsk Peninsula in 1930. These averaged 22 inches at the withers but ranged from 20 to 24 inches. They were short coupled, averaging only 23.1 inches, as compared to 27 inches required for the "standard" sled dog. Also there is one description of the Kolyma-Chukchi dog from the Arctic coast near Alaska in 1902 as having "relatively short and thick legs, an exceptionally deep and well-developed chest, and short, thick hair." The wolflike appearance, like that of all arctic breeds, was also noted. Far too much has been made, however, of the wolf heritage. Although the Chukchi reportedly crossbred their dogs with wolves, both accidently and experimentally, the resulting pups generally lacked the obedience qualities of their purebreds.

Although it would be ridiculous to assume the Chukchi breeding program resulted from any concept of linebreeding, the customs of the dog-breeding Chukchi nevertheless effected a breeding program that would be hard to match today. During the summer months all the dogs were allowed to run free, hunting their own food and returning sleek and fat at the sign of first snow. During the rest of the year, which included the heat seasons of the bitches, all the dogs, except the lead dogs and other obedient dogs that had been taught not to steal food, were tied up. The well-trained dogs were tied up only for a couple of days before a long trip in order to conserve energy. Any new dogs acquired by a village required at least two or three days before they were accepted by the pack and had to be watched carefully for their safety. This assured a certain kind of linebreeding and inbreeding since the free-running lead dogs controlled the breeding of the bitches.

During periods of famine many dogs died, although observers noted that, at least in the Anadyr Region, those that died were usually killed by the natives to prevent them from suffering during the last weeks of starvation. And it is probable that the natives would not kill their best dogs since they were always careful to maintain their best for breeding stock. In fact, so high a premium was placed on these dogs that, according to one report, in 1822 when famine and the accompanying distemper threatened to destroy the entire pack of the westernmost Arctic Coastal Chukchi, a Chukchi woman managed to keep the line from dying out by nursing two pups at her own breast.

The bitches were selected by the simple method of killing all but the most promising at birth or as young pups, those that the women, who were largely in charge of such matters, wanted to keep for breeding. The males were selected only after several months in harness. At the age of one year, or after the first winter in harness, whichever came first, all males were gelded to keep fat on them and make them more tractable as team dogs. The leaders and particularly strong dogs, however, were left ungelded to be used for breeding. The majority of these dogs usually belonged to the village leader who could afford to maintain dogs primarily for breeding.

Among the Samoyed peoples, the bitches were tied up when in heat and excused from work in order to prevent indiscriminate breeding. This was unnecessary among the Chukchi because the bitches were tied up during their heat anyway, and the only ungelded dogs having access to them were the ones selected precisely for breeding. Bitches in whelp were never permitted to work on a team. This "downtime" of the bitches was, in fact, one of the principal reasons why the Chukchi preferred to keep a ratio of only one bitch to every seven males.

The American sled dog expert, Olaf Swenson, noted from his years of observation in the Chukchi region that the best dogs were not produced by conscious selective breeding, but resulted from selection among many pups based entirely upon performance. Nevertheless the practices of the traditional Chukchi villages produced a "dog-breeding ecology" that probably could not be surpassed or even equaled in the best modern dog-breeding circles. And, contrary to early Russian observations, the perpetuation of these pure native breeds was in no way threatened by the mere presence of outside dogs in the Russian villages visited by the Chukchi teams.

The introduction of outside dogs, in fact, was common along the trade route from Gizhaga north from Kamchatka five hundred miles to Markovo in the heart of the Anadyr District for more than a century before Russian observers noted a distinct breed of dog being bred by the dog-breeding Chukchi who visited this trade center. One of the most common of these outside dogs was a collielike dog with a long shaggy coat. This dog resulted from crossing the original large dog of the Itelman with smaller dogs imported by the Russians. A group of these dogs were, in fact, imported to run in the All Alaska Sweepstakes, and one of them, Russky, actually served as one of Seppala's best lead dogs. These collielike dogs were bobtailed, were very probably neutered before export and, at any rate, according to Seppala, were never used for breeding.

Today it would probably be impossible to find a purebred Chukchi sled dog anywhere in Siberia. The last of these dogs succumbed to the ravages of collectivization during the 1920s on the Pacific coast and during the 1930s along the Arctic coast. In order more readily to synthesize the native tribes by breaking down old tribal hierarchies, the Soviets managed to either starve or kill the village leaders, known as *kulaks*, since these men were always the richest in the villages. What the authorities, who were simultaneously perplexed by the grave decline in the quality of local dogs, failed to realize was that these kulaks were wealthy primarily because they kept and saw to the breeding of the best dogs in the villages, thus ensuring successful hunting.

Witnessing the decline of the native breeds, the Soviet administration, on the recommendation of various fact-finding missions into the territory, launched a large-scale program of collectivized breeding based on the standard of the "Leningrad factory breed." The final blow was the establishment, in 1935, of a political indoctrination center on the Arctic coast at Chaun with traveling teams of political activists and a "nursery for the breeding of pedigreed dogs." By the late 1930s all major Chukchi villages had permanent Russian residents to oversee the implementation of Soviet modernization programs.

THE LAST EXPORTATION TO AMERICA

These programs, however, probably did not seriously affect the last holdouts among the Chukchi villages until almost one hundred years after the Treaty of 1837 had recognized the Chukchi lands as a semiautonomous country within the Russian Empire. This is significant because the fourth and last group of purebred Chukchi sled dogs exported to America were selected in 1929 from the Chukchi villages near the North Cape on the Arctic Coast of Siberia to form the personal team of Arctic trader, Olaf Swenson.

Swenson had spent most of his life establishing a legendary reputation as a friend of the Chukchi and as a connoisseur of their purebred sled dogs, and he managed to ship four of the best Arctic Coast Chukchi dogs in the summer of 1930 directly to the East Coast of America. The most famous of these dogs, Kreevanka and Tserko, started their contributions to modern AKC Siberian Husky pedigrees, first at Mrs. Elizabeth Ricker's Poland Spring Kennels in Maine and later at Harry Wheeler's Grey Rocks Inn at St. Jovite, thirty miles north of Montreal. The others, Laika's Bilka and Volchok, went to Mrs. Ricker and were interbred with the Siberians that Leonhard Seppala had brought south with him from Alaska.

Swenson had spent a quarter of a century working especially with the Chukchi because he said he had developed a special fondness for them as a people. He was the last contact of the Chukchi with the outside world, because he had obtained an exclusive five-year contract with the Soviet government in 1926 to bring supplies into Siberia and take out furs collected

Lorna Taylor with Burka of Seppala and Sapsuk of Seppala, 1938.

Champions Belka, Panda, Kira—pictured in 1947.

by the Soviet government from the natives. Swenson knew sled dogs as well as, if not better than, anyone in the Arctic at the time, and he had no use at all for mixed breeds.

After his ship became locked in the ice near Cape North in the center of the Arctic Coast Chukchi area in October 1929, Swenson achieved fame by escaping overland 4500 miles to the Trans-Siberian railroad at Irkutsk just north of Mongolia. He set out on his trip with a Chukchi dog team which was returned to his ice-bound ship from the Kolyma River and then picked up the following spring for export to New England.

Although Swenson paid no attention to the markings of his dogs, he was a master in judging both conformation and behavioral characteristics, or "attitude." He commented that, "I have paid as high as $150 each for good dogs and found them hard to find, whereas I could have bought all the ordinary animals I wanted for $10 apiece." He spoke of the innate dignity of a good Chukchi working dog and of the close personal and lifelong relationship between these dogs and their master, contrasting it with the cruel treatment of dogs suffered in most other tribes.

The key to the close personal relationship observed by Swenson between the Chukchi dogs and their master no doubt is the role of the dog in the Chukchi religion. Swenson corroborates earlier observations that the Chukchi had a highly sophisticated and monotheistic religion, and he emphasizes the central importance of a divine man who was perfect and ascended to heaven in order to give the Chukchi good hunting and a good death. This religion required strict moral behavior and was so strongly adhered to that during the first two centuries of Christian missionary efforts not a single Chukchi was converted. The Chukchi believed that the gates of heaven were guarded by their Chukchi dogs, and that any Chukchi who mistreated a dog would never get past this dog on the way to heaven.

The Chukchi dogs, unlike those of almost all other arctic tribes, often slept in the snow houses as cushions for the Chukchi children at night. No doubt the older women, who were so influential in picking the puppy bitches to carry on the breed, placed importance on good personality in their dogs so they would be well suited to harmonious communal living. The affection of the bitches, together with the qualities of obedience and intelligence that determined which male dogs would be used for breeding, combined to produce the personality traits for which the AKC Siberian Husky is still well-known.

Swenson devotes an entire chapter in his book, *Northwest of the World: Forty Years Trading and Hunting in Northern Siberia,* to one dog, and the story of his efforts over a period of two years to buy this dog, named Bilkov (Snowball), at almost any price. After he finally gave up, the dog's master one day gave him Bilkov as a present and was insulted when Swenson wanted to pay for him. Such was the inherent dignity of the Chukchi. And of their dogs, he wrote:

38

A working dog in Siberia has none of the insipid, fawning tricks of the pet house dog. He has a dignity which is frequently unapproachable, and Bilkov had this to a high degree. . . . When I started out to work with the dog . . . for six months he was the worst dog I had ever known. He simply refused to accept me as his boss and constantly took matters in his own hands. Finally, however, he gave up the struggle and from then on until the day he died several years later he was the best dog I had ever seen in any man's team. When we were on the trail, with Bilkov leading, there was never any trouble. I could put into the team the most stubborn fool cur in the world, the kind of dog who will tangle the whole team by refusing to follow the leader, but when the leader was Bilkov, he had only to take command, go to the right or to the left, and every dog in the team would follow him, so that they acted and looked like one unit.

Further on Swenson states:

It is absolutely impossible to place a price on a good dog, especially if he is a leader. Buying one is almost like buying a human being who is going to undertake a joint venture with you. You know that before your trip is over the dog may have saved your life by his intelligence, instinct and courage. It is he and his team who will often lead you through a snowstorm when every guide which you have has failed. Many a time when I have been on the trail, fighting my way back to camp through blinding, driving snow, I have turned the job completely over to the dogs; they could smell the way back to camp, pick up an old trail which even a native would be unable to find, and bring me safely in. Sometimes, when you are traveling on ice and the sled breaks through, a good leader who minds instantly and accurately, will get you out without difficulty, whereas a poor one will simply increase your hazard and, likely as not, send you to your death. This is the kind of dependability on which it is impossible to place any market value. You try to find the animals you want, that you can believe in and depend upon, and once you have found them, you buy them (if you can) for whatever price you can arrange.

We are fortunate that the last of the purebred Chukchi dogs exported as foundation stock for the present day Siberian Husky were selected by a man who both knew and appreciated them and could obtain the best.

Dog Sled showing driver's stand.

This interesting 1929 photo shows the legendary Arthur Tredwell Walden with a coy "Short" Seeley smiling in the sled.

Seppala Siberians at St. Jovite, 1932; driver, Harry Wheeler.

40

3

The Early Siberian in New England

IRONICALLY, ACTIVITIES THAT IN ONE PART OF the world constitute a grueling way of life, can—in another part and under different circumstances—become a matter of pleasure and sport. Such became the case when, in 1922, the Brown Paper Company of Berlin, New Hampshire, sponsored a three-day, point-to-point sled dog race covering 123 miles. The winner of this first International Race was Arthur Walden of Wonalancet, New Hampshire, driving a single hitch of nine dogs with his famous dog Chinook on lead.

Walden had become interested in sled dogs while prospecting in Alaska and had returned to Wonalancet Farm (which his wife ran as an inn) determined to establish a line of sled dogs based upon Chinook, his large yellow mixed-breed dog. Chinook was bred to a number of bitches, including a large German Shepherd named Erica. From these breedings, puppies that resembled Chinook were kept and bred until Walden virtually established a line of large, yellowish, lop-eared dogs that bred true to type. These dogs, which he called "Chinooks," became something of a tourist attraction at Wonalancet Farm, and visitors would come for the opportunity of riding behind a real dog team. Indeed, the team was so superbly trained, legend has it that one of Walden's favorite tricks was to send Chinook, his teammates, and a driverless sled out into an open field across from Wonalancet Farm and put them through their paces by issuing "Gee" and "Haw" commands by megaphone from the porch of his home. This expertise with dogs undoubtedly was the factor in his win of the First International Race, and was later (in 1928) to earn Walden appointment as head driver on the first Byrd Antarctic Expedition.

THE NEW ENGLAND SLED DOG CLUB

This first race sparked so much enthusiasm that, largely through the efforts of Walden himself, the New England Sled Dog Club was formed in 1924 and began sponsoring its own races in the winter of 1925. Its other organizers included Fred Lovejoy, a Boston businessman; Walter Channing, a well-known real estate man, also from Boston; Moseley Taylor, whose family owned (and still does) *The Boston Globe*; and Milton Seeley, about whom more will be said later. Walden was the first president. The vice presidents were Dr. Harry Souther of Boston, Charles DeForest of New Haven, Everett Rutter and Percival Estes of New Hampshire, Styles Oxford of Maine, and Dustin White of Vermont. Claude Calvert of Meredith, New Hampshire, became the club's first secretary-treasurer.

The early New England racing scene was quite different from that of today. In the first place, the races were generally longer. Also, since the roads were generally not plowed, many of the courses could be along the main streets of towns. The crowds were large and the newspaper coverage extensive. The towns where the races were held were eager to play host and even paid the club a nominal amount for the honor of holding the race. The drivers themselves were paid three dollars a day expense money and were, by and large, a tighter-knit group than today. This was in part because they were fewer, normally less than twenty-five, and because, due to more primitive modes of travel, they spent more time together. There were no superhighways, and in winter even a journey of twenty miles was an undertaking. Consequently, most drivers arrived at the course on the day before the race and stayed in guesthouses, tourist homes, or the local hotel; there were no motels. The dogs were often brought in on trucks—not pickups, but large, covered trucks—and bedded down in various barns, the use of which had been prearranged. Every Saturday night the host town would hold a "Mushers' Ball" and crown a "Mushers' Queen"—an honor usually accorded the girl who managed to sell the most buttons, one of the ways in which the towns raised the money to hold the event.

The races themselves were in some ways more exciting for the spectator than those of today. Because there were fewer teams, there was usually a handicap division, which of course gave the race a handicap winner as well as an elapsed-time winner. Each team was given a handicap based upon its previous performance time, calculated so that each team should theoretically finish at the same time. As a result, there were often very exciting finishes and even the slower teams had a chance at a trophy. Emile

St. Goddard, driving his Canadian hounds, was one of the few drivers ever to win both the elapsed time and the handicap races. Since he started last, he had to pass every other team on the course to accomplish this feat.

The early races sponsored by the New England Sled Dog Club were largely dominated by Arthur Walden and his Chinooks. In fact, so handily did he win these races it was felt he just couldn't be beaten. In 1927, however, Leonhard Seppala came to race at Poland Spring, Maine.

After the famous Serum Drive, Seppala had been touring the United States with a team of Siberians, and when it was known that he would be in the area, he was challenged to race against Walden.

The impression that Seppala and his dogs made upon the New England sled dog enthusiasts was not particularly overwhelming. "Siberian rats" they had been originally dubbed in Alaska, and the New Englanders' viewpoint was not much different. In fact, the Siberians appeared so small next to the huge New England sled dogs that some people objected, on humanitarian grounds, to the Siberians being allowed to race at all.

The Siberians' first performance in New England has become something of a legend, no doubt richly embellished with time and telling. But since the legend is by now more accessible than any bare assemblage of facts, we tell it in its entirety.

In the first place, the cards seemed stacked against the Siberian entry from the beginning. For one, while Walden's Chinooks were in excellent racing condition, the little Siberians had been on exhibition and marching in parades, and were soft. Consequently, when Seppala and Walden traveled the ninety miles from Wonalancet Farm to the race site at Poland Spring together, the Chinooks spent the three-day trip considerably outdistancing the Siberians, and word got around that the Siberians were small and slow.

Furthermore, on the day of the race, Seppala, who had brought some forty-odd dogs with him, was informed that he would be allowed to race only seven. He vigorously argued that since his dogs weighed only 50 to 55 pounds, as opposed to the 100-pound dogs that were being used by the majority of drivers, he should be allowed to use at least eleven dogs to equal their pulling power. The judges, however, ruled otherwise.

And things went from bad to worse. On the morning of the race, the noise of the crowd frightened the Siberians at the starting line; when the starter said "Go," they plunged over a stone fence and down a hill behind the line itself. With the clock already running, it was all Seppala could do to get the team back up the hill and over the fence.

Once back on the trail, things went smoothly for about two miles until the team suddenly bolted into the front door of a house they were passing. As it turned out, it was the aroma of frying mutton chops that had overcome the dogs. As the woman who was frying the chops looked up and saw what she believed was a pack of wolves descending upon her,

Leonhard Seppala with Bonzo at Lake Placid, 1932.

Sapsuk of Seppala.

White Water Lake Knight, owned by Ronald Bowles' Calivali Kennels.

she let out a piercing scream and fainted. The chops fell to the floor but were too hot for the dogs to handle and Seppala managed to untangle them and get underway again.

About ten miles out, Seppala overtook a team of Chinooks driven by the Poland Spring Hotel owner's wife, Mrs. Elizabeth Ricker. A few minutes after passing the team, Seppala felt something touching his leg. It proved to be Mrs. Ricker's team without Mrs. Ricker. This put Seppala in a dilemma. Should he stop and untangle her team, and wait for her to catch up and thereby lose the race, or should he continue? As he later put it, he felt "they would likely kill each other and her too" if they were not untangled. The race was not worth such a risk, so Seppala stopped his dogs and left them standing on the trail—an extremely risky act since they might take off at any moment—and went back to straighten out the badly tangled team. Mrs. Ricker came running up and thanked him but said the delay would surely lose him the race. Seppala concurred but was determined to give it his best and got underway again.

As if enough ill fate had not befallen the Siberians, a skunk crossed their trail shortly before the finish line, and the dogs, picking up the scent, began running for all they were worth. Fortunately for Seppala, the skunk hid in an old sled track by the side of the trail and the dogs did not see him as they passed.

The result turned out to be a shocker. For despite the many mishaps, the Siberian team came in first, seven minutes ahead of Walden. The crowd went wild and that night Seppala was interviewed and the dogs photographed.

It also rained that night, and cars cut deep ruts in the road. Then it froze and the trails became icy and rough. These conditions favored Seppala, who knew that with his lighter dogs with their tough feet he would surely win the next day's conclusion of the race. Unfortunately, the other drivers and the judges decided to cancel the remainder of the race in order to save the dogs' feet for the big New England point-to-point race of 133 miles to be run the following month. As it turned out, Seppala won that race as well.

THE SIBERIAN HUSKY CLUB OF AMERICA

As the Siberians continued to dominate the New England racing scene, more and more sled dog enthusiasts began switching from the local large freighting dogs to the Siberians. Not only were they faster, but they were far less inclined to fight, required less food, and were much more attractive.

This attractiveness, however, was relative, for it should not be assumed that these early Siberians possessed the uniformity of structure, coat, and markings they do today. It is true that the Chukchi had spent centuries perfecting these dogs as long-distance, low-energy-consuming sled dogs possessing incredible endurance and a degree of uniformity that was obvious to even the most untrained eye. The goal of the Chukchi breeders, however, had always been function; and where the rudiments of survival are hard come by, aesthetics seldom enter the picture. Even the dogs bred in different regions of the Chukchi domain, although similar, differed somewhat in structure and coat length.

Seppala, although obviously also concerned with function, had already begun breeding with an eye toward greater uniformity. His color preference was light gray, while his wife's was white. Normally it was she who chose the puppies while he did the training; in the years to come, they would prove to be a formidable team, especially when working with Earle Snodie at his Bow Lake Kennels in Washington where some very fine white Siberians were produced.

But at the time the first Siberians were seen in New England, there was quite a variety in the specimens. Some were long and leggy, others shorter coupled and heavier boned; some were marked symmetrically, many were not. The job of modifying this existing breed of moderately attractive, moderately uniform sled dogs into a dual-purpose breed—one that could not only perform its original function in harness, but could also conform to a detailed standard of uniformity that would enable it to compete in the conformation ring on equal footing with breeds that had been specifically bred for the show ring for decades—was a monumental task. The fact that this feat was largely accomplished within a few short years speaks for the energy, know-how, and dedication of the pioneers of the breed.

Not the least of the problems facing these early breeders was the need to create a standard of conformation. After the breed was officially recognized by the American Kennel Club in 1930, the first Standard was published in *The American Kennel Gazette* in April of 1932. It read as follows:

General Appearance—For hundreds of years the Siberian Husky has been used as a sled dog in northeastern Asia. He should be exceptionally active, quick and light on his feet, able to run in harness with a load, at a speed of twenty miles an hour for short distances. He should be strong, courageous and tireless on the trail. He should have a deep strong chest, heavy bone, strong legs and feet, straight powerful back and well-muscled hindquarters. A grown dog should stand about 23 inches at the shoulders and weigh about 60 pounds. A bitch should be smaller and weigh about 10 or 12 pounds less.

Head—The size of the head should be in proportion to the body, but not clumsy or too large. It should be of medium width between the ears. The ears should be erect, set high on the head, medium in size, pointed at the tops and well covered with hair on the inside. It should be of medium length and slightly wedge shaped. The jaws and teeth are very strong, and should be neither overshot nor undershot. The eyes may be either blue or brown, with a keen, friendly, and intelligent expression. Eye rims dark. The nose may be either light brown or black. The muzzle should be strong, the lips dark and firmly fitting together.

Chest and Ribs—Chest should be deep and strong, but not too broad. The ribs should be well arched and deep.

Back, Quarters and Stifles—The loins should be slightly arched and especially well muscled. The stifles should be well let down and very muscular. The back should be straight, not too long, and strongly developed.

Legs—Straight of good length, well muscled and good bone.

Feet—Strong, not too compact, with exceptionally tough pads protected with hair.

Tail—Long, and usually carried over back but sometimes dropped down, especially when tired. Should be well protected with fur and hair, but bushy tails not desirable.

Size and Weight—Dogs, 22 to 23½ inches at shoulder, 54 to 64 pounds; bitches, 21 to 22½ inches, 44 to 54 pounds.

Color—All colors permissible from white to black including many variations of grays and mixed wolf colorings.

Coat—Should be thick with a very soft and warm underfur next to the skin. The guard hairs should not be too long, and should be straight, not too coarse, and fairly close to the body so that the graceful lines of the dogs are not obscured. A bushy or shaggy coat is not desirable.

Scale of Points—Size and general appearance, 25; head and neck, 10; coat and color, 10; chest and ribs, 10; quarters and stifles, 15; back, 10; legs, 10; feet, 5; tail, 5. **Total**—100.

The only odd thing about this Standard is the request for heavy bone, and a weight range heavier than any of the earlier dogs actually were. The only explanation seems to be that although the biggest of these early dogs weighed 55 pounds, and all had quite moderate bone, there was an assumption that a slightly bigger dog might actually perform better. In subsequent years this assumption proved untrue.

Apart from this it should be noted how closely this Standard resembles the one used today. Except for phrasing, various clarifications, and changes in minor details, the only change has been to drop the point scale. The degree to which the basic tenets of this Standard have survived indicates the kind of in-depth study that went into its composition. This Standard and, perhaps even more so, the Standard submitted after the formation of the Siberian Husky Club of America in 1938 were the results of years of intensive study of various breed characteristics found in several generations of Siberians. And although there were some differences of opinion on some details, there was, by and large, a surprising degree of agreement among these early fanciers. When difficulties developed over these details, it was often Seppala himself who was called upon for advice. It was he, for instance, who described the majority of Siberian tails that he had seen as being like a "fox brush" rather than like a plume. Although a variety in coat length and coupling could be observed among the early imports, he stated that his preference, and those he felt to be most typical, were the relatively short-coupled, medium-coated dogs.

The first official meeting of the Siberian Husky Club of America was held at Milton and Eva Seeley's on June 10, 1938. Dean C. F. Jackson served as the club's first president, with Mrs. Samuel Post as vice president and Mrs. Seeley as secretary-treasurer. On the board of standards were Dean and Mrs. Jackson, Mrs. Moseley Taylor, Mr. and Mrs. Seeley, Miss Margaret Dewey, Miss Millie Turner, and Charles Roberts. The advisory committee consisted of Mrs. Kaare Nansen (formerly Mrs. Elizabeth Ricker), Leonhard Seppala, judge Coke Hill, Clarence Grey and Mrs. Birdsall Darling. It was at this meeting that the 1938 Standard was drawn up; it was adopted by the AKC two months later, in August.

FOUNDATION KENNELS OF THE BREED

Insofar as the formation of the Siberian Husky Club of America established a channel of communication among breeders, provided a more comprehensive Standard of conformation, and fostered greater interest in the show ring—an interest not easily fostered among many of the early dyed-in-the-wool dog drivers—1938 represents a milestone in the history of the breed. However, much of the work toward greater standardization had already taken place in the decade prior to the founding of the club.

The absence of records, and the vagueness of memory, make it impossible to acknowledge everyone who, in one way or another, contributed to the development of the breed during these formative years. Immunization was not developed to the extent it is today, with the result that many good dogs died young. This and other quirks of fate caused some of the early lines to die out completely and explains why some top-quality dogs of the time have had little influence on the breed except as a treasured memory in the minds of some old-timers.

NORTHERN LIGHT

Such was the case, for instance, with the line of the predominantly white Siberians bred by Julian Hurley of Alaska. Hurley, a lawyer and judge, purchased his first dogs from Frank Dufresne, onetime head of the Alaskan Game Commission, and an avid racing enthusiast. Many of these dogs were imported to Michigan and New England. Most of them were white, and one—Northern Light Kobuck—in September 1932 became the first Siberian Husky AKC champion of record. Kobuck, whelped in 1928, was owned by Oliver R. Shattuck of Alton, N.H., who, along with Hurley, registered many of the first Siberians.

The first Siberian Husky to be registered by the American Kennel Club was listed in the December 1930 Stud Register as follows: Fairbanks Princess Chena, 758,529—by Bingo II ex Alaska Princess (by Jack Frost ex Snowflake). Jack Frost by Scotty ex Vasta. Bingo II by Bingo ex Topsy. Owner—Mrs. Elsie K. Reeser. Breeder—Julien A. Hurley, Fairbanks, Alaska. Whelped 9/16/27. White. Then in the January 1931 Stud Register, twenty-one Siberians bearing the Northern Light prefix were listed, all bred by Mr. Hurley. Unfortunately, the Northern Light strains have all but disappeared.

But some strains of this pioneer period have left their impact. In turning to them now, we first note that two of them take on such importance that we have chosen to tell the story of the Chinook Kennels of Milton and Short Seeley, and of the Monadnock Kennels of Lorna Demidoff, in a chapter to themselves. It follows this chapter.

ELIZABETH RICKER AND THE SEPPALA SIBERIAN KENNELS

The meeting of Leonhard Seppala and Elizabeth Ricker, the Poland Spring Hotel owner's wife, on the trail of that first New England race which Seppala entered was a fortuitous one in terms of the breed's subsequent history. So impressed was Mrs. Ricker with the performance of these little dogs that she immediately sold her entire stock of crossbred sled dogs and bought all forty-odd Siberians that Seppala had brought with him. Although many of these dogs were neutered, as was the custom with the majority of sled dogs, her breeding program was extensive, and at times there were over 160 dogs, including puppies, at her kennel.

Although she remained an active breeder only a relatively short time, from 1926 to 1932, Elizabeth Ricker's contribution to the breed was an extremely significant one. Among the outstanding dogs bred or housed at this first New England kennel were the famous Togo (presented to Mrs. Ricker by Seppala as a token of his esteem); Kreevanka, Tserko, Volchok and Laika's Bilka, all selected and imported from Siberia by Olaf Swenson, the fur trader; and Bonzo and Tosca, littermates, whelped in July 1925, and imported from Alaska. Bonzo became an outstanding leader, first on Mrs. Ricker's team and later on Harry Wheeler's, and Tosca proved an outstanding brood bitch, producing some of the best of the early specimens, especially when bred to Kreevanka.

Kingeak, a Togo son, was also at this kennel. Another Togo son, Sepp III, was acquired from Mrs. Ricker by Dean Jackson and went on to produce the famous Ch. Shankhassock Lobo, second AKC registered Siberian Husky to attain championship and the dog that for many years

Two early Siberians shown here are the all-white Nurmi and Jean.
Warren Boyer

Elizabeth Ricker (later Nansen) with a group of famous early sled dogs. In the foreground, from left, are Sugruk, Mukluk and Sapsuk II. In the background the dogs are Jean (left) and Sepp I.
Warren Boyer

50

was used to illustrate the breed in the AKC's publication, *The Complete Dog Book.*

In 1932, when Mrs. Ricker—divorced from Ted Ricker—was married to Kaare Nansen, son of the famous polar explorer, her dogs were acquired by Harry Wheeler of St. Jovite, Canada; and from there they influenced the breeding program of almost every New England kennel. Mrs. Ricker's (or Mrs. Nansen's) influence on the breed, however, was not limited to her role as a breeder and driver. She served for many years on the advisory committee of the Siberian Husky Club of America. She is also the author of *Seppala, an Alaskan Dog Driver* and *Togo's Fireside Reflections*, both invaluable to the student of the early days of sled dog driving and racing. Mrs. Nansen died in 1991.

HARRY WHEELER

Harry Wheeler's kennels at the Grey Rocks Inn in St. Jovite was based upon the stock he obtained from Mrs. Ricker as well as upon numerous dogs that came directly from Alaska. Like many of the early breeders, Mr. Wheeler's primary concern was racing, but he did provide influential stock to many of the early New England kennels. To Mrs. Frothingham's Cold River Kennels went several dogs including Ch. Vanka of Seppala II, an offspring of Kreevanka and Tosca and an outstanding stud. William Shearer's Foxstand Kennels was also based upon Wheeler stock.

In the late 1940s, when the responsibilities of managing his Grey Rocks Inn became too time-consuming, Wheeler sold his dogs to Don McFaul of Maniwaki, Quebec, who thus established his Gatineau Kennels which continued to exert an influence on the breed until the early 1960s.

Wheeler, like Seppala and Ricker before him, often used the suffix "of Seppala" when naming his dogs. Renowned for their racing ability, Wheeler dogs were highly prized by many early fanciers of the breed, and today some people still speak of the "pure Seppala strain" that emanated from this kennel. In all fairness, however, it should be pointed out that, given the fact that almost all the early stock came directly from Seppala or related breeding, the dogs coming from this kennel were no more "pure Seppala" than those from most other foundation kennels, the only difference being that Wheeler perpetuated the name longer.

MRS. MARIE LEE FROTHINGHAM AND THE COLD RIVER KENNELS

Established in 1936 by Mrs. Marie Lee Frothingham and her daughter, Marie Turner (now Mrs. M. Turner Remick) in Beverly Farms, Massachusetts, the Cold River Kennel was named after the river that flowed behind their property in Sandwich, New Hampshire.

Although Mrs. Frothingham, known to her friends as "The Duchess," never drove a team, she oversaw the training and masterminded the racing strategy of some of the most successful teams of that era. For many years the Cold River Kennel team number one was driven by Don Shaw, a professional driver, while Cold River Kennel team number two was driven by Millie Turner. While Shaw won the majority of races entered in both the United States and Canada, Miss Turner's team placed consistently, very often being the highest-placing team driven by a woman. For those who think the red, or copper, Siberian is a fairly recent development, it is interesting to note that one of Millie Turner's early dogs, which had been bred by Moseley Taylor, was a red (appropriately named "Red").

After Miss Turner, who is also a well-known animal portraitist, married and moved to Alaska, Mrs. Frothingham hired a number of drivers, the last of whom were Lyle and Marguerite Grant. The Grants trained and drove the Cold River teams from 1949 until 1956, when they acquired the last of Mrs. Frothingham's dogs as the foundation for their own Marlytuk Kennels in Carlisle, Massachusetts.

Although Cold River Kennels was primarily oriented to turning out top racing dogs, some of their dogs were shown by Miss Turner on a limited basis. In 1940, Ch. Vanka of Seppala II, known as "Cossack," completed his championship. He, his full brothers Vanka of Seppala and Burka of Seppala, as well as Sapsuk of Seppala, Ch. Helen of Cold River (an outstanding lead dog), Duchess of Cold River, Valuiki of Cold River, Rola, Bugs, Delzeue of Cold River, Enara of Cold River and a bitch named Sky of Seppala all appear often in pedigrees.

Mrs. Frothingham's many contributions on behalf of the breed included service as president of the Siberian Husky Club of America. She died in September 1969 at the age of 82.

OTHER FOUNDATION KENNELS

Margaret Dewey's Komitik Kennels bred many of the early outstanding dogs. Miss Dewey was a very conscientious student of the breed, and was an active member—and secretary for several years—of the Siberian Husky Club of America. But unfortunately, although it is possible to find the Komitik name far back in some of today's pedigrees, it is rare.

Other kennels that got their start during this period were Roland Bowles's Calivali Kennels, Dr. Roland Lombard's Igloo Pak Kennels and the kennels of Alex Belford in Laconia, New Hampshire. During these formative years, Belford—whose enthusiasm for sled dog racing has been carried on for many years by his son, Dr. Charles Belford—owned one of

Millie Turner Remick with Cold River Kennels' team. L.to r: Juneau, Tongass, Ch. Vanka of Seppala II, Putsa of Seppala and Surgut.

Two very influential Cold River bitches:

			Unknown
		Unknown	
	Kreevanka		Unknown
			Unknown
		Unknown	
Ch. Vanka of Seppala II*			Unknown
			Fritz
		Harry	
	Tosca		Shika
			Putza
		Shika	
			Duska

CH. HELEN OF COLD RIVER (Whelped 11/6/42)
DUCHESS OF COLD RIVER

			Togo
		Kingeak	
	Smokey of Seppala		Rosie
			Nutok
		Pearl	
Sky of Seppala			Czarina
			Unknown
		Wolf	
	Nanna		Unknown
			Unknown
		Nan	
			Unknown

*Brother of Vanka of Seppala and Burka of Seppala.

53

Bill Belletete in Laconia Race. Izok of Gap Mountain, a very influential stud, is at right point.

Ch. Aleka of Monadnock and Chort of Monadnock, owned by J. August Duval.

the most influential dogs in the breed, Belford's Wolf, another dog from Mrs. Ricker's kennel.

Others, not kennel owners per se but who nevertheless owned dogs that made significant contributions to the breed included Walter Channing, who owned a Togo daughter named Toto, and Leonard Chapman, who owned an outstanding gray male out of John "Iron Man" Johnson's kennels in Alaska named Duke.

Somewhat later, in the early 1940s, William Belletete and J. August Duval came upon the scene. Both had worked with sled dogs during the war and both were avid racing enthusiasts. Belletete acquired his dogs primarily from William Shearer, who had acquired them from the army after the war. The most significant of these was Duchess of Cold River out of Mrs. Frothingham's breeding, who, when bred to Ch. Wonalancet's Baldy of Alyeska, produced two outstanding specimens: Kiev of Gap Mountain and Izok of Gap Mountain. Kiev was used to illustrate the Standard for many years and Izok went on to become one of the most influential studs in the breed.

Duval purchased two dogs from Monadnock Kennels, Chort of Monadnock and Aleka of Monadnock, and a mating of these produced one of the most impressive matched teams in the history of the breed, as well as some very important dogs in terms of genetic influence. All named for their dam, this litter consisted of Aleka's Czar, Czarina, Khan, Oka, Ruska and Sonya. Jean Lane (now Jean Bryan) later acquired this team and showed both Aleka of Monadnock and Aleka's Czarina to their championships. When the time came to breed Aleka's Czarina, Izok of Gap Mountain was chosen as a stud, and out of this mating came the famous and highly influential Mulpus Brook's The Roadmaster.

Short Seeley with Ch. Wonalancet's Baldy of Alyeska and Ch. Wonalancet's Disko of Alyeska.

56

4

Chinook and
Monadnock

$\mathbf{A}$LTHOUGH ALL OF THE BREEDERS MENTIONED
in the preceding chapter contributed greatly in furthering the cause of the
Siberian Husky, two of the foundation kennels, whether because of circumstance, or greater dedication or perseverance managed to produce such
consistently outstanding stock that their names have become synonymous
with excellence in the breed. And, indeed, it is extremely difficult today
to find a Siberian Husky whose background cannot be traced back to one
or, in most cases, both of these kennels.

More than any other of the foundation kennels, Chinook and Monadnock remained dedicated to the concept of a dual-purpose Siberian,
one who could win in the show ring as well as on the trail. Too often today
one hears the argument of show dogs versus sled dogs and forgets that not
only did Chinook and Monadnock produce the foundation stock for almost
every show kennel in the country, they also fielded some of the top racing
teams of their day. Indeed, even today when the sport of sled dog racing
has grown so popular, Mrs. Seeley and Mrs. Demidoff—the women behind
these two kennels—are ranked among the top women drivers of all time.
And the teams they drove contained many bench show champions, many
of them outstanding leaders.

CHINOOK KENNELS

When Eva, known to her friends as "Short," and Milton Seeley were married in May of 1924, they elected to spend their honeymoon mountain climbing in New England. There they witnessed their first sled dog team in action, a team of Arthur Walden's Chinooks, and were so impressed, particularly by Chinook himself, that they immediately ordered one of his puppies to become their house pet in their home on the Hudson River near Nyack, New York, where Milton owned a successful chemical business.

And this might have been the extent of the Seeleys' involvement with the world of sled dogs had not Milton, stricken with diabetes in the days before insulin, been advised by his doctors to give up the world of business and move to the mountains. The year of this prescribed early retirement was 1928, the same year Arthur Walden was preparing to accompany the first Byrd Antarctic expedition as head dog driver. Walden needed someone to manage Wonalancet Farms during his absence, and the Seeleys were available. Out of these circumstances developed one of the most impressive careers in the world of sled dogs.

In the winter of 1929, "Short" learned to drive a dog team composed of Chinooks. Having been a physical education teacher, she took to the rigors of the sport naturally, although for years she was the only woman to actively participate. And even though she was small, she was probably foremost among all women drivers in her ability to handle a sled.

It was also in the winter of 1929 that the Seeleys saw their first team of Siberians at a race in Poland Spring and decided to eventually own and breed some of their own. Subsequently they also became involved with Alaskan Malamutes. Today, these two breeds—although not invented by the Seeleys—are acknowledged to have become what they are largely because of the foundation breeding at this kennel.

When Walden returned from the Antarctic he sold his share of the kennel to the Seeleys, who moved it to its present site in Wonalancet and named it Chinook in honor of Walden's great leader, who died in the Antarctic. In the years that followed, the Seeleys were an active force in getting both the Siberian and the Alaskan Malamute recognized by the AKC and in forming the Siberian Husky Club of America.

It was also at Chinook that the dogs were trained for the second and third Byrd expeditions, and that the training of many of the sled dogs used in the Second World War took place. Originally the army planned to use sled dogs to assist the Ski Troops in the reinvasion of Norway. But when this plan was abandoned, the dogs were used in Greenland, Labrador, Alaska, Italy, and to rescue the wounded in the Battle of the Bulge.

The Arctic Search and Rescue Unit, found to be so much more effective than mechanized transport in saving the lives of pilots downed in frozen arctic wastes, and the first Dog Ambulance Corps, assigned to rescue

Milton Seeley with Toska of Wonalancet (right) and her sister
Cherie. Toska was the dam of Ch. Wonalancet's Baldy of Alyeska.

Cheeyak of Alyeska, foundation bitch of the Chinook Kennels.

the wounded of the Third Army from the snow-buried fields of France in 1945, both contained dogs trained at Chinook.

But although Chinook Kennels has been active in every phase of the sled dog world, from training to racing to developing more nutritional food formulas, it was the Seeleys' painstaking care in determining what was ideal in both the Siberian Husky and the Alaskan Malamute, and breeding toward that ideal, that has made the kennel the shrine of these breeds it is today.

In creating their Siberian line, the Seeleys managed, through the help of Mrs. Ricker, to lease Toto, a Togo daughter, from Walter Channing. They then succeeded in getting her approved by the AKC as a trial bitch, this being in the days when the Siberian was first getting recognized. Toto was then bred to Moseley Taylor's Tuck and produced one lone female, Tanta of Alyeska. Tanta was first shown at Manchester, New Hampshire, where, as the only bitch entry, she went Best of Breed over nine males. Tanta was then bred to Leonard Chapman's Duke and produced nine puppies. Two of these, Yukon and Sitka, eventually went to William Shearer's Foxstand Kennels. Seven of the puppies went to Moseley Taylor to form his wife's highly successful matched racing team. Although Mr. Taylor succeeded in talking the Seeleys into selling six outright, the seventh, Cheeak of Alyeska (the Seeleys choice of the litter) was only leased and had to be returned each year to Chinook for breeding.

In 1934 Cheeak was bred to Belford's Wolf, and out of this great combination came many of the first AKC registered Siberian Husky champions. Among these was Ch. Laddy of Wonalancet, who went on to sire some of the first dogs registered with the Igloo Pak kennel name, and Ch. Turu of Wonalancet. Out of the combination of Mrs. Frothingham's Sapsuk of Seppala and Tosca of Alyeska (a littermate of Cheeak of Alyeska) came Toska of Wonalancet who, when bred to Ch. Turu of Wonalancet produced perhaps the first really exceptional specimen of the breed, Ch. Wonalancet's Baldy of Alyeska. Baldy attained his championship in 1941 and shortly thereafter became the first Siberian Husky to win the Working Group (at the North Shore Kennel Club). Baldy was also shown with his brother, Wonalancet's Disko of Alyeska, in brace competition. Together they won several Best Brace in Group awards, and at the Eastern Dog Club Show in Boston went all the way to Best Brace in Show.

Baldy turned out to be not only a great show dog but a great stud as well, siring many outstanding dogs including the famous Izok of Gap Mountain.

From the beginning, the Seeleys were staunch supporters of the Standard and recognized the weaknesses as well as the strength of their dogs. Although Cheeak of Alyeska was an excellent example of the breed, and although she was the shortest coupled of the litter, the Seeleys realized that the tendency of her parents and the rest of her otherwise outstanding litter was toward ranginess. For this reason, after being bred to Belford's

Ch. Wonalancet's Baldy of Alyeska.

					Unknown
				Smoky	
					Unknown
			Belford's Wolf		
					Harry
				Tosca	
					Kolyma
		Ch. Turu of Alyeska			
					Ici
				Duke	
					Wanda
			Cheeak of Alyeska		
					Tuck
				Tanta of Alyeska	
					Toto
CH. WONALANCET'S BALDY OF ALYESKA (Whelped 6/10/40)					
					Unknown
				Tserko	
					Unknown
			Sapsuk of Seppala		
					Bonzo
				Dushka	
					Nanuk
		Toska of Wonalancet			
					Ici
				Duke	
					Wanda
			Tosca of Alyeska		
					Tuck
				Tanta of Alyeska	
					Toto

61

Wolf and producing Turu and Laddy, she was bred to Dean Jackson's Sepp III, a Togo son who, like his father, was quite close coupled. This mating produced Ch. Cheenah of Alyeska who, in 1938, became the first Siberian Husky female to attain her championship. Cheenah was then bred to a male of Harry Wheeler's kennels, a grandson of both Kingeak and Tserko named Wolfe of Seppala. Out of this breeding came Bonzo of Taku who, when bred to Kituh of Taku, a granddaughter of Ch. Wonalancet's Baldy of Alyeska, produced one of the all-time greats of the breed—a black and white, blue-eyed male named Ch. Alyeska's Suggen of Chinook.

For many years Suggen was Mrs. Seeley's personal companion and official greeter of all visitors to Chinook Kennels. For many years, his portrait was the one used to head the Siberian column of the *AKC Gazette*. Not only was Suggen a great show dog and stud, he was an extremely long-lived one, siring litters well into his teens and being bred, at least on one occasion, to his great-great-granddaughter, Ch. Yeso Pac's Aurora. And not to be outdone by his kennelmate, Ch. Wonalancet's Baldy of Alyeska—who could claim among his influential progeny his grandson Mulpus Brook's The Roadmaster, of later Monadnock fame—Suggen was grand-sire of the other mainstay of that illustrious breeding program, Ch. Monadnock's Pando.

Milton Seeley died in 1944, but "Short" continued to remain a dominant force in both Malamutes and Siberians until she died in 1985. She was an active breeder, judge, and Honorary Life President of the Siberian Husky Club of America and remained an ardent and outspoken teacher of newcomers and a vigilant protector of these breeds she all but invented over half a century ago. Honored at a banquet in 1971 on her eightieth birthday, where she received greetings from such people as Richard Nixon and Sherman Adams, she received this salutation from the noted judge, Maxwell Riddle:

"For me you have long been America's First Lady of Dogdom. And surely you rank as the world's first lady of sled dogs."

Few would disagree.

THE CHINOOK MEMORIAL by *Peggy Koehler*

After the death of Short Seeley, James Wall, the gentleman who bought the Chinook Kennel property from Short's estate, conceived the idea of a special monument, a memorial to Milton and Eva B. Seeley. Mr. Wall has a reverence for the past and a keen awareness of the historical significance of his property. After considerable thought, he devised a plan which would permit those devoted to the arctic breeds and to sled dog racing to visit the "shrine of these breeds" and still allow him to maintain his privacy. A raised terrace was to be built between the stone wall and the road (formerly a parking area) on which would be set the original and

One of the first outstanding black and white Siberians and a highly influential stud:

                                                    Kingeak
                                    Smokey of Seppala
                                                    Pearl
                        Wolfe of Seppala
                                                    Tserko
                                    Sigrid of Seppala
                                                    Dushka
            Bonzo of Taku
                                                    Togo
                                    Sepp III
                                                    Unknown
                        Ch. Cheenah of Alyeska
                                                    Duke
                                    Tosca of Alyeska
                                                    Tanta of Alyeska

CH. ALYESKA'S SUGGEN OF CHINOOK   (Whelped 6/2/49)

                                                    Ch. Turu of Alyeska
                                    Ch. Wonalancet's Baldy of Alyeska
                                                    Toska of Wonalancet
                        King Husky of Wonalancet
                                                    Belford's Wolf
                                    Tcheeakio of Alyeska
                                                    Cheeak of Alyeska
            Kituh of Taku
                                                    Ch. Laddy of Wonalancet
                                    Igloo Pak Chuckchee
                                                    Tchuchis of Wonalancet
                        Igloo Pak's Kresta
                                                    Ch. Laddy of Wonalancet
                                    Igloo Pak Vixen
                                                    Tchuchis of Wonalancet

Short Seeley with leader Woska followed by (r. to l.) Ch. Turu of Alyeska, Ch. Wonalancet's Disko of Alyeska, Tosca of Wonalancet and Laddy of Wonalancet.

63

restored Chinook Kennel signs, a flagpole, and the Admiral Byrd stone with the bronze plaque dedicated to "All noble dogs . . ." which Mr. Wall was willing to move from the center of his property.

In the meantime Nancy Cowan had been petitioning the State of New Hampshire Department of Historical Resources to place an official State Historical Marker at the roadside of Chinook Kennels. When word came down that this could be accomplished in 1988, it made one more item to place on the terrace. Jim and Nancy also felt that a granite monument inscribed with the number one sled motif would be the final jewel in the crown. But from where was the money to pay for all this going to come? Peggy Koehler volunteered to be the fund-raiser, and through the very generous support of breed, kennel and racing clubs and friends and admirers from all across the country, the goal was accomplished.

The date for the dedication ceremony *had to be* October 8, 1988, because this was the exact date that Admiral Byrd had dedicated *his stone* fifty years before. Much work had to be done to clean up the property from the devastation caused by the Hurricane of 1988. For the occasion there was gently falling snow, which everyone was sure Short Seeley had ordered as "special effects." Nearly 150 people braved the cold and sat under the tent at roadside to hear the many tributes to the Seeleys and Chinook Kennels.

Former Governor Melrim Thomson spoke fondly of Short's "terroristic activities" in Republican politics and said that she had always reminded him of a pie . . . crusty on the outside, but inside filled with all the sweetness and goodness in the world. Nancy Cowan introduced many of the veterans of the Byrd Antarctic expeditions, men who had spent months at Chinook Kennels learning how to drive dog teams or teaching others this fine art. Dick Moulton, himself a BAE veteran, spoke of Milton Seeley as "the finest man ever to walk the face of the earth."

Then Mr. Moulton called upon Carol Williams and Taku to help him dedicate the monument. Taku was an eleven-year-old Alaskan Malamute bitch, coowned by Carol and Eva B. Seeley, from the last litter ever bred at Chinook Kennels. A line from her harness had been attached to the drape over the monument, and when Carol gave her the come command she unveiled the beautiful granite stone. Then, as "Taps" was played, a six-dog Siberian Husky team came down the road with an empty number one sled in tow; an emotional moment and the finale of the Chinook Memorial Dedication Ceremony. "Short would have loved it!"

Lorna B. Taylor and Short Seeley racing at Manchester, Vermont, 1936.

Lorna Taylor (Demidoff) with Ch. Togo of Alyeska (finished in 1939) and Short Seeley with Ch. Cheenah of Alyeska (finished in 1938), two of the earliest AKC champions of the breed.

MONADNOCK KENNELS

Among the early breeders no kennel has had quite the impact upon the Siberian Husky breed as Monadnock Kennels.

For old-timers and newcomers alike, there was always a certain excitement at ringside when a dog bearing the Monadnock prefix was to be exhibited. But ironically, the name has become such an institution as to occasionally dwarf the rather quiet, unassuming, albeit stately woman behind it. This fact was brought home to me at a show some years ago. I had been admiring the dog of an intense young exhibitor, who was obviously new to the breed, and asked her about its background. She replied that although she was uncertain of its more immediate background, further back it was "mostly Monadnock." She then asked if I knew anything about the judge. I assured her, "No matter what happens, with Mrs. Demidoff judging, one knows that the dog who will eventually take the honors will be a good one." To which the young lady, rather challengingly, responded, "Well, I only hope she appreciates a Monadnock type of dog." In my shock, I could barely get out: "But Mrs. Demidoff *is* Monadnock!"

Almost anyone who has ever owned a Siberian Husky knows the name Monadnock. But I doubt that many are aware of the incredible dedication that has gone into the building of the Monadnock success.

There was, for example, the nightmarish summer that Mrs. Demidoff suffered when some thirty of her puppies died from distemper as she valiantly tried to save even one and failed.

Then there is the story of Ch. Otchki of Monadnock, four-time National Specialty winner, and the only Siberian of his time to have the triple distinction of being a bench show champion, an Obedience title holder, and a racing leader. Otchki was unquestionably one of the best dogs produced at Monadnock Kennels, but today few know his name—for Otchki turned out to be sterile.

These and other setbacks would have made anyone with less fortitude and determination take up basket weaving or some other less harrowing hobby. But Lorna Barnes had had a dream.

The story of Monadnock Kennels really had its start in Tenafly, New Jersey, over eighty years ago, when a little girl of six got her first ride in a dog cart behind a small collie-shepherd type dog named "Beans." So thrilled was she by the experience that Lorna Barnes began reading everything she could find about sled dogs. And when she was lucky enough to get a glimpse of one in a movie, she nearly fell out of her seat with excitement. Finally, when she was sixteen and living with her family in Fitzwilliam, New Hampshire, her father arranged for her to ride behind a real dog team. This was a team of Eskimo dogs belonging to a man named Ed Clark who, for a publicity stunt of some kind, was driving them from Woodstock, N.H., to Boston and back. They were being kenneled for the

The Monadnock matched team in action at Sandwich, New Hampshire, 1937.

Lorna Taylor with Ch. Togo of Alyeska, first Siberian to place in the Group (at Newport, Rhode Island, 1939).

67

night in a stable in Keene, and while they were there, Mr. Barnes drove his daughter over by horse and sleigh and she got to ride behind the dogs on a run of some five miles. From that day on, it was her dream to one day own a team of her very own.

In 1929 at Laconia, she got to see her first race. Although she was not overly impressed with the motley appearance of most of the dogs, she was very much so with their performance. She also learned a very valuable lesson in training and conditioning. It seems that one of the first teams to start that day took off at such incredible speed that she naturally assumed it to be one of the better teams, if not the very best. Shorty Russick's team, on the other hand, down from Flin Flon, Manitoba, starting later, actually began at a walk, and seemed "really rather pathetic." In those days, the Laconia race consisted of thirty miles a day for three consecutive days, and Russick's team, trained for long distances and in excellent condition, won the race, while the team that had started so fast finished well back in the field. It was a lesson Lorna never forgot, and in the twenty years of active competition that followed, the teams fielded by Monadnock Kennels were always in excellent condition, regularly covering as much as thirty-five miles a day during midwinter training.

In 1930, Leonhard Seppala drove a team of Siberians in the Laconia race, and Lorna saw for the first time what she had found lacking the year before: dogs of outstanding beauty and uniformity who were also excellent in harness. Seppala, of course, won the race with ease, and from that day on Lorna was a devotee of the Siberian.

In 1931 she married Moseley Taylor, son of the publisher of the *Boston Globe* and an avid sled dog enthusiast. Lorna learned to drive a team and for a year or so drove the dogs considered not fast enough for Moseley's first-string team. These dogs were mostly crossbreds, for Moseley was not particularly concerned with the looks of his dogs so long as they were fast. But Lorna did such a commendable job with his second-string team and obviously enjoyed it so much that Moseley, knowing her weakness for the beautiful little Siberians, bought her the Seeleys' matched team. This team, consisting of Togo of Alyeska, Anvik of Alyeska, Cheeak of Alyeska, Tosca of Alyeska, Flash, Laska and Toto, were young but had been beautifully trained at the Seeleys' by Nate Budgell. It was with this team that Lorna entered the ranks of sled dog racing's top drivers, becoming the first woman driver ever to win a race and placing consistently near the top in races she didn't win.

It was also in the 1930s that Mrs. Taylor began showing her dogs, simply to have something to do in the warmer months when she was not driving. Later, as a seasoned judge, she always had considerable sympathy for the occasional moments of embarrassment experienced at one time or another by most novice handlers, for she vividly remembered her first show in which, having shown horses as a girl, she followed the standard procedure for horse shows and entered every class for which her dogs were eligible.

The litter that started it all at Monadnock. L. to r. are: Anvik of Alyeska, Ch. Togo of Alyeska, Waska (spayed), Toto (spayed), Tosco of Alyeska (foundation bitch of Monadnock) and lying down, Cheeak of Alyeska. Pictured in 1935.

The most historically significant members of the first well-known matched team in the history of the breed:

			Unknown
		Thor	
			Unknown
	Ici		
			Unknown
		Unknown	
			Unknown
Duke			
			Unknown
		Unknown	
			Unknown
	Wanda		
			Unknown
		Unknown	
			Unknown

CH. TOGO OF ALYESKA
CHEEAK OF ALYESKA   (Whelped 7/2/32)
TOSCA OF ALYESKA
also SITKA OF FOXSTAND

			Unknown
		Unknown	
			Unknown
	Tuck		
			Unknown
		Unknown	
			Unknown
Tanta of Alyeska			
			Suggen
		Togo	
			Dolly
	Toto		
			Jafet
		Nome	
			Alma

69

To make matters worse, hers were the only two Siberians entered. And so, for four straight classes, she and the friend who was handling her other dog trotted in and out of the ring, feeling very foolish but accumulating quite a number of ribbons. She always remained grateful to judge Louis Murr, who, she said, never cracked a smile or became impatient, but approached each class with the same air of seriousness.

Togo of Alyeska completed his championship in 1939 but was never used extensively at stud, since, at the time, Mrs. Taylor did not fully realize what a remarkable dog he was. In retrospect, this is regrettable, for she later felt he might well have been the best all-round Siberian she ever owned. Exceptionally loyal for a Siberian, he was also what could only be described as a truly gifted leader. Once, on a bet, for instance, Mrs. Taylor was able to write her name in a field of new snow with a three dog team simply by issuing directional commands to Togo.

An incident in Togo's life demonstrates not only the incredible instinctive drive of these dogs, but how the instinct for their particular kind of work, once properly nurtured, gains supremacy over all others. It has been mentioned that Togo was exceptionally loyal for a Siberian—loyal almost to a fault. Once, for instance, when Mrs. Taylor was forced to leave him at home with her parents, he refused to eat and going to her closet pulled down a pair of her ski pants, curled up on these and did not budge until she returned several days later. Knowing the degree of his devotion, which, of course, was reciprocated, Lorna seldom went anywhere without Togo. So when she went to visit friends some sixty to seventy miles from where she was then living in Fitzwilliam, she naturally took him along. Most of her dogs were at this time on temporary loan to a young man named John Chase; but there were a few dogs left at home in Fitzwilliam, including a bitch in season. Being an unusual Siberian, Togo could be let out of the house wherever Lorna happened to be and could be counted upon to come immediately when called. So on the first morning of the visit, Togo was let out. This time, however, he did not come when called. The area was searched, the police were informed, but all to no avail. Finally, after several hours, a call came from John Chase saying that, by way of an extraordinary set of circumstances, he had Togo there. By good luck, he had happened to be driving on a highway about twenty miles from where Lorna was visiting and had seen the dog running for all he was worth, apparently trying to get back to the bitch in season. He called to the dog, but Togo never even broke stride. Finally, after driving several miles alongside the dog, trying frantically to figure out how he might apprehend him, he remembered that they were approaching a turnoff to the right that ended in a dead end at a high fence. Remembering also that Togo was a lead dog, Mr. Chase leaned out of the car window and gave the command, "Togo, Gee." Togo took the turn, found himself at the fence, and gave up the chase.

Although seldom bred, as leader of the most impressive matched

Ch. Vanya of Monadnock III, BB at the SHCA Specialty in 1946. His dam, Ch. Panda of Monadnock was BOS.

Ch. Belka of Monadnock II, 1950 SHCA Specialty winner.

```
                                              Unknown
                                 Kreevanka
                                              Unknown
                   Burka of Seppala
                                              Harry
                                 Tosca
                                              Kolyma
        Valuiki of Cold River
                                              Tserko
                                 Sapsuk of Seppala
                                              Dushka
                   Delzeue of Cold River
                                              Tserko
                                 Chuchi of Seppala
                                              Bilka of Seppala
```

CH. VANYA OF MONADNOCK III   (Whelped 12/15/44)

CH. BELKA OF MONADNOCK II

```
                                              Unknown
                                 Smoky
                                              Unknown
                   Belford's Wolf
                                              Harry
                                 Tosca
                                              Kolyma
        Ch. Panda
                                              Ici
                                 Duke
                                              Wanda
                   Tosca of Alyeska
                                              Tuck
                                 Tanta of Alyeska
                                              Toto
```

71

team of the era, a team that was not only a top contender on the course but the one that elicited the greatest response from the spectators off the course, Togo made many friends for the breed, and so was not without influence. His litter sister, Tosca of Alyeska, on the other hand, was bred, and it is from her that Monadnock Kennels descends.

The name Monadnock was not actually registered until 1940, the year before Lorna, having divorced Moseley Taylor, married Prince Nikolai Alexandrovitch Lopouchine-Demidoff, a Russian prince who had emigrated to the States after the Revolution and a top sled dog driver in his own right until a back injury forced him to retire from competition. So not until 1940 do dogs bred by Lorna bear the Monadnock prefix.

In 1938, Tosca was bred to Belford's Wolf to produce Lorna's first homebred champion and an excellent racing leader, Ch. Panda. In 1940 Tosca was bred to Millie Turner's Ch. Vanka of Seppala II and produced outstanding dogs including Ch. Kira of Monadnock (not to be confused with Monadnock's Kira), and Ch. Kolya of Monadnock (not to be confused with Monadnock's Kolya), who became the foundation male at the Nagle's Kabkol Kennels.

Ch. Panda was then bred to Millie Turner's Valuiki of Cold River to produce two very outstanding specimens of the breed, Ch. Vanya of Monadnock III and Ch. Belka of Monadnock II (not to be confused with a later bitch belonging to Katherine Hulen named Ch. Monadnock's Belka). Belka was also a racing leader and, although bred only once, produced Ch. Aleka of Monadnock who, along with Chort of Monadnock and their offspring, composed the famous matched team of J. August Duval.

At this point Mrs. Demidoff felt that she had what she wanted in the way of outside influences and confined her breeding, for the most part, to within her own kennel. Ch. Vanya of Monadnock III was bred many times to Ch. Kira of Monadnock, producing such dogs as Pando of Monadnock, who, owned by the McInnes' Tyndrum Kennel in Alaska, greatly influenced the Siberian in that part of the country; Chort of Monadnock, sire and member of Duval's matched team; and Ch. Monadnock's Otchki CD who, although sterile, gave the Siberian world something to shoot for in terms of all-around excellence.

What might be considered the final phase of the Monadnock breeding program came some years later. In 1954 Jean Lane (now Jean Bryar), having acquired Duval's matched team, bred Ch. Aleka's Czarina to the famous Izok of Gap Mountain. From this litter she elected to keep a very striking black and white, blue-eyed male whom she named Mulpus Brook's The Roadmaster (after the latest top-of-the-line Buick). Although his dam, Czarina, continued her show career and went on to take Best of Opposite Sex at three consecutive National Specialties, The Roadmaster was to see the inside of the ring only once in his life. This was at the Manchester

Mulpus Brooks the Roadmaster.

                                    Belford's Wolf
                          Ch. Turu of Alyeska
                                    Cheeak of Alyeska
                Ch. Wonalancet's Baldy of Alyeska
                                    Sapsuk of Seppala
                          Toska of Wonalancet
                                    Tosca of Alyeska
        Izok of Gap Mountain
                                    Kreevanka
                          Ch. Vanka of Seppala II
                                    Tosca
                Duchess of Cold River
                                    Smokey of Seppala
                          Sky of Seppala
                                    Nanna

MULPUS BROOK'S THE ROADMASTER   (Whelped 5/31/54)
                                    Valuiki of Cold River
                          Ch. Vanya of Monadnock III
                                    Ch. Panda
                Chort of Monadnock
                                    Vanka of Seppala I
                          Ch. Kira of Monadnock
                                    Tosca of Alyeska
        Ch. Aleka's Czarina
                                    Ch. Togo of Alyeska
                          Nicholas of Monadnock
                                    Ch. Kira of Monadnock
                Ch. Aleka of Monadnock
                                    Valuiki of Cold River
                          Ch. Belka of Monadnock II
                                    Ch. Panda

(N.H.) Kennel Club Show, where he went all the way to Best of Breed from the puppy class. Unfortunately, it was at this show that he contracted distemper, which left him totally blind in his right eye.

At the time, Mrs. Lane was in the process of building a fast racing team and felt a dog with impaired vision might be a liability. Mrs. Demidoff, on the other hand, had just retired from racing after twenty years of competition and thought the young dog might not only be able to function adequately on her pleasure team but be an asset to her breeding program. Thus, The Roadmaster took up residence at Monadnock.

During this same period Ch. Alyeska's Suggen of Chinook had been bred to Monadnock's Kira, an Izok of Gap Mountain daughter. Out of this litter Lorna selected an attractive black and white, blue-eyed male whom she named Monadnock's Kolya. Unfortunately Kolya died very young of distemper, but not before siring two litters. Bred in 1954 to Ch. Monadnock's Nina, he sired Monadnock's Zora who, when later bred to Roadmaster, produced the very influential Ch. Monadnock's Konyak of Kazan. Nina was a double Izok granddaughter and an outstanding bitch. She was, in fact, the first Siberian bitch ever to place in Group, which she did three times. The breeding was repeated in 1955, shortly before Kolya's death, and produced what is usually somewhat disappointing to a breeder— a litter of one. But with that one puppy, in whom it seems all the right genes had congregated after years of selective breeding, the course of Siberian Husky history was drastically changed. For he was Ch. Monadnock's Pando.

The name "Pando" was the suggestion of a friend, and Lorna later somewhat regretted not thinking of something more original or dignified. But because of the dog who wore it, the name has come to have a majesty it might not otherwise have had; for what Togo had been to the trail, Pando was to the show ring. Although never extensively campaigned, he was, nevertheless, rarely defeated in breed competition and was winning and placing in the Working Group at a time when Siberians were rarely even looked at. From 1957 through 1961, he won four Specialty Shows and five consecutive Bests of Breed at Westminster.

But Pando's greatness lay not only in his outstanding record as a show dog, but in his ability to produce. An extremely prepotent sire, he was able to consistently produce offspring who were not only good specimens of the breed, but remarkably like himself in appearance. This was most strikingly the case with his son Ch. Monadnock's King, who was so similar to his father that even Mrs. Demidoff occasionally confused them. Shown as a brace only in large shows, they were Best Brace in Show at every major show in which they were entered, including the International and Eastern dog shows twice. When teams of four were still being shown, Pando and three sons, usually Ch. Monadnock's King, Ch. Monadnock's Savda Bakko, and Monadnock's Czar, often stole the show. This was especially true when the competition consisted of four dogs handled by

Ch. Monadnock's Pando.

Wolfe of Seppala
Bonzo of Taku
      Ch. Cheenah of Alyeska
Ch. Alyeska's Suggen of Chinook
      King Husky of Wonalancet
Kituh of Taku
      Igloo Pak's Kresta
Monadnock's Kolya
      Ch. Wonalancet's Baldy of Alyeska
Izok of Gap Mountain
      Duchess of Cold River
Monadnock's Kira
      Ch. Vanya of Monadnock III
Panda Girl
      Nadejda

CH. MONADNOCK'S PANDO   (Whelped 4/4/55)
and MONADNOCK'S ZORA   (Whelped 10/26/54)

      Ch. Wonalancet's Baldy of Alyeska
Izok of Gap Mountain
      Duchess of Cold River
Monadnock's Petya
      Ch. Vanya of Monadnock III
Tanya of Monadnock
      Ch. Kira of Monadnock
Ch. Monadnock's Nina
      Ch. Wonalancet's Baldy of Alyeska
Izok of Gap Mountain
      Duchess of Cold River
Monadnock's Laska
      Ch. Vanya of Monadnock III
Panda Girl
      Nadejda

four different handlers. When it came time for the Monadnock team to move and Lorna single-handedly gaited all four dogs in perfect unison around the ring, there was never any doubt in the spectators' minds as to who should win.

In addition to Ch. Monadnock's King, a National Specialty Winner and the first Siberian Husky in the continental United States ever to win a Best in Show, Pando's outstanding offspring included Ch. Monadnock's Dmitri, the first Siberian to win two Best in Show awards and the foundation stud of Koryak Kennels; Ch. Frosty Aire's Alcan King, a Best in Show winner and foundation stud of Fra-Mar Kennels; and Specialty winners—Ch. Monadnock's Prince Igor, CD, Ch. Foxhaunt's Tovarisch, CD, Ch. Monadnock's Rurik of Nanook, and Ninaki of Monadnock. Among his grandsons to have won Specialty Shows are Ch. Savdajaure's Cognac, Ch. Kronprinz of Kazan, Ch. Dichoda's Yukon Red, and Ch. Fra-Mar's Soan Diavol, who is also a Best in Show winner.

So extensive has been Pando's influence, however, that it is impossible to enumerate all the dogs produced by him who have had in turn been an influence on the breed. Suffice it to say that at the 1966 Specialty Show held in Philadelphia, it was discovered that of the 103 dogs being exhibited, 100 were direct descendants of Pando. Pando himself made his final ring appearance at this show, winning the Veteran Dog class at eleven years of age and receiving a standing ovation from ringside.

The final phase of the Monadnock breeding program can then be seen as a process of amalgamating the assets of these two great studs, Pando and Roadmaster. From Pando came class, bearing, elegance, while Roadmaster provided his beautiful head and his somewhat more robust, deep-chested structure. And although Pando's influence may have been more far reaching, since he was in greater breeding demand outside of the kennel, Roadmaster produced around a dozen champions in his own right, including the last great Monadnock stud, Ch. Monadnock's Akela, who, along with Ch. Frosty Aire's Banner Boy, Ch. Savdajaure's Cognac, Ch. Baron of Karnovanda and Ch. Frosty Aire's Beau-Tuk-Balto, ranked for many years as one of the breed's top producing studs of all time.

In retrospect, Mrs. Demidoff consistently downplayed her role of mastermind of probably the most consistently successful breeding program in the history of the breed. Her first love, she insisted, was driving: not winning per se, but the sheer pleasure of working with a team of beautiful, excellently trained animals. If she managed to produce beautiful specimens, she said, it was because she enjoyed working with beautiful animals, not because she had her heart set on the accumulation of ribbons. And there has never been a dog at Monadnock who was only a show dog. Even Pando, for all his success in the ring, spent many more hours as leader of the Monadnock pleasure team than he did at shows. And, of course, enviable as the Monadnock show record is, Lorna's racing record still places her among the best women drivers in the history of the sport, a career that

Ch. Monadnock's King and Ch. Monadnock's Pando, Best Brace in Show at the Eastern Dog Club, 1961, under judge Virgil Johnson.

Best in Show team: Champions Monadnock's Savda Bakko, Serge, King and Pando. The judge is Walter Reeves making the awards at Chicago International.

Ch. Monadnock's King with Mrs. Demidoff following a BIS win at
Mohawk Valley in 1961.

Ch. Monadnock's Akela (left), a distinguished Roadmaster son. Ch. Monadnock's Zita (right), a
Pando daughter and an outstanding producer in her own right.

hit its peak in 1945 with firsts at Fitzwilliam, Newport, and East Jaffrey, New Hampshire.

When asked about her mistakes, or what she might have done differently, Mrs. Demidoff said that she probably should not have let Pando be used on so many outside bitches. In explanation, she said temperament was a far greater problem in earlier days, as many of the early Siberians were shy. So when a bitch was brought to be bred to Pando, she often accepted it if it exhibited a friendly, outgoing nature, even though it might have been less than perfect structurally. In this respect, it was Marie Turner Remick who once made the statement that future breeders could thank Lorna Demidoff for the beautiful temperament of the contemporary Siberian. When one considers that Lorna is also credited with bringing the Siberian to its highest level of physical perfection, it is no wonder that the name Monadnock carries the prestige it does today.

The only other regret that Mrs. Demidoff occasionally voiced was

The bitch most frequently bred to Ch. Monadnock's Pando, Czarina was the dam of such champions as Monadnock's King, Serge, Prince Igor, CD, Tasco del Norte, Red Tango of Murex and Rurik of Nanook.

<pre>
                                              Wolfe of Seppala
                              Bonzo of Taku
                                              Ch. Cheenah of Alyeska
                Ch. Alyeska's Suggen of Chinook
                                              King Husky of Wonalancet
                              Kituh of Taku
                                              Igloo Pak's Kresta
   Monadnock's Nikko
                                              Ch. Wonalancet's Baldy of Alyeska
                              Izok of Gap Mountain
                                              Duchess of Cold River
                Monadnock's Kira
                                              Ch. Vanya of Monadnock III
                              Panda Girl
                                              Nadejda
MONADNOCK'S CZARINA (Whelped 10/14/54)
                                              Ch. Togo of Alyeska
                              Nicholas of Monadnock
                                              Ch. Kira of Monadnock
                Sasha of Monadnock
                                              Belford's Wolf
                              Ch. Panda
                                              Tosca of Alyeska
   Monadnock's Nadya
                                              Czar of Alyeska
                              Chinook's Alladin of Alyeska
                                              Tcheeakio of Alyeska
                Akiak of Anadyr
                                              Chinook's Alladin of Alyeska
                              Dirka of Anadyr
                                              Candia
</pre>

that Pando started such a craze for black and white, blue-eyed Siberians that many newcomers thought of this as the only criteria for excellence. Fortunately the presence of the beautiful copper and white, bicolor-eyed male, Ch. Monadnock's Akela at Monadnock, did much to dispel the myth that the only good Siberian was a black and white, blue-eyed one. And for the record, Pando's show record would probably have been exactly the same had he been gray and white and brown-eyed.

Nor was Pando simply a show and working dog. For many years he was the house pet and official greeter at Monadnock. He was also the mascot of the Monadnock Regional High School, whose senior yearbook is still called the *Pandorian*. In his advanced years he suffered from nephritis, and Lorna was afraid that his activities as mascot might be more than he was up to. But not wanting to disappoint the kids, she simply sent King along as his stand-in, and the student body never knew the difference.

The last of the Monadnock studs, Akela, a son of Roadmaster and Ch. Monadnock's Norina (a double Pando granddaughter), died unexpectedly in December 1976. But with his champion get numbering some thirty-one at last count, it is unlikely he will be forgotten any sooner than any of his remarkable forebears.

When I visited Monadnock Kennels for the first time, after standing and marveling at Akela and the handful of beautiful Monadnock bitches, all well past ten and beautifully cared for, I was invited inside by Lorna, who by now had grown fairly accustomed to having her afternoons interrupted by intense young fanciers of the breed eager to have some particle of knowledge bestowed on them. Once inside and past the almost overwhelming array of trophies, I sat under the beautiful wall-size photograph of Pando, King and Roadmaster lying in the snow in harness and listened as she talked dogs and showed old photographs in her quiet, moving way. When I finally managed to tear myself away, knowing I had taken up her entire afternoon, but knowing it was not one I'd soon forget, I happened to notice the license plate on the station wagon outside. It read PANDO, above which was written the motto of the state of New Hampshire, "Live Free or Die." And I thought how for a little girl in Tenafly, New Jersey, a dream had surely been realized.

5

Outstanding Kennels

$\mathbf{O}$F THE 132 BREEDS CURRENTLY RECOGNIZED by the American Kennel Club, the Siberian Husky consistently ranks among the top 20 in popularity. Despite this popularity, the fact that the majority of dogs exhibited today still evidence the qualities of type, temperament and soundness found in previous generations speaks well for the dedication of the fanciers who nurtured this once-obscure breed into its present position of popularity.

What follows is a description of what might be called the "second generation" of Siberian kennels which fostered the breed during its slow growth during the 1940s and 1950s and even into the 1960s and 1970s. While all of these kennels were established prior to 1960, many are still active today. But even those now defunct have left an indelible mark on the breed.

In all fairness, however, it should be emphasized that today, throughout America (and even abroad) there are more kennels than ever dedicated to producing top-quality Siberians, kennels that are alert to the dangers engendered by the breed's fantastic popularity and that are zealously guarding the qualities that make the breed the unique one it is today. May their success continue.

ALAKAZAN

The real beginning of Alakazan Kennels was a vacation trip to the Adirondacks in 1954. There Paul and Margaret Koehler saw their first Siberians and brought back to their home in Pittsford, New York, near Rochester, a black and white puppy bitch whom they named Laska of Kazan. Kazan was chosen as a kennel name because of its Siberian associations. Years later, however, when the Koehlers decided to register the name with the AKC, they were informed that proper nouns were no longer allowed. To circumvent the problem, they simply appended the expression "a la" to the name and Alakazan became a registered kennel name.

At the time they bought Laska, the Koehlers knew nothing about Siberian bloodlines. Fortunately for them, Laska was from the very best. Her sire was Aleka's Ruska (Chort of Monadnock out of Aleka of Monadnock) a member of Tat Duval's famous matched team, and her dam was Monadnock's Laska (Izok of Gap Mountain out of Panda Girl).

The Koehlers' next acquisition was a large wolf-gray male named Nordholm's Jonas. Jonas was purchased from Joel Nordholm, some of whose dogs came from William Shearer's Foxstand lines. Jonas was shown to his championship, bred to Laska to produce Agfa of Kazan and then bred to Agfa to produce the Koehlers' first homebred champion—the bitch Peggy considers the real foundation bitch of Alakazan—Ch. Kira of Kazan. Kira's show record was outstanding. Finishing her championship by taking the points in four out of the six shows in which she was entered, she went on to take Best of Opposite Sex to Ch. Monadnock's King at the 1962 National Specialty.

Kira was then bred to Ch. Monadnock's Serge, a Pando son whom the Koehlers acquired from Frosty Aire Kennels, to produce Ch. Kronpinz of Kazan, a great team dog, the 1965 National Specialty Winner, Best of Breed winner at Westminster in 1966, and a Working Group winner.

In 1960 the Koehlers acquired another young male from Monadnock Kennels, a son of Roadmaster and Pando's sister, Monadnock's Zora, who went on to become Ch. Monadnock's Konyak of Kazan, probably the most influential of all Alakazan studs and the one who is largely responsible for the kind of exciting physical presence associated with Alakazan dogs. Among his more famous offspring are Ch. Alakazan's Satan Sitka, Ch. Yankee Czar's Yogi, Ch. Alakazan's Nikki, Ch. Snoridge's Lorelei, and the very influential Kameo of Kazan, through whom Konyak maintained his influence in the Alakazan breeding program.

Kameo's dam was Czarina Alexandria, a double Pando granddaughter and litter sister of Ch. Monadnock's Norina. Although never shown, Kameo was an outstanding bitch. Bred four times to Ch. Frosty Aire's Banner Boy, she produced such dogs as Ch. Alakazan's Kossak, Ch. Alakazan's Kio Kam of Snoana, Ch. Alakazan's Saanki, Ch. Alakazan's Banner Blue, and Ch. Alakazan's Nikolai. And today, Nikolai himself can claim

Ch. Monadnock's Volcana, a top copper bitch of the Alakazan Kennels.

Ch. Alakazan's Banner Blue.

around a dozen champion offspring so far to his credit, including the multi Best in Show winner Ch. Dudley's Tavar of Innisfree.

The bitch that has served largely to complement the strengths of Kameo in the Koehlers' breeding program is Alakazan's Kristi, a daughter of Ch. Savdajaure's Cognac and Ch. Yeso Pac's Tamara, purchased from the Poseys' Yeso Pac Kennels. Like Kameo, Kristi was never shown, but like Kameo she has made her presence felt. More delicate than her kennelmate, she is responsible for much of the "classiness" of Alakazan dogs. Bred to Banner Boy, she produced Alakazan's Gunnar who, when bred to Kameo, produced Ch. Alakazan's Kira. Kristi also produced several champion offspring in her own right.

But the dog which Peggy feels most closely resembles her ideal of all the dogs she has bred is the strikingly beautiful copper and white daughter of Ch. Monadnock's Akela and Alakazan's Tia Valeska named Ch. Monadnock's Volcana. Among her impressive wins, Volcana took Best of Opposite Sex to her half brother Ch. Marlytuk's Red Sun of Kiska at the 1971 National Specialty.

Impressive as the Alakazan show record is, however, it is only part of the story. Seven years as one of the top drivers in the Arctic Sled Dog Club, Paul's racing career peaked in 1964 when he won the coveted Siberian Husky Club of America's racing trophy with an extremely impressive team composed of five bench show champions and two pointed dogs. He also served as president of the Siberian Husky Club of America from 1962 to 1964. Jointly the Koehlers were putting out the Siberian Husky Club of America's *Newsletter* for many years and are largely responsible for its current award-winning format. They have also provided the foundation stock to kennels all over the United States and sent dogs to such places as Finland, Germany, France and Italy.

Although it was Paul who first got the Koehlers into Siberians and whose enthusiasm and eye for dogs put them on the road to being one of the top kennels in the country, his business responsibilities have required more and more of his time in recent years, and it is now Peggy who is most closely associated with the activities of the kennel. She too has held various offices in the Siberian Husky Club, including first vice president, member of the board of directors, editor of the *Newsletter*, and head of the Standards committee set up to revise the Standard in 1971.

Impressive as her official activities have been, however, her greatest influence has probably been in a subtler capacity. Trained as an English teacher and librarian, although absent for many years from the classroom, over the past thirty-odd years she has devoted her particular talents to the meticulous study and teaching of her favorite subject, the Siberian Husky. And whether from her chair at ringside, in her capacity as writer of various columns and articles, or over coffee in her kitchen, she has probably disseminated as much down-to-earth, commonsense information about the breeding, raising and appreciation of the Siberian Husky as anyone alive.

Ch. Alaskan's Bonzo of Anadyr, CD, was the breed's first BIS winner. To his great credit, he was also an outstanding racing leader. Bonzo was owned by Alaskan Kennels of Earl and Natalie Norris.

Asked about the theories behind her own breeding program, she considers her own "recipe for stew" to be an attempt to synthesize the strengths of three of the great dogs of the breed: Pando, Roadmaster, and Banner Boy. Over the years her particular concerns, beyond maintaining the basic requisites of type, have been movement; strong, well-angulated fronts and rears; sufficient length of neck; a silhouette that is somewhat longer than tall; small, high-set ears; a muzzle that is somewhat longer than that sought by some breeders (and thus more compatible with the Standard); and, above all, that a Siberian should be a delight to be with.

ALASKAN KENNELS

Earl and Natalie Norris's Alaskan Kennel is probably better known to Siberian fanciers by the Anadyr prefix which they use in naming their Siberians. Nevertheless, the kennel name is *Alaskan*.

To the Norrises, raising and driving sled dogs had been a way of life long before they met each other in Alaska. Natalie started driving dogs at the age of ten in Lake Placid, New York, where she made sufficient money to support her dogs by giving rides to wealthy tourists. Her reputation as a dog driver became such that in 1940, at the age of sixteen, she exhibited her dog team at a sport show in Madison Square Garden. During the war she sold her dogs to the Seeleys to be used by the Army Search and Rescue Units. After the war, when she had finished college, she went to work as a kennel helper at the Seeleys' Chinook Kennels. This was in 1945.

In 1946, she decided to go to Alaska and, after consulting with Short Seeley, took along two dogs to act as foundation studs of the kennel she proposed to set up there. These were Chinook's Alladin of Alyeska (Czar of Alyeska out of Tcheeakio of Alyeska) and a dog named Terry who was subsequently discarded. Arriving in Alaska with eleven dogs, she met Earl Norris, whose kennel at that time contained fifteen dogs, and the rest is history.

Earl himself began driving dogs at the age of ten in his hometown, Orofino, Idaho, and by the age of twelve owned his first Siberian. Determined to be where the action was in the world of sled dogs, Earl moved to Alaska in 1945 and started a small but high-caliber racing kennel. The primary interest of both Earl and Natalie was to develop a kennel of high quality purebred dogs, both Siberians and Malamutes. In 1946, however, when Natalie arrived in Anchorage, no one in Alaska seemed to be breeding registered Siberians, so the Norrises virtually had to start from scratch. Basically, three dogs are responsible for what became their Anadyr line: Chinook's Alladin of Alyeska, and two bitches, Bayou of Foxstand and Candia.

Bayou of Foxstand was bred by Joe Booth of Massachusetts and registered by William Shearer. Bred to Alladin she produced Ch. U-chee

Chinook's Alladin of Alyeska, a foundation stud for Earl and Natalie Norris' Alaskan Kennels.

of Anadyr who, along with Pando of Monadnock (not to be confused with Ch. Monadnock's Pando) became the foundation of Charles and Kit McInnes's Tyndrum Kennels in Anchorage. A breeding of these two subsequently produced Ch. Tyndrum's Oslo, CDX from whom came the foundation stock of Bob and Lou Richardson's S-K-Mo Kennels, Frosty Aire Kennels, and in turn Innisfree, Snoana, Chotovotka and many others.

Candia, sired by Bugs of Cold River out of Foxstand's Sukey, was obtained directly from Foxstand Kennels. Bred to Alladin in 1947, she produced the first homebred Anadyr bitch, Dirka of Anadyr, who in turn produced Ch. Noho of Anadyr, who was undefeated in the conformation ring during his five-year career.

Ch. Bonzo of Anadyr, CD, however, is probably the most famous dog produced by the Norrises. A grandson of Alladin, he was an outstanding lead dog, the fourth champion Siberian in the United States to earn an Obedience degree, and, in 1955, became the first Siberian in the world to win a Best in Show.

Alladin was the foundation stud of Alaskan Kennels, and Nanuk the foundation bitch of Kabkol Kennels.

			Kingeak
		Smokey of Seppala	
			Pearl
	Wolfe of Seppala		
			Tserko
		Sigrid of Seppala	
			Dushka
Czar of Alyeska			
			Togo
		Sepp III	
			Unknown
	Ch. Cheenah of Alyeska		
			Duke
		Tosca of Alyeska	
			Tanta of Alyeska

CHINOOK'S ALLADIN OF ALYESKA
NANUK OF ALYESKA (Whelped 5/9/44)

			Unknown
		Smoky	
			Unknown
	Belford's Wolf		
			Harry
		Tosca	
			Kolyma
Tscheeakio of Alyeska			
			Ici
		Duke	
			Wanda
	Cheeak of Alyeska		
			Tuck
		Tanta of Alyeska	
			Toto

Unique among Siberian kennels who can boast a Best in Show winner, Alaskan Kennels is and always has been first and foremost a racing kennel. Indeed it is Earl's boast that while others race their show dogs, the Norrises show their racing dogs. While this may be something of an oversimplification, it does serve to underline the Norrises' primary orientation. And, indeed, their racing record and record as producers of top lead and team dogs that have been exported all over the world is probably incomparable.

DICHODA

It was at their first dog show in 1945, while living in Alexandria, Virginia, that Frank and Phyllis Brayton saw their first Siberian Huskies. Earl Nagle told them what kind of dogs they were, and when the Braytons returned home to California in 1946 they took with them a male from the Nagles' Kabkol Kennels named Dingo Dmitri of Kabkol. Unfortunately Dingo was struck by a car at eight months of age and died in Frank's arms, but he nevertheless played a significant role in the kennel. From him comes the *Di* in Dichoda, and from his unfortunate death comes the rule that no Dichoda dog is sold to anyone without an adequately fenced yard, no matter what.

The rest of the Dichoda name came from the next two Siberians acquired by the Braytons, Echo of Kabkol and Gouda of Kabkol. Echo, a bitch out of Ch. Kolya of Monadnock and Nanuk of Alyeska, provided the *cho* while Gouda, a male out of Ch. Kolya of Monadnock and Kabloona, provided the *da*. A litter out of these two in 1948 provided the Braytons with their first homebred champion, Ch. Dichoda's Aurelia, CD, who in 1952 became the third Siberian in the United States to earn both her bench show championship and an Obedience title.

In 1953, Noho of Anadyr was purchased from Earl and Natalie Norris's Alaskan Kennels. Noho, a son of Yaddam of Huskie Haven and Dirka of Anadyr, completed his championship in 1958 and was undefeated in breed competition during the five years he was shown. Bred to Aurelia, he produced the first of the Dichoda reds, and in 1960, Dichoda's Gjoa, the bitch the Braytons kept from this litter, became the second red Siberian Husky to attain championship status, and the first female.

In 1960 Noho sired a litter out of Lou Richardson's Ch. Atu of Glacier Valley, and Frank chose a beautiful bitch out of this litter who was named Dichoda's Beauty of S-K-Mo. Shown on a very limited basis, she nevertheless acquired seven points and went on to produce some of the best known Dichoda dogs.

In 1961 the Braytons acquired Ch. Monadnock's Rurik of Nanook from Virginia Emrich. Rurik was a son of Ch. Monadnock's Pando and Monadnock's Czarina, and, like Noho before him, he was never defeated

Ch. Dichoda's Yukon Red, one of the most outstanding copper Siberians in the history of the breed. Owned by Dichoda Kennels.   *Joan Ludwig*

```
                                          Ch. Alyeska's Suggen of Chinook
                           Monadnock's Kolya
                                          Monadnock's Kira
              Ch. Monadnock's Pando
                                          Monadnock's Petya
                           Ch. Monadnock's Nina
                                          Monadnock Laska
Ch. Monadnock's Rurik of Nanook
                                          Ch. Alyeska's Suggen of Chinook
                           Monadnock's Nikko
                                          Monadnock's Kira
              Monadnock's Czarina
                                          Sasha of Monadnock
                           Monadnock's Nadya
                                          Akiak of Anadyr
```

CH. DICHODA'S YUKON RED   (Whelped 1/18/65)

```
                                          Charney of Seppala
                           Yaddam of Huskie Haven
                                          Nony of White Water
              Ch. Noho of Anadyr
                                          Chinook's Alladin of Alyeska
                           Dirka of Anadyr
                                          Candia
Dichoda's Beauty of S-K-Mo
                                          Pando of Monadnock
                           Ch. Tyndrum's Oslo, CDX
                                          Ch. U-Chee of Anadyr
              Ch. Atu of Glacier Valley
                                          Yaddam of Huskie Haven
                           Cawkick of Lakota*
                                          Nabesna of Polaris
```
*Poko Bueno of Lakota's sister.

was shown. He also
...d a litter that contained
...erlative red and white

...re owner-handled by
...f his points from the
..., was a victim of mul-
...ronounced, the Bray-
...edience trainer, Tom
...won his first Working
...der the noted judge
...up twelve times.
...Siberian Husky in the
...ined in the top five.
...od specimen but one
...e year he was ranked

...eir dogs extensively.
...mber of dogs. Rather
...more than a dozen
...s contribution to the

...a and one of the first
...eders in the country
...the years they have
...the Siberian in the
...b as well.
...Phyllis continues the
...in recent years has
...piness and beautiful
...h. Dichoda's Yukon
...y more with points.
...to some of the best-

...ding president and

Bella

Rescuing
Alaskan

...mstead Falls, Ohio,
...ebred dogs in 1954
...X degree in Obe-
...became interested
...t her eye at several

shows and this was Ch. Kenai Kittee of Beauchien, CD. Finally, in 1959 she contacted the Fosters and obtained from them a young Pando son out of a bitch named Kura.

Marie's intention had been to work the puppy in Obedience. Instead, although he did get the first two legs toward his CD degree, he became Ch. Frosty Aire's Alcan King, the second Pando son to win a Best in Show. He also became the first American Best in Show winning Siberian to sire an American Best in Show winner.

The next important dog the Wamsers acquired was a bitch from the Fosters, sired by Ch. Frosty Aire's Beau-Tuk-Balto out of Laika of Monadnock, who became Ch. Fra-Mar's Misarah. Missy, in turn, was bred to Ch. Frosty Aire's Eric to produce their first homebred champion bitch, Ch. Fra-Mar's Karo Mia Diavol. It is upon these three dogs that the Fra-Mar breeding program was based. Essentially it entailed linebreeding on Ch. Monadnock's Pando, with Karo Mia being used as a partial outcross.

The most famous dog to come out of Fra-Mar Kennels was a product of Alcan King and Misarah—American, Bermudian and Canadian Ch. Fra-Mar's Soan Diavol. Not only was he, like his father, a Best in Show winner, but he was ranked as the top winning Siberian in the country in 1966, 1968, and 1969 and the top Siberian in Canada in 1970.

Like many of the better kennels in the country, Fra-Mar is a relatively small kennel whose breeding program is conducted slowly and carefully. Among the impressive dogs to come out of this kennel are Ch. Fra-Mar's Czarina Diavol, Ch. Fra-Mar's Troisk Diavol, Ch. Fra-Mar's Challa Diavol, Ch. Fra-Mar's Shiva Diavol, Ch. Fra-Mar's Aja-Tu Diavol, Ch. Fra-Mar's Cherry Puff Diavol, and Ch. Fra-Mar's Nicholai Diavol. Diavol means devil and has always been used in naming dogs of Marie's own breeding. As she says, "All the little devils are mine."

FROSTY AIRE

Jack and Donna Foster's interest in Siberians began in 1955 in Alaska where Jack was stationed in the army. Upon returning to Indiana, they brought with them a male, later Ch. Kenai Krystee of Lakota, CD, and immediately sent back to Alaska for a bitch who was to become Ch. Kenai Kittee of Beauchien, CDX, Frosty Aire's foundation bitch and a very important bitch to the history of the breed.

A daughter of Ch. Tyndrum's Oslo and Tyndrum's Shiva, Kittee had an outstanding show career (going either Best of Breed or Best of Opposite Sex over 80 percent of the time she was shown) and an equally outstanding career in Obedience (winning the *Dog World* Award of Distinction for three consecutive scores of 195 or better). Bred three times, to Sonya's Torger, to Ch. Stoney River's Ootah and to Ch. Red Tango of Murex, she produced such offspring as Ch. Frosty Aire's Tofty, Ch. Frosty Aire's

Ch. Frosty Aire's Alcan King, a BIS winner, owned by Fra-Mar Kennels. Pictured at his final show ring appearance one month prior to his twelfth birthday.

Am., Can., Berm. Ch. Fra-Mar's Soan Diavol (Alcan King ex Ch. Fra-Mar's Misarah) was the first BIS progeny for a BIS Siberian. Bred and owned by the Wamsers' Fra-Mar Kennels, here shown in a good win at the Detroit KC under judge William L. Kendrick. *Evelyn Shafer*

Ch. Kenai Kittee of Beauchien, CDX, foundation bitch of Frosty Aire
Kennels, pictured at 10 months.

```
                                         Valuiki of Cold River
                              Ch. Vanya of Monadnock III
                                         Ch. Panda
                    Pando of Monadnock
                                         Belford's Wolf
                              Ch. Panda
                                         Tosca of Alyeska
          Ch. Tyndrum's Oslo, CDX
                                         Czar of Alyeska
                              Chinook's Alladin of Alyeska
                                         Tcheeakio of Alyeska
                    Ch. U-Chee of Anadyr
                                         Surgut of Seppala
                              Bayou of Foxstand
                                         Duchess of Huskyland

CH. KENAI KITTEE OF BEAUCHIEN, CDX   (Whelped 5/27/56)

                                         Ch. Igloo Pak's Anvik
                              Snow Storm
                                         Nadejda
                    Misha of Breezymere
                                         Dichoda's Akimo Kio
                              Sikha
                                         Doonah of Monadnock
          Tyndrum's Shiva
                                         Ch. Vanya of Monadnock III
                              Pando of Monadnock
                                         Ch. Panda
                    Tyndrum's Comanchee
                                         Keetna of Monadnock
                              Gretel of Tyndrum
                                         Ch. U-Chee of Anadyr
```

Susitna and Frosty Aire's Suntrana, all of whom figure in contemporary pedigrees. Among her most outstanding grandsons were Ch. Frosty Aire's Beauchien, CD, and Ch. Frosty Aire's Banner Boy, CD.

Much of the breeding at Frosty Aire was aimed at producing dogs of the type and caliber of the famous Izok of Gap Mountain, whom the Fosters saw on a trip to the East. Sonya's Torger was chosen as a stud for Kittee because he was an Izok son. Marina of Mulpus Brook Farm was then purchased because she was a daughter of Baldy of Gap Mountain, an Izok brother. Laika of Monadnock was also purchased because she was linebred to Izok. Another of the Frosty Aire foundation bitches was Kura, who, when bred to Pando, produced Marie Wamser's Best in Show winner Ch. Frosty Aire's Alcan King.

One breeding, that of Kittee to Ch. Monadnock's Red Tango of Murex, was done specifically to obtain red puppies. There were, however, no red puppies in the litter; but a great-grandson, Ch. Frosty Aire's Eric, did become the foundation sire for reds, producing such dogs as Ch. Frosty Aire's Red Devil Beau and Ch. Frosty Aire's Jolly Red Giant as well as a number of black and white and gray titled dogs. And subsequently Red Beau himself became a top producing sire.

Perhaps the real peak in the Frosty Aire breeding program began in 1960 when Ch. Frosty Aire's Beauchien, a Kittee grandson, was bred to Ch. Klutuk's Carrie, owned by Dr. Mary Helen Cameron, to produce the famous "Beau-Tuk" litter, the only litter in the history of the breed in which all became champions. They were Ch. Frosty Aire's Beau-Tuk Balto, Ch. Frosty Aire's Beau-Tuk Belka, Ch. Frosty Aire's Beau-Tuk Katrina, CD, Ch. Beau-Tuk Beauvallon and Ch. Frosty Aire's Beau-Tuk Evil One, CD. And this was only the beginning. Balto finished at eight months, twenty-three days and then proved to be what all breeders hope for—that truly prepotent sire capable of producing get that are consistently as good or better than himself. Balto produced twenty-four champions, which once ranked him among the five or ten top producing studs in the history of the breed. But his most outstanding offspring was Ch. Frosty Aire's Banner Boy, CD, owned by the Piuntis, who was not only a truly great specimen of the breed but the sire of some thirty-five champions to date, making him for some time the breed's number one champion-producing sire.

Balto was not the only member of his litter to exert a strong influence on today's Siberians. Belka was the granddam of Ch. Frosty Aire's Bittersweet, Ch. Frosty Aire's So Cold and Ch. Frosty Aire's Persimmon, all by Ch. Frosty Aire's Red Devil Beau. And Persimmon is still the youngest Siberian to attain her championship, doing so at seven months, twenty-one days, and with three strikes against her: she was a red in a day when reds were still rare in the show ring, a bitch, and a puppy. Shown out of the puppy class only, she amassed three Best of Breed, three Best of Opposite Sex, three Best of Winners, two Winner's Bitch and one class

The historic Beau Tuk all-champion litter. L. to r. back row: sire, Ch. Frosty Aire's Beauchien, CD; Ch. Frosty Aire's Beau-Tuk Balto (d); Ch. Frosty Aire's Beau-Tuk Belka (b) and dam, Ch. Klutuk's Carrie. Front, Ch. Beau-Tuk Evil One, CD (b); Ch. Beau-Tuk Katrina, CD (b) and Ch. Beau-Tuk Beauvallan.

Ch. Frosty Aire's Beau-Tuk Balto finished at under nine months and went on to sire 24 champions, making him one of the breeds top producers.

Ch. Frosty Aire's Banner Boy, top stud for Art and Mary Ann Piunti's Snoanna Kennels. He was the sire of some 35 champion offspring.

The famous "Beau-Tuk" litter, the only sizable litter in the history of the breed in which all finished to their championships:

<pre>
                                                      Izok of Gap Mountain
                                    Sonya's Torger
                                                      Aleka's Sonya
                     Frosty Aire's Tobuk
                                                      Ch. Tyndrum's Oslo, CDX
                                    Ch. Kenai Kittee of Beauchien, CDX
                                                      Tyndrum's Shiva
        Ch. Frosty Aire's Beauchien, CD
                                                      Ch. Igloo Pak's Anvik
                                    Snow Storm
                                                      Nadejda
                     Snow Bird
                                                      Dichoda's Akimo Kio
                                    Sihka
                                                      Doonah of Monadnock

CH. FROSTY AIRE'S BEAU-TUK BALTO
CH. FROSTY AIRE'S BEAU-TUK BELKA
CH. FROSTY AIRE'S BEAU-TUK KATRINA, CD
CH. FROSTY AIRE'S BEAU-TUK BEAUVALLON
CH. FROSTY AIRE'S BEAU-TUK EVIL ONE, CD
        (Whelped 12/9/60)
                                                      Torr of Seppala
                                    Little Sepp of Bow Lake
                                                      Leda of Bow Lake
                     Snow Sepp of Bow Lake
                                                      Igloo Pak's Chukchee
                                    Mitzy of Bow Lake
                                                      Malinka of Bow Lake
        Ch. Klutuk's Carrie
                                                      Valuiki of Cold River
                                    Ch. Vanya of Monadnock III
                                                      Ch. Panda
                     Klutuk of Long's Peak
                                                      Izok of Gap Mountain
                                    Alaskan Twilight of Long's Peak
                                                      Tanya of Monadnock
</pre>

first awards in twelve shows, and went third in Working Group the day she finished.

Over the years Frosty Aire has remained a dominant force in the Midwest, from where their meticulous breeding program has influenced kennels all over the country, including Sihu, Susitna, Snoana, Alakazan, Innisfree, Chotovotka, Weldon, So-Huck, Wintersett, Klutuk, Sno-Mound and others.

IGLOO PAK

Dr. Roland Lombard's career as a sled dog driver has been so remarkable that his career as a breeder of registered Siberians is occasionally overlooked. Nevertheless, the Igloo Pak prefix is frequently found in the pedigrees of outstanding show dogs and running dogs in the breed today, and their names are pointed to with great pride.

Igloo Pak (pronounced to rhyme with cake) was registered by Roland and his wife, Louise, about 1940 and was one of the first Siberian kennels to become registered. It means, simply, "the house of the white man." But the story of Igloo Pak really goes back to the 1920s when Roland, then a high school student, first saw and fell in love with Siberian Huskies. His first Siberians were given to him by Seppala and Mrs. Ricker and were named Arctic, Paddy and Frosty.

After he completed his education, and after the war, he was able to acquire Helen of Cold River from William Shearer. Helen was the daughter of Ch. Vanka of Seppala II and Sky of Seppala and was a sister of Duchess of Cold River. She had been in the Army's Search and Rescue unit and proved to be an outstanding lead dog. The Lombards also showed her to her championship.

Another of the outstanding dogs to have come to Igloo Pak was Monadnock's Vickie of Igloo Pak, a trained tracker and racing leader. Before the age of superhighways when the drivers gathered together the night before the races, it was often Vickie who kept them entertained by putting on demonstrations of scent discrimination that included picking up dimes placed on the floor among various other objects. Unfortunately she died very young.

Ch. Sitka's Wona of Alyeska was also an Igloo Pak dog and winner of a Group Fourth in an age when Siberians were rarely even looked at in Group. A Wona son, Igloo Pak's Anvic, was Best of Breed at the 1947 SHCA Specialty under Mrs. Seeley.

For the most part Igloo Pak stock was based upon Chinook, along with some Monadnock, Foxstand, Belford and Cold River dogs. But undoubtedly the most influential dog to have come out of Igloo Pak in terms of contemporary pedigrees was Igloo Pak's Tok, a son of Alyeska's Sugrut of Chinook and Igloo Pak's Misty, and the sire of many outstanding dogs. Tok has proved influential in many lines, especially in the Yeso Pac breeding program.

While "Doc" was in the spotlight of the racing world for over seventy years, Louise also contributed a great deal to the world of sled dogs. Her first love was Alaskan Malamutes, and she showed a pure white one and then proceeded to make him the first individual of a northern breed to hold a CD. For many years she also raced Malamutes, but later changed to Siberians. Among her achievements was a second in the Women's Championship race in Alaska in 1969, coming in just fifteen seconds behind the winner.

But the real contribution of Igloo Pak goes far beyond the various outstanding specimens that have been produced there. Rather, in their lifelong commitment to the breed, the Lombards have kept the Siberian lifelong commitment to the breed, the Lombards have kept the Siberian "on the map" as a running dog for, although they ran quite a few crossbreds, there was always a number of purebred Siberians on their teams, and in 1957 "Doc" won the North American Championship race with a team composed entirely of registered Siberians. It is this sort of example that has served as an inspiration to fanciers of the breed for so many years.

"Doc" died in October of 1990.

An early Igloo Pak dog who was influential on the East Coast, especially through his daughter, Igloo Pak's Kresta, and later on the West Coast at Earl Snodie's Bow Lake Kennels:

				Smoky	Unknown
					Unknown
		Belford's Wolf			
				Tosca	Harry
					Kolyma
	Laddy of Wonalancet				
				Duke	Ici
					Wanda
		Cheeak of Alyeska			
				Tanta of Alyeska	Tuck
					Toto
IGLOO PAK CHUCKCHEE (Whelped 7/1/45)					
				Sapsuk of Seppala	Tserko
					Dushka
		Suggen of Wonalancet			
				Tosca of Alyeska	Duke
					Tanta of Alyeska
	Tchuchis of Wonalancet				
				Sepp III	Togo
					Unknown
		Lassie of Wonalancet			
				Cheeak of Alyeska	Duke
					Tanta of Alyeska

INNISFREE

Lieutenant-Colonel Norbert Kanzler and his wife, Kathleen's, involvement with purebred dogs goes well back into the 1950s when they bred Miniature Schnauzers which they showed both in conformation and Obedience. And although they only obtained their first Siberian in 1960, they were the originators of one of the most broadly based and influential breeding programs in the country, and it is impossible to give an accurate picture of the development of the Siberian without including the Kanzlers.

Having been located in Michigan, Kansas, California and Maryland, Innisfree has been among the most mobile of Siberian kennels, and its record in the show ring has been one of the most impressive. However, when asked to write something about the history and specific character of her kennel, Kathleen tends to minimize the individual accomplishments of her dogs in favor of discussing some of the more crucial issues in establishing a breeding program. As she once said, she can often recall the precise set of a given dog's shoulders without recalling whether or not he completed his championship. What she has written provides such an incisive picture of the concerns that a breeder has, a picture that in so many ways is more important than a given breeder's show record, we feel it should be included in its entirety. What follows, then, are her words:

Innisfree Siberians are based on two foundation brood bitches purchased in Alaska. Innisfree's Rashiri of A-Baska and Tanio were whelped in 1960–61 in Alaska. Both these bitches were bred by people that were racing purebred Siberians in the heyday of registered Siberians in Alaska.

Innisfree's Rashiri of A-Baska was bred to Frosty Aire stud dogs. Rashiri's first litter with Ch. Frosty Aire's Beauchien, CD, produced two females that became the foundation bitches of two Michigan kennels. Rashiri's second breeding was with Ch. Frosty Aire's Beau-Tuk Balto and produced Ch. Frosty Aire's Masked Bandit, the foundation of Chotovotka Kennels, Bob and Dorothy Page; and Ch. Innisfrees' Lobo, our Siberian companion on our travels around the world.

Innisfree's initial breedings were aimed toward preserving the soundness and type of our two original bitches, and toward introducing the showiness and eye appeal of the Frosty Aire studs. At this point in the breed it seemed important to linebreed to stabilize the traits we felt were important. American and Canadian Ch. Frosty Aire's Starfire, a Balto daughter, Group placer, top-producing brood bitch of the year, and undefeated by any other Siberian in Canada, was bred to her sire, Ch. Frosty Aire's Beau-Tuk Balto. This mating produced three champions. One of these, Ch. Innisfree's Beau-Tuk, was the foundation of Weldon Kennels, Nancy T. Perkins. This linebred Balto son in turn was a keystone of Innisfree. Ch. Weldon's Beau-Buck, a son of Ch. Innisfree's Beau-Tuk, and Ch. Weldon's Beau-Tukker, a grandson of Beau-Tuk, are current studs at Innisfree.

Ch. Innisfree's Beau-Tuk was bred to Innisfree's Rashiri of A-Baska and produced Ch. Innisfree's Chilka, producer of many champions for her owner, Nancy Perkins. Most notable of these are Ch. Weldon's Enuk Balto, producer of two Best in Show winners, Ch. Weldon's Beau-Phunsi and Ch. Innisfree's O'Murtagh. Innisfree's Banshee, a sister of Chilka's, also produced many champions, among them Ch. Innisfree's Banshee Tu, American and Canadian Ch. Kler's Rosie and most notably, Ch. Innisfree's Oomachuk.

Tanio, bred to Ch. Innisfree's Beau-Tuk, produced Ch. Innisfree's Kitka,

Ch. Innisfree's Oomachuk and Ch. Innisfree's Barbarossa.

A truly outstanding bitch in her own right, Oomachuk figures significantly in contemporary pedigrees.

			Izok of Gap Mountain
		Sonya's Torger	
			Aleka's Sonya
	Ch. Frosty Aire's Tofty		
			Ch. Tyndrum's Oslo, CDX
		Ch. Kenai Kittee of Beauchien, CDX	
			Tyndrum's Shiva
Ch. Innisfree's El Ferro			
			Poko Bueno of Lakota
		Ch. Kenai Kristyee of Lakota	
			Tyee
	Ch. Frosty Aire's Chena		
			Ch. Stoney River's Ootah
		Kura	
			Stony River's Kayenta

CH. INNISFREE'S OOMACHUK   (Whelped 8/31/65)

			Ch. Frosty Aire's Beauchien, CD
		Ch. Frosty Aire's Beau-Tuk Balto	
			Ch. Klutuk's Carrie
	Ch. Innisfree's Beau-Tuk		
			Ch. Frosty Aire's Beau-Tuk Balto
		Am. & Can. Ch. Frosty Aire's Starfire	
			Frosty Aire's Starina
Innisfree's Banshee			
			Ch. Tyndrum's Oslo, CDX
		Siya of A'Baska	
			Cheena of Nobilis
	Innisfree's Bashire of A'Baska		
			Loki
		Takla of Ananen	
			Tyone of Anadyr

101

Winners' Bitch and Best of Winners at the Siberian Husky Club of America Specialty, and the foundation bitch for another Michigan kennel. Another Tanio daughter, Arctic's Angel of Innisfree (Tanner) produced Ch. Innisfree's Sierra Beau-Jack (Burnside) and Ch. Innisfree's Beau-Kara and Innisfree's Beau-Biddy. Angel was sired by Ch. Innisfree's Krimbo. Krimbo was a Balto son bred to a Balto daughter out of Rashiri.

Our consistent use of Balto, inbred to one of his daughters out of Rashiri or his linebred son, Ch. Innisfree's Beau-Tuk, produced one major line that exists at Innisfree today. However, an enduring kennel must have several options. All breeding cannot go in one direction. A breeder must have other ways to go if his original plans do not materialize. Even if the original linebreeding is going successfully, outcrosses must be introduced regularly. Many great lines in a breed are apt to fade away when one great producing dog ages. A viable kennel must consistently produce good dogs year after year, with the offspring produced being as good as, or hopefully better than, the foundation stock. These offspring, besides being good or great specimens of the breed, must be capable of producing quality if one's kennel is to remain significant on the breed scene. Adhering to this theory of developing compatible lines that could be introduced to each other as outcrosses, Innisfree worked on two more strains.

The most important of these was the offspring of Ch. Innisfree's El Ferro. El Ferro was a small in stature, black and white, brown-eyed male. He was a beautiful-headed dog with lovely movement. El Ferro bred to Innisfree's Banshee produced the great producing bitch Ch. Innisfree's Oomachuk who, when bred to Ch. Alakazan's Nikolai, produced American and Canadian Ch. Dudley's Tavar of Innisfree's two time Best in Show Winner, Ch. Innisfree's Pegasus, current important stud at Innisfree, and Ch. Alakazan's Dak Rambo. El Ferro, bred to Zucane's Puna of Bluebell, produced American, Canadian and Bermudian Ch. Innisfree's King Karl (Weir). King Karl was the first Bermudian champion Siberian and the first Siberian to earn three championships.

The crossing of offspring of Ch. Innisfree's Beau-Tuk with Ch. Innisfree's El Ferro continues to be an important part of Innisfree's breeding programs.

The third option we used was the introduction of reds into the breeding program. Breeding for one trait should always be approached with caution. In the early 1960s red Siberians were a phenomenon. It was a challenge to develop dogs that would produce quality red Siberians. Zucane's Puna of Bluebelle was bred to Ch. Frosty Aire's Eric (red) and produced Ch. Innisfree's Barbarossa, a red. Barbarossa was used as an outcross for more leg and his offspring brought this back, successfully, into the lines of Beau-Tuk and the original bitches. Ch. Innisfree's Royal Purple, a Barbarossa son, is currently used for this purpose. Royal's dam, Innisfree's Fireweed, was a surprise indeed. A mating with Innisfree's Rashiri of A-Baska and her grandson, Innisfree's Tonto, out of Ch. Innisfree's Lobo and Tanio produced Fireweed. A light red, she was not recognized as a red until she was five weeks old. She opened up many directions for the reds to go. Through Fireweed we discovered that Rashiri was a red carrier and of course many

Ch. Weldon's Beau-Buk, bred by Nancy Perkins' Weldon Kennels and owned by Innisfree Kennels.

Ch. Weldon's Beau-Tukker, bred by Nancy Perkins and owned by Innisfree Kennels.

Ch. Innisfree's Pegasus, bred by Peggy Koehler and Kathleen Kanzler and owned by Innisfree Kennels.

of her offspring carried the red gene. This was good news for the red Siberians of the time. The few available reds were closely related and the introduction of a strong outcross red line was of value.

The current top studs at Innisfree are Ch. Innisfree's Pegasus and Ch. Weldon's Beau-Tukker, with Ch. Innisfree's Sierra Cinnar, becoming, we hope, the ideal coming-on young stud, along with Innisfree's Import and Innisfree's Targhee.

The outstanding bitches are Ch. Innisfree's Meghan, Ch. Innisfree's Beau-Kara and Innisfree's Beau-Biddy. These are third-generation bitches bred here who, together with outcross bitches, Innisfree's Kathleen and Innisfree's Kismet (a product of Ch. Monadnock's Akela, Ch. Koonah's Red Kiska), Ch. Marytuk's Red Sun of Kiska and Ch. Dichoda's Yukon Red, will enable Innisfree to continue building on the near forty Innisfree Champions produced so far.

Our breeding philosophy and concerns are to utilize the best dogs available at any given time. No kennel stays in the running by using their own dogs exclusively. Pride in your dogs is misplaced if you build a line on anything less than the best available.

Many dogs that are fine animals in themselves are not capable of reproducing themselves, because their four grandparents were not exceptional animals. The longer one looks at dogs, the more one sees that a grandmother with no outstanding virtues that was used out of misplaced emotion by a fond owner has undue influence on her grandchildren. How much further ahead a breeding program would be if that fond owner had looked with less love and more awareness at the bitch. Perhaps then the mature decision would have been to love her as a pet and buy the best-bred female available to build upon.

The other basic breeding principle is to never compromise on temperament. The unique, friendly personality of the Siberian cannot take second place to quality. Aggressive or shy traits are inherited and cause nothing but heartache for the sincere breeder. You have to live with a dog first, then show him. A dog's temperament is basically aggressive or soft. A decided tendency to too aggressive (vicious) or too soft (shy) are judgments a breeder must consider in breeding animals. Personality is an offshoot of temperament. Personality traits are the traits that make a dog an individual. A happy, outgoing, willing-to-please Siberian that takes correction with no resentment is our picture of breed temperament.

The original Innisfree bitches were very sound and typey. Both were grays and not flashy—plain jane types, perhaps. When they were bred, it was the soundest that were kept. Often these were not the flashiest. When building for future generations, it is imperative that soundness and breed type be the first considerations in selecting puppies for breeding stock.

Pitfalls are falling for that dramatic black and white, blue-eyed pup or the darkest red one and perhaps overlooking the superior soundness that may be present in the gray or dilute black pup with bicolored eyes or a white break in his coat.

The breed is not yet at a stage where one can breed all top-quality, dark

Ch. Dudley's Tavar of Innisfree (Ch. Alakazan's Nikolai ex Ch. Innisfree's Oomachuk), owned by Clarence and Gladys Dudley, was twice a BIS winner.
William Gilbert

Ch. Dudley's Varska (Ch. Dudley's Tavar of Innisfree ex Ch. Dudley's Tava of Innisfree), bred by the Clarence Dudleys and co-owned by them with Ginger Scott, had eight Bests in Show scored in the U.S. and Canada.

black or red dogs with blue eyes. Serious breeders must still pursue perfection through the soundest animals of proper type regardless of color.

Another pitfall that entraps breeders is searching for more size, more specifically a bit longer leg. This is a nagging problem. Many of our greatest producing dogs would have been closer to the ideal if they were a bit higher on leg. The way to ruin your breeding program is to breed the small, typey, refined bitch to the big, long-stationed, long-backed male. Genes do not mix. Some pups will be small, some large and long. Two different types of dogs are not going to produce the ideal. If you are going to genetically outcross for size, breed phenotypes (dogs that look alike). Then breed back toward the family lines that work for you. Outcrosses, for whatever reason, are usually most useful in a breeding program when bred back into the original family. Your results are in the second generation, not the outcross itself.

Although Innisfree doesn't have a name in racing, all of the original dogs through 1968 were raced in Michigan. The team was composed of six champions on the seven-dog team. The will to work is an important facet of Siberians that should be preserved. The dogs are harness trained and run for fun by Norb, Trish, John and Sheila. The terrain and climate of southern Maryland are not conducive to serious running.

Innisfree is a family affair. Trish, John and Sheila are most often seen in the ring handling the dogs while Norb gets the kennel moved, built and set up at whatever spot the army sends us. So far Innisfree has been in Michigan, Maryland, New York State, Kansas, California and then returned to Maryland.

KARNOVANDA

Judy Russell has probably never done anything halfway in her life when it comes to animals. An animal "nut" as a child, she had dogs, cats, hamsters, mice, rabbits, birds, fish or whatever happened along. She began riding at seven, competing in saddle horse events at nine, owned her first horse at ten, and by the time she retired from competition in the late 1950s, she had won just about every Saddle Horse or Horsemanship championship open to a juvenile, a woman or an amateur, including the "good hands" championship at the Kentucky State Fair in 1954, 1955 and 1956. And much of her success in Siberians she feels is probably directly attributable to her background in horses.

It was actually her longtime trainer, Chris Reardon, who gave her her first Siberian for her nineteenth birthday. He had first seen some at the American Royal Horse Show in Kansas City, Missouri, and had ordered a pair. He offered Judy her choice of puppies and she chose the bitch who became Ch. Eska's Nonie, UD. Nonie became Judy's constant companion through college and presented her with a litter of eight puppies in her senior year. Judy kept a bitch, which she named Karen. Karen completed her championship and attained a UD degree in Obedience. She later pro-

Foundation bitch of Karnovanda Kennels:

<pre>
                                        Aleka's Khan
                        Baloo of Komatik
                                        Waska of Komatik
            Misha of Monadnock
                                        Izok of Gap Mountain
                        Tamara
                                        Aleka's Sonya
        Baron von Richthoven
                                        Czar of Alyeska
                        Chinook's Alladin of Alyeska
                                        Tcheeakio of Alyeska
            Alaskan Cheeakio of Anadyr
                                        Chinook's Alladin of Alyeska
                        Dirka of Anadyr
                                        Candia

  CH. ESKA'S NONIE, UD   (Whelped 11/18/58)
                                        Ch. Wonalancet's Baldy of Alyeska
                        Izok of Gap Mountain
                                        Duchess of Cold River
            Sonya's Torger
                                        Chort of Monadnock
                        Aleka's Sonya
                                        Ch. Aleka of Monadnock
        Eska of Timberland
                                        Ch. Igloo Pak's Anvik
                        Snow Storm
                                        Nadejda
            Akia's Kenai of Timberland
                                        Gouda of Kabkol
                        Dichoda's Akia
                                        Echo of Kabkol
</pre>

Ch. Karnovanda's Ivan Groznyi became a champion at eight months, Won 15 Group placements and sired 20 champions.

duced Ch. Karen's Token of Karnovanda, CD, who produced some nice puppies. Nothing at Karnovanda today, however, descends from her.

Nonie, on the other hand, was bred again and from her Karnovanda Kennels descends. It was after Judy had married Joel Russell and while they were both doing graduate work at Berkeley that Nonie was bred a second time. This time she was shipped all the way across the country for a mating with Pando, and out of this breeding came the last two syllables of the name Karnovanda, Ivan and Zenda. *Kar* for Karen, *no* for Nonie, *van* for Ivan and *da* for Zenda. The two important puppies from this litter were Ch. Baron of Karnovanda, CD, and Ch. Karnovanda's Zenda, CD. Baron amassed some sixteen Group placings during his career and sired twenty-five champions, while Zenda became a top ranking brood bitch, producing ten champions in her own right, the record in the breed to date.

The next step in the Karnovanda breeding program came after the Russells had moved to Michigan. Once there, they purchased an inbred son of Ch. Frosty Aire's Eric and his daughter, Frosty Aire's Miss Erica, who became Ch. Frosty Aire's Jolly Red Giant. He was acquired specifically to be bred to Zenda, a breeding which produced Ch. Karnovanda's Zenzarya, who, when bred back to her uncle, Ch. Baron of Karnovanda, produced a total of six champions. The most important of these was Ch. Karnovanda's Lara Baronovna, dam of six champions herself, the most famous of which is Ch. Karnovanda's Wolfgang, whelped March 11, 1970 and winner of six Group firsts and a Best in Show.

Meanwhile, back in 1966, Zenda had been bred to Ch. Foxhaunt's Glacier Blu and had produced a bitch who became Ch. Karnovanda's Koyukuk. This litter also contained the second of the Russells' Ivans, Ch. Karnovanda's Ivan Groznyi. Finishing his championship at eight months, which is a breed record for males, Ivan won some ninety Best of Breed awards and placed fifteen times in Group. Extremely useful when bred to daughters and granddaughters of Baron, he produced twenty champions, and five of his get reside at Karnovanda today.

Karnovanda is a relatively large kennel, housing usually between twenty and thirty dogs at a time. Since her divorce in 1971, Judy teaches full-time, raises her three children, takes care of several horses and ponies, and, with the help of friend and fellow Siberian enthusiast, Nancy Hanes, operates the kennel. As if these activities weren't enough, Judy, Nancy and the three children all race with the Great Lakes' Sled Dog Association, so that the fall and winter months are taken up entirely with training and racing. The rest of the year is devoted to showing, which Judy approaches with the same energy and singleness of purpose, as attested by the fact the number of champions owned or bred by Karnovanda now stands at over one-hundred-fifty.

Ch. Karnovanda's Wolfgang, a BIS winner bred and owned by Karnovanda Kennels.

```
                                        Ch. Frosty Aire's Beau-Tuk Balto
                          Ch. Frosty Aire's Banner Boy, CD
                                        Frosty Aire's Suntrana
            Ch. Foxhaunt's Glacier Blue
                                        Igloo Pak's Tok
                          Foxhaunt's Kaytee
                                        Yeso Pac's Sandy
Ch. Karnovanda's Ivan Groznyi
                                        Monadnock's Kolya
                          Ch. Monadnock's Pando
                                        Ch. Monadnock's Nina
            Ch. Karnovanda's Zenda, CD
                                        Baron von Richthoven
                          Ch. Eska's Nonie, UD
                                        Eska of Timberland
```

CH. KARNOVANDA'S WOLFGANG   (Whelped 3/11/70)

```
                                        Monadnock's Kolya
                          Ch. Monadnock's Pando
                                        Ch. Monadnock's Nina
            Ch. Baron of Karnovanda, CD
                                        Baron von Richthoven
                          Ch. Eska's Nonie, UD
                                        Eska of Timberland
Ch. Karnovanda's Lara Baronovna
                                        Ch. Frosty Aire's Eric
                          Ch. Frosty Aire's Jolly Red Giant
                                        Frosty Aire's Miss Erica
            Ch. Karnovanda's Zenzarya
                                        Ch. Monadnock's Pando
                          Ch. Karnovanda's Zenda, CD
                                        Ch. Eska's Nonie, UD
```

KORYAK

The story of Dr. James Brillhart's Koryak Kennels is a story of determination. Losing the first three purebred dogs he purchased to hereditary and congenital defects, Jim became interested in Siberians, whose looks, temperament and intelligence appealed to him and who seemed free of many of the hereditary defects he had found in other breeds.

His run of bad luck however, was not over, and he lost the first three Siberians he purchased as well. Through a freakish set of circumstances, two were shot, and the third, well on his way to his championship, contracted distemper and died.

At this point he was ready to give up dogs altogether, but hearing that Monadnock Kennels had a promising puppy for sale, he decided to take one last chance. Driving all the way to New Hampshire from Indiana, he returned with a black and white, blue-eyed puppy who, indeed, was to bring a change of luck. For he grew up to be Ch. Monadnock's Dmitri, the first Siberian to win two Best in Show awards and the top ranked Siberian in the country in 1964 and 1965. In his best year, he was also ranked among the Top Ten Working Dogs. He then went on to become what too few top winners manage to become, a top producer. In 1967 and 1968 he was ranked the number one producing Siberian sire in the country and in 1968 tied for eleventh place among the twenty-five top producing Working Group sires.

Bred to Monadnock's Kira of Koryak, a Roadmaster daughter acquired from Monadnock Kennels, Dmitri produced the first homebred Koryak champions, Ch. Mikhail of Koryak and Ch. Galya of Koryak. Shown as a brace, Dmitri and Mikhail won five Best Brace in Show awards, including the International Kennel Club show in Chicago in 1968. And Galya, bred back to her grandfather, Pando, provided the first red in the Koryak line, Ch. Tova II of Koryak.

Although Koryak's breeding and showing activities have ceased, its influence remains strong in the breed as a taproot source of influential stock to kennels all over the country. Among Dmitri's more famous progeny are Mikhail, Galya, Ch. Romka Koryak of Bolshoi, Ch. Kincki of Koryak, and his granddaughter, Ch. Koryak's Scarlet Scandal, who, in 1968, tied for first place with Ch. Karnovanda's Zenda, as the top producing dam in the country.

MARLYTUK

Lyle and Marguerite Grant began their career in Siberians in 1950 as trainers of Mrs. Frothingham's Cold River Kennel racing team. While Lyle did the actual competing, Peggy did much of the training during the week. This arrangement continued through the winter of 1956 when Mrs.

Frothingham found she could no longer keep her kennel and offered the Grants any of her dogs and equipment they wanted. Thus began Marlytuk Kennels: *Mar* for Marguerite, *ly* for Lyle and *tuk* for Ahkeetuk, the first Siberian pup owned by the Grants.

From Mrs. Frothingham's dogs the Grants selected one male, Ninga of Cold River, and four females, Lena of Cold River, Enara of Cold River, Tongass of Cold River and Rola. Of these Rola proved the most significant. A daughter of Igloo Pak's Blui and Ch. Helen of Cold River, Dr. Lombard's famous lead dog, she was bred to Izok of Gap Mountain to produce two very influential dogs in the Marlytuk breeding program, a bitch named Wanee of Marly and a dog named Ch. Noonok of Marly.

While Wanee, bred to a Roadmaster son, Monadnock's White Xmas, produced Marlytuk's Ahrigah Nakoo, dam of both Ch. Koonah's Red Kiska and Ch. Koonah's Red Gold, Noonok produced such offspring as Ch. Marlytuk's Ahkee, Marlytuk's Tukki and Ch. Marlytuk's Nonah who, in turn, were influential in the Savdjaure and Doonauk lines as well as in the Marlytuk breeding program.

Acquired from the Dennisons, Koonah's Red Kiska became one of the truly outstanding copper bitches in the breed. Completing her championship at the age of nine months, she enjoyed a highly successful and extremely long show career, going Best of Opposite Sex, for instance, at Westminster Kennel Club in 1973 at the age of nine years.

Over the years, largely because of Kiska and her sister Ch. Koonah's Red Gold, Marlytuk became particularly well-known for its red Siberians, although all colors were produced there. When the time came to breed Kiska, Ch. Monadnock's Akela was chosen as the stud, and this breeding was done five times. Among the many truly outstanding offspring produced by this combination, the most famous has undoubtedly been Ch. Marlytuk's Red Sun of Kiska, known in the Siberian world as "Sunny." Completing his championship in 1968 by winning four out of five shows, all of them four-point majors, Sunny went on to win two National Specialty Shows and to accumulate well over fifty Best of Breed ribbons, feats which kept him near the top in both Phillips System and *Kennel Review* rankings for a number of years. Not only was Sunny a great show dog, however, but a highly prepotent stud who has left an indelible mark on the breed, especially at Marlytuk where a great deal of work has been done to ensure that his soundness, type, and above all, his beautiful movement are maintained.

It is not surprising, however, that both Sunny and Kiska were renowned for their movement, since Marlytuk has always been a top working dog kennel as well as a show kennel, and most of their top show dogs have spent a number of years in harness. In fact, Marlytuk is the only kennel to win the Siberian Husky Club of America's racing trophy four times.

It was probably due in part to the fact that Marlytuk dogs were worked in harness that Peggy always took a great interest in brace and team com-

Ch. Koonah's Red Kiska, one of the most outstanding copper bitches in the history of the breed. She produced Ch. Marlytuk's Red Sun of Kiska, a breed legend in his own right.

Ch. Marlytuk's Red Sun of Kiska stepping out at the 1975 Specialty at 9½ years.

```
                                        Ch. Wonalancet's Baldy of Alyeska
                          Alyeska's Kobuk of Chinook
                                        Tcheeakio of Alyeska
              Alyeska's Sugrut of Chinook
                                        Ipuk of Alyeska
                          Keo of Alyeska
                                        Tcheeakio of Alyeska
        Columbia's Admiral
                                        Monadnock's Kolya
                          Ch. Monadnock's Pando
                                        Ch. Monadnock's Nina
              Monadnock's Flash
                                        Monadnock's Nikko
                          Monadnock's Czarina
                                        Monadnock's Nadya

CH. KOONAH'S RED KISKA       (Whelped 10/19/63)
CH. KOONAH'S RED GOLD
                                        Izok of Gap Mountain
                          Mulpus Brook's The Roadmaster
                                        Ch. Aleka's Czarina
              Monadnock's White Xmas
                                        Kita Kituh of Chebacco
                          Dama of Monadnock
                                        Star of Chebacco
        Marlytuk's Ahrigah Nakoo
                                        Ch. Wonalancet's Baldy of Alyeska
                          Izok of Gap Mountain
                                        Duchess of Cold River
              Wanee of Marly
                                        Igloo Pak's Blui
                          Rola
                                        Ch. Helen of Cold River
```

petition: Marlytuk braces have won eight Best Brace in Show awards, five of which were won by Sunny and Kiska. In fact, in 1975, they took Best Brace in Show at all three specialty shows, Sunny at the age of nine and a half and Kiska at the age of twelve, a feat for which they became known at Marlytuk as "the Geritol twins." So not only were Marlytuk's racing and show records remarkable, but their record for endurance was equally enviable.

Peggy Grant died in July 1990, but as later chapters will show, the Marlytuk legacy will long be enjoyed in kennels throughout the country. The last of Peggy's dogs and the Marlytuk name itself have been inherited by Peggy's longtime protégé, Carol Nash of Canaan Kennels, who will no doubt keep the tradition alive for many years to come.

SAVDAJAURE

Situated in Ashland, Massachusetts, Savdajaure Kennels is the result of the combined efforts of three people, Ragnar and Ingrid Forsberg and their daughter Anna Mae. In the mid 1950s the Forsbergs began raising Norwegian Elkhounds, and their dogs carried the kennel name Lapp. When the family moved to Ashland where their kennel could be larger, they decided to add another breed. And it was at a dog show shortly thereafter that they saw the Monadnock brace of King and Pando and decided then and there that this was the breed.

From Monadnock they acquired two dogs, a bitch who became Monadnock's Savda Pandi and shortly thereafter, a male named Monadnock's Savda Bakko. Pandi had been bred by Muriel Stumpfer and was out of Ch. Monadnock's Red Tango of Murex, a copper and white son of Pando, and Monadnock's Eb'ny Lass of Murex. This being in the days when bitches were frequently left home to produce puppies while the males were shown, Pandi did not complete her championship. Bred only to Bakko, however, she did produce six champions and has certainly left her stamp on the breed.

Bakko, on the other hand, was shown. Bred by Ella H. Shovah out of a mating of Pando and Ch. Sintulata, he, like Pandi, was born in September of 1958. He won his first five points at the National Specialty in Washington in 1959 at the age of six months and went Best of Winners at the Specialty Show in Philadelphia nine months later. In all he completed his championship in only ten shows, never placing lower than Reserve Winners' Dog. He was also a member of the famous team of Pando, King, Bakko and Monadnock's Czar and was a Group winner in 1964. During his career he sired nine champions and was twice winner of the Stud Dog Class at National Specialties.

As impressive an animal as Bakko was, however, he had the capacity to produce better than himself. And, indeed, in July of 1960, there was a

Ch. Savdajaure's Cognac, twice a National Specialty winner and the sire of 24 champions.

Ch. Monadnock's Savda Bakko, sire of Ch. Savdajaure's Cognac.

puppy born at the Forsbergs who, like Togo and Pando before him, was the only live puppy in the litter. In 1958 the name Savdajaure, meaning "mountain lake" in the Swedish Lapp language, had been registered by the AKC, and this puppy became Ch. Savdajaure's Cognac, Best of Breed at two National Specialties, three Area Supported Shows, and three-time winner of the Working Group. He also lived to produce twenty-four champions to make him one of the top producing Siberian sires of his time.

Among Cognac's most influential offspring has been Ch. Savdajaure's Miuk, CD, a copper and white male by Cognac out of Ch. Snoridge's Lorelei, bred by Anna C. Schmale and sent to the Forsbergs as a stud fee puppy. Winner of the Stud Dog Class at the National Specialty in Philadelphia in 1970, Miuk himself sired twelve champions.

Other influential dogs to have resided at Savdajaure have been Ch. Savdajaure's Keema Tova, Ch. Savdajaure's Mekki, Ch. Savdajaure's Vackra Dockra, Ch. Savdajaure's Bushka, Ch. Savdajaure's Tanni and Miuk's son Ch. Savdajaure's Kalle Brun (Swedish for Charlie Brown).

As large a contribution to the breed as Savdajaure has made, however, it is interesting to note that it was quite a small kennel where breeding was done very rarely. Each dog was in effect a family pet—and a testimonial to the research, dedication and teamwork that has made Savdajaure what it was when it was when it was active.

While being a full-time nurse and now an AKC licensed judge, Anna Mae has also managed to serve in almost every capacity in the Siberian Club of America including official historian and AKC delegate.

S-K-MO

Robert and Lou Richardson's interest in Siberians began in the mid 1950s while Bob was serving in the air force in Alaska. Returning to southern California in 1957, they brought with them down the Alcan Highway a small ball of gray fur who subsequently became Ch. Sassara's Ozera, their first champion and longtime racing leader.

Finding the sport of sled dog racing already established in southern California, the Richardsons began acquiring and breeding dogs for their team. And like other Siberian enthusiasts in the area, they also began showing their dogs. From 1959 to 1966, they finished fifteen champions, ten of which were bred by themselves, and acquired the enviable racing record of never having been beaten by any team of any breed trained in southern California.

Out of Ch. Sassara's Ozera, their first champion, came what was perhaps the best-known of S-K-Mo dogs, Ch. S-K-Mo's Charney Sambo and his sister Ch. S-K-Mo's Charney Sooka. Not only did this team win five Best Brace in Show awards, but they won four of them consecutively the first four times they were shown together.

Five time Best Brace in Show winners, Ch. S-K-Mo's Charney Sooka and her brother, Ch. S-K-Mo's Charney Sambo.

Ch. S-K-Mo's J.P. McMorgan, owned by John and Laurel Tanner.

Basically, however, the S-K-Mo breeding program can be seen to be based primarily upon two dogs: Ch. Tyndrum's Oslo, CDX, and Ch. Kola of Anadyr. The influence of Oslo comes from two dogs brought down from Alaska, Ch. Bennett's Digger and an outstanding bitch named Ch. Atu of Glacier Valley; the influence of Kola, also brought down from Alaska and a brother of the very influential Ch. Noho of Anadyr owned by Dichoda Kennels, comes down through a number of progeny including Ch. Dichoda's Udacha of S-K-Mo, Ch. S-K-Mo's Kolyema Snova, Ch. S-K-Mo's Matushka Katrina and Ch. S-K-Mo's Charney Korsar.

Having tried unsuccessfully to introduce Eastern stock into their lines, the Richardsons finally leased Dr. Brillhart's Ch. Mikhail of Koryak in 1968 and were successful in introducing him into the S-K-Mo breeding program. This line with some stock introduced from Martha Lake Kennels served to complement the carefully linebred stock that descended from the Richardsons' original Alaskan imports.

For many years Lou was very influential in the Siberian Husky Club of America and in 1966 became an AKC licensed judge. Since that time there has been very little breeding done at S-K-Mo Kennels. Nevertheless, the influence that this kennel has exerted on the Siberians of the Far West is probably rivaled only by that of Dichoda.

YESO PAC

In 1954 Charlie and Carolyn Posey established their Yeso Pac (C. A. Posey spelled backward) Kennels with the intention of raising Boxers. No sooner had they moved into their new kennel property, however, than a friend offered them a Siberian bitch whose cat chasing and fence jumping he had found too much to cope with. Carolyn was against acquiring this scrawny, out-of-coat troublemaker who had already had five different owners at the age of four. Charlie, on the other hand, either out of curiosity, or a sense of challenge, or because even then he had a keen eye for dogs, wanted to take her. And so Kara came to live with the Poseys and the Boxers somehow got lost in the shuffle.

Kara, who came from Kabkol stock behind which was both Chinook and Monadnock breeding, turned out to be considerably more than the scrawny troublemaker she at first appeared. Not only did she rapidly win the affection and respect of both the Poseys, but, once back in coat and in good weight, she completed her championship with dispatch and then presented the Poseys with their first litter, one that contained three champions: Ch. Kara's Idyl, Ch. Kara's Aral, and Ch. Kara's Umlak.

Indeed, Kara, who Charlie said greatly resembled the Seeleys' Ch. Wonalancet's Baldy of Alyeska, became the foundation of Yeso Pac and produced a number of litters. Among them, the result of a mating with

Pando, was one that contained another very significant birth, Ch. Checkers of Yeso Pac.

The next important step in the Poseys' breeding program was the acquisition of a young male from Monadnock Kennels who became Ch. Monadnock's Prince Igor, CD. A Pando son and the Posey's only Obedience title holder, Igor went Best of Breed at Westminster in 1958 and was the 1961 National Specialty winner. Bred to Ch. Kara's Idyl, he produced Yeso Pac's Sandy who, when bred to the famous Igloo Pac's Tok, produced a number of exceptional dogs including Ch. Yeso Pac's Reynard who finished his championship at eleven months.

Bred to Checkers, Igor produced Ch. Yeso Pac's Aurora, a double Pando granddaughter who, when bred back to her great-great-grandfather, Ch. Alyeska's Suggen of Chinook, produced a truly outstanding bitch Ch. Yeso Pac's Tamara. Tamara in turn was bred three times to Ch. Savdajaure's Cognac to produce such dogs as Alakazan's Kristi, extremely influential in the Alakazan line, Yeso Pac's Reddy Kilowatt and Ch. Yeso Pac's Minx, both reds, and, perhaps most significantly, Ch. Yeso Pac's Vodka, an extremely important stud at Yeso Pac. During his lifetime Igor sired twelve champions while Vodka sired ten.

To complement this line of dogs, the Poseys introduced Igloo Pak stock, primarily through Igloo Pak's Tok, along with an intermingling of Calivali and Foxstand lines. Among their most outstanding show dogs was a bitch named Ch. Chebco's Tashinka. Acquired from Walter Shanks, this exceptionally beautiful copper and white daughter of Ch. Monadnock's Akela and Ch. Chebco's Copper Prestige was shown only seven times and finished with four majors.

But showing has only been part of Yeso Pac's commitment to the world of Siberians, and over the years their record on the trail was just as remarkable as their record in the ring. For over a dozen years Charlie was one of the top contenders in the New England Sled Dog Club, and in 1974 the Yeso Pac racing team, led by Yeso Pac's Satan, winner of the Sled Dog Class at the Canadian Specialty in 1974, was ranked number two in the club, attesting to the fact that the Poseys' breeding program was still based on producing the same dual-purpose Siberian they first came to know and believe in.

Charlie Posey died in 1988 and that year's national Specialty was dedicated to his memory. Carolyn is now an honorary life member of the Siberian Husky Club of America.

BALTIC, FOXHAUNT, STONEY RIVER AND KABKOL

Four other kennels operating during the middle-generation period of the breed, although no longer active today, contributed greatly to the

Ch. Monadnock's Prince Igor, CD, owned by Yeso Pac Kennels, was BB at the 1961 SHCA National Specialty.

Ch. Yeso Pac's Reynard (lying down) and Ch. Yeso Pac's Tamara.

progression of the breed. They were Baltic, Foxhaunt, Stoney River and Kabkol.

Baltic Kennels was established in the early 1950s in Commerce City, Colorado, by John and Ruth Cline. Their first bitch, Baltic Chilla Chima, was acquired from Jerry Nemecek in 1955. Sired by Cheechako of Timberland out of Stoney River's Chima, she proved to be a foundation bitch in the truest sense of the word.

Bred to Ch. Stoney River's Jet Siobhan, Chilly provided the Clines with their first homebred champion, a bitch named Ch. Baltic Chilla's Gay Charmer, as well as another champion, Ch. Stoney River's Shutka. Charmer was then bred to Ch. Stoney River's Ootah to produce Teko Zema, an outstanding stud. Bred to Panda of Clear Creek, a Chilly daughter, he produced perhaps the most famous of Baltic dogs, Ch. Ty Cheeko of Baltic, CD, the number one Siberian in the country in 1963 and sire of such dogs as Ch. Loki Easter of Baltic and Ch. Stashi's Ganya of Baltic. In a mating with another Chilly daughter, Baltic Chilla's Hao-Chi-La, Teko then produced the outstanding and influential bitch, Ch. Alapah Oonik of Baltic. And finally, bred directly back to Chilly for her last litter, he produced Ch. Reginald of Baltic who, in turn, sired Ed Samberson's Best in Show winner Ch. Darbo Domeyko of Long's Peak.

The Clines are both dead now, but the distinctive silver and gray dogs that descend from their line can be found in kennels all across the country, especially in the Rocky Mountain area where Baltic dogs and their descendants continue to be a dominant force to this day.

Foxhaunt Kennels was founded in the mid 1950s by Mr. and Mrs. Richard Williams. During its formative years the kennel was located in New Jersey before being moved to Algonquin, Illinois.

The Williams foundation stock came from Monadnock Kennels and consisted of a daughter of Pando and Czarina named Ninaki of Monadnock, who was later a National Specialty winner, and Monadnock's Kootenai, a son of Roadmaster and Monadnock's Zora and a full brother of Ch. Monadnock's Konyak of Kazan. A mating of these two produced Foxhaunt's first champion, Ch. Foxhaunt's Ziok. This breeding also produced a bitch named Foxhaunt's Sinopah who, when bred back to Pando, produced Ch. Foxhaunt's Tovarisch, the 1961 National Specialty winner.

Before leaving the East, the Williams acquired two more bitches, Foxhaunt's Ondine and Foxhaunt's Kaytee. Ondine came from Monadnock Kennels, was a double Pando granddaughter from a breeding of Frosty Aire's Chenik and Monadnock's Natasha, and was a full sister of Ch. Monadnock's Norina and Czarina Alexandria. After moving to the Midwest, she was bred to Ch. Frosty Aire's Banner Boy to produce Ch. Foxhaunt's Czarina. Kaytee, bred by Yeso Pac Kennels out of Igloo Pak's Tok and Sandy, was also bred to Banner Boy, a breeding which resulted in the last major step in the Foxhaunt breeding program. Out of it came both Ch. Foxhaunt's Glacier Blu and Foxhaunt's Suggen. Glacier Blu went Best of Breed at the International Dog Show in Chicago, while Suggen, although never campaigned to his championship, was a National Specialty winner.

Throughout their career, the Williams' primary concern was in breeding a standard Siberian who could also run on a team, and their racing record both in the East and the Midwest has been outstanding. Although other responsibilities have curtailed their activity in Siberians, the Williams still own a last son of Suggen.

Kabkol Kennels, although active only a short time during the late 1940s and early 1950s, has had an influence on today's Siberians. Owned by Earl and Margaret Nagle, the foundation stock consisted of three dogs, a stud named Ch. Kolya of Monadnock, out of Ch. Vanya of Monadnock III and Ch. Kira of Monadnock, and two bitches, Nanuck of Alyeska and Kabloona. Nanuck was a product of Chinook Kennels sired by Czar of Alyeska out of Tcheeakio of Alyeska, and Kabloona was unregistered. Out of these three dogs and their offspring came all the Siberians carrying the Kabkol name, some of which appear in the pedigrees of some of the most influential kennels in the country, particularly in those of Dichoda and Yeso Pac.

Stoney River Kennels belonged to James and Lucille Hudson and was in existence from 1952 to 1961, during which time they finished seven champions. Their foundation bitch was a daughter of Ch. Vanya of Monadnock III and Ch. Kira of Monadnock named Tanya of Monadnock. Their foundation stud was Aleka's Khan, a son of Chort of Monadnock and Ch. Aleka of Monadnock. A breeding of these two produced Ch. Stoney River's Frosty Boy. A breeding of Tanya back to her father produced, among others, Ch. Stoney River's Gay Panda, Stoney River's Chima and Stoney River's Nanuk. When Stoney River's Chima was bred to Cheechako of Timberland, she produced Baltic Chilla Chima, the foundation bitch of Baltic Kennels. The breeding of Khan to Nanuk produced Ch. Stoney River's Karluk, the first Siberian to place in the Group in Colorado. Tanya bred to Frosty Aire's Tobuk produced Ch. Stoney River's Tikki-tue and Ch. Stoney River's Taiki-O. Bred to Czar of Anadyr she produced the influential Ch. Stoney River's Ootah and the equally outstanding Ch. Stoney River's Rinda. Shown for the first time at the age of six months and three days, Rinda took a five-point major and proceeded to complete her championship in the next three shows, finishing at the age of nine months, six days—for many years the youngest bitch in the breed to have finished her championship. For a time, the Hudsons also owned and showed Ch. Monadnock's Nina, the dam of Pando and a three-time Group placer.

Ch. Baltic Pacesetter and Baltic Tor-Na-Do's Inuijak, bred by John and Ruth Cline and owned by Mr. and Mrs. R. B. Conyers' Taiga Kennels.

Dick Williams driving Foxhaunt's all Siberian racing team, 1968-69. Double lead: Foxhaunt's Suggen and Trina. Point: Ch. Foxhaunt's Zorina and Foxhaunt's Glacier Blu.

MORE RECENT KENNELS

Demavand/Sno-Den

Michael Jennings established his Demavand Kennels in upstate New York in 1972, and by the late 1970s had formed a sort of casual partnership with Dr. Peter Perez of Sno-Den Kennels in order to produce a truly dual-purpose Siberian—Mike, and later Johanna DuWaldt, doing most of the showing, Pete doing most of the racing. Most of their current stock descends from Ch. Demavand's Sa Shunka of Sno-Den, an animal as much admired by racers as by show enthusiasts, and their oustanding pure white, Demavand's Wiska. Their dogs combine Marlytuk, Monadnock, Alakazan, Innisfree and Yeso Pac lines, along with a smattering of Canadian racing stock.

In addition to Shunka and Wiska, their well-known animals include Ch. Demavand's Shabdiz, Ch. Goldspur's Ahzrahk Bannu, Ch. Demavand's Ahtesh, Ch. Demavand's Czar of Adaconda, Ch. Innisfree's Sahar of Demavand, Ch. Innisfree's Aktar of Demavand, Ch. Demavand's Quequeg, Ch. Demavand's Shiva, Ch. Sno-Den's Nagi of Stormwake, Ch. Sno-Den's Isaac, Ch. Demavand's Chekhov (RWD at the 1990 National Specialty) and Ch. Demavand's Liyaza Cassandra—co-owned with Mike by Johanna DuWaldt and Tom Zirnheld, and winner of Best of Opposite Sex at the 1988 National Specialty.

Indigo

Dr. David and Mrs. Sheila Qualls formed Indigo Kennels in the mid 1970s based primarily on Innisfree stock along with a smattering of Karnovanda. Although they have finished numerous champions of various backgrounds, the real cornerstone of their breeding program proved to be Ch. Innisfree's Newscents Niavar, a daughter of Ch. Innisfree's Sierra Cinnar and Ch. Innisfree's Canadian Export, and producer of seventeen champions to date, including three Best in Show winners. Her most famous offspring, Ch. Indigo's Intity, became the winningest bitch in breed history, owner-handled all the way, with 20 all-breed Bests in Show, 96 Group firsts, 57 other Group placements and 201 Bests of Breed. She was also BOS and BB, respectively, at the 1985 and 1986 National Specialties.

David, a veterinarian, was also instrumental in the formation of the Siberian Husky Ophthalmic Registry (SHOR) for the Siberian Husky Club of America.

Itaska

Paul Wilhauk began his involvement with Siberians in 1964 with Doonauk's Kiak, bred by Ray and Viola Akers, whom he finished easily, as he did a number of subsequent dogs such as Ch. Chebco's Eemah,

Ch. Demavand's Sa Shunka of Sno-Den, owned by Michael Jennings. *Klein*

Ch. Demavand's Liyaza Cassandra, a granddaughter of Sa Shunka, and like him, she has done well in the show ring and demonstrated a real talent for working before a sled. *Janet Ashbey*

Ch. Innisfree's Newscents Niavar, owned by Indigo Siberians of Dr. and Mrs. David Qualls. "Newscents" is the top brood bitch in Siberian history. *Ritter*

Ch. Indigo's Intity, a "Newscents" daughter, is the breed's top-winning bitch. Talent runs in families!

bought from Walter Shanks, Ch. Itaska's Ah-New, Ch. Pokey Itaska and Ch. Charro's Copper Cha-Lee.

As Paul became increasingly in demand as a handler, he stopped breeding Siberians for many years until he married in 1981. At that time his Itaska Siberians joined forces with wife Wendy's Frostfield Alaskan Malamutes.

Recent Itaska dogs of note include brothers Am. & Can. Ch. Itaska's Marvelous Marvin and Ch. Itaska's Good Time Charlie, along with an up-and-coming Marvin son, Itaska's Mighty May.

Kaila

Richard and Pauline Price founded their Kaila Kennels in the early 1970s in Boulder Creek, California, based on Innisfree stock plus Marlytuk crosses through Ch. Arctic Rogue O'Innisfree (shown to Best of Breed at the 1977 National Specialty by Richard). Careful attention to head type, temperament, movement and the correct height-to-length proportions has characterized their breeding over the years, resulting in such animals as Ch. Kaila's Beau Blue of Rusojhn (Winners Dog at the 1979 National Specialty), Ch. Kaila's Cashmere (WB, BW and Award of Merit Winner at the 1985 National Specialty) and Group Winners Ch. Dudley's Kaila of Innisfree, Ch. Kaila's Tom E. Wolfe, Ch. Kaila's Sno-Mate Connection, Ch. Kaila's Encore and Ch. Runamuck's Kaleetan of Kaila.

Apart from Innisfree and Marlytuk lines, the Prices also introduced stock from Baltic and Anadyr (Alaskan Kennels).

Other noteworthy Kaila Siberians include Ch. Kaila's Red Zinger, Ch. Kaila's Temujin of Innisfree, Ch. Kaila's Winter Eve of Rusojhn, Ch. Kaila's Katta's Kate, Ch. Kaila's Kinda Katta, and Ch. Kaila's Mountain Mist (Reserve Winners Bitch at the 1984 National Specialty).

Kontoki

Pointing out that the AKC Standard for the Siberian Husky uses the words "moderate" and "medium" eighteen times, Thomas Oelschlager and Marlene DePalma have combined Innisfree and Savdajaure lines to produce highly consistent Siberians that are among the winningest in the show ring today—by some measures, perhaps, the winningest of all time. Favoring slow-maturing animals that maintain the refinement of type that allows for long show careers, they've produced such standouts as Ch. Kontoki's Natural Sinner (Nate), winner of nine Best in Show Awards and seventeen Specialty Best of Breeds (a record for the breed), his grandson Ch. Kontoki's One Mo Time, winner of thirty-three Bests in Show (also a breed record), Ch. Kontoki's Hot Lips (also a Best in Show winner) and Ch. Kontoki's Dennis the Menace (also a Nate grandson, and a multiple Best in Show winner).

Am., Can. Ch. Itaska's Marvelous Marvin, a Specialty, Group and BIS winner and an important stud dog. *Chuck Tatham*

Ch. Kaila's Cashmere, owned by Richard and Pauline Price, was BW at the 1985 SHCA Specialty enroute to her championship.

Ch. Kaila's Kinda Katta. *Missy Yuhl*

Ch. Kontoki's Natural Sinner, owned by Thomas Oelschlager and Marlene DePalma, was awarded Best in Show at the Old Dominion KC show under the English judge Gwen Broadley.

Ch. Kontoki's One Mo' Time, owned by Thomas Oelschlager and Marlene DePalma, is the breed's top BIS-winner with 35 all-breed bests to his credit. Owner-handled throughout his career, he topped the breed entry at Westminster 1987 under judge Arthur Reinitz.

Chuck Tatham

Kontoki has also bred or owned the most Specialty Sweepstakes winners: Ch. Kontoki's One Mo Time, Ch. Kontoki's Natural Sinner, Ch. Kontoki's New York Times, Ch. Kontoki's Elizabeth Claiborne, Ch. Innisfree's Gonna Fly Now, Ch. Kontoki's Second Time Around, Ch. Kontoki's The Gospel Truth, Kontoki's Church Lady, Ch. Kontoki's Hot Lips and Ch. Kokomo's Claim to Fame.

Other Kontoki champions include Ch. Kontoki's Once Upon a Time, Ch. Kontoki's Step in Time, Ch. Kontoki's Sing N in the Rain, Ch. Kontoki's Missionary Man, Ch. Kontoki's A Mark in Time, Ch. Kontoki's Jumpin Jack Flash and Ch. Kontoki's Moonstruck.

Kossok

Alice Watt began her Kossok Kennels in 1968, but it was not until she acquired a red, blue-eyed bitch, Am. & Can. Ch. Kohoutek's Kia of Kristland, in 1976 that her current breeding program began. Based on offspring of Kia and Am. & Can. Ch. Innisfree's Sierra Cinnar, Kossok Siberians now contain various blendings of Innisfree, Kaila and Sno-Fame stock. And seventeen have become champions.

The goal at Kossok is to produce healthy, beautiful dogs with stable temperaments that can be successful winners and loving pets, and that retain the body structure that would enable them to perform in harness.

Of the Midnight Sun

"Whatever that is, it's what I want," remarked Janis Church of the first Siberian she ever saw at a match in Wichita, Kansas, thereby bringing into being the Siberians of the Midnight Sun, established in 1960 on Monadnock stock with later infusions of Innisfree.

Although she has successfully competed in all aspects of Siberian performance—Janis's racing teams of the late sixties and early seventies containing leaders Ch. Tonkova of the Midnight Sun, CD, and Ch. Kroshka of the Midnight Sun, along with foundation bitches Ch. Monadnock's Midnight Sun, Ch. Monadnock's Midnight Musya and Ch. Koritza of Kettle Moraine—she realized early that most puppies are inevitably sold as pets. So temperament and soundness are of paramount importance in the breeding program.

Others of their significant animals include Ch. Akkani of the Midnight Sun, his son Ch. Kokoda of the Midnight Sun, daughter Ch. Soka of the Midnight Sun and more recently a bitch owned but not bred by them, Ch. Zaimar's Scarlet Ribbons, a Group and Specialty winner who later became the number one Siberian in Japan with seven Bests in Show.

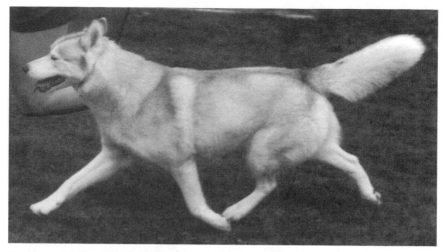

Ch. Kossock's Good as Gold (Ch. Innisfree's Sierra Cinnar ex Ch. Kohoutek's Kia of Krisland).

Ch. Kossock's Patch of Bleu (Ch. Kaila's Beau Bleu of Rusojhn ex Ch. Kossock's Buttercup Bouquet).

Bubbleup of the Midnight Sun.   *Cott/Daigle*

Ch. Dimondust of the Midnight Sun (Ch. Kaila's Beau Bleu of Rusojhn ex Spice N' Ice of the Midnight Sun), owned and bred by Janis R. Church.   *Wayne Cott*

Ch. Innisfree's Pagan Sinner, owned by Sandra James, is a multiple BIS winner and a noteworthy stud dog.   *Alverson*

Ch. Saroja's New Era of Camarade (Ch. Innisfree's Pagan Sinner ex Innisfree's Saroja Treasure), owned by Sandra James.   *Earl Graham*

Saroja

After years of owning Siberians purely for companionship, Ronald and Sandra James established their Saroja (sah-row-hah) Kennels across Lake Pontchartrain from New Orleans in 1979 with the purchase of Ch. Innisfree's Pagan Sinner (a son of Ch. Innisfree's Sierra Cinnar and an inbred daughter of Ch. Weldon's Beau Tukker). Owner-handled to three Best in Show awards, he was among the top ten Siberians for three years and among the top producers for six years.

Concentrating on combining the best of Innisfree with the best of Marlytuk, the Jameses combined Pagan with offspring of Ch. Demavand's Sa Shunka of Sno-Den, Ch. Innisfree's Red Roadster and Ch. Arctic Rogue O'Innisfree in order to keep plenty of leg and athleticism, as well as type. And in ten years of moderate breeding, the Jameses produced thirty champions, including Ch. Saroja's September Schervari, Ch. Saroja's Stonemartin (a Specialty winner), Ch. Saroja's Kissyfur, Ch. Saroja's September Jilgre (Best Brood Bitch at both the 1989 National Specialty and the 1989 Atlanta Specialty), Ch. Saroja's New Era of Camarade (another Specialty winner), Ch. Saroja's Symphony in Blue, Ch. Saroja's Sarsaparilla, Ch. Saroja's Joint Venture, Ch. Saroja's Simply Marvelous and Ch. Saroja's Special Souvenir.

Snoking

Richard and Janice MacWade formed their Snoking Kennels when they married in 1976. But each had already spent many years in the breed, primarily with Fra-Mar dogs: Jan having finished Ch. Jo-L's Leea, Ch. Jo-L's Stormy, Ch. Jo-L's Baby George and Ch. Fra-Mar's Mr. Nimo; Richard having finished a son of Ch. Fra-Mar's Soan Diavol, Ch. Fra-Mar's Arctic Challenger, and Ch. Eu-Mor's Copper Warrior.

Since joining forces they've introduced Baltic, Innisfree, Karnovanda and Telemark (Canadian) stock to produce such animals as Ch. Snoking's Snowdrift, Ch. Snoking's Ice Princess, Ch. Snoking's Coal Miner, Ch. Snoking's Gold Rush, Ch. Snoking's Cotton Candy, Ch. Snoking's Satisfier and Ch. Snoking's Sugar Baby. They were also co-owners of Ch. Bolshoi's Grey Sinner, purchased from Canada, who was Best of Breed at the 1982 National Specialty and sire of Ch. Snoking's Cotton Candy.

After experiencing the tragedy of inherited cataracts with Ch. Innisfree's On the Road Again, who at eighteen months had already won three Specialty Bests in Show and five all-breed Bests in Show, they founded SEARCH (Siberian Husky Eye Anomaly Research Committee) in what they describe as "an effort to reduce the incidence of inherited eye disease so all may enjoy the breed for many years to come."

Snowfire

Linda and George Lehman's Snowfire Kennels was established in 1974 and has evolved out of two foundation bitches purchased from Alakazan Kennels, Ch. Alakazan's Snowfire and Ch. Alakazan's Liberty Belle. Out of these came Ch. Snowfire's Viva, Ch. Sudo's Shokalodka, and Ch. Snowfire's Tovarish (a Group winner) and Ch. Snowfire's Reprint, respectively. Later champions include Ch. Snowfire's Kerashive Yvar, Ch. Snowfire's April Edition, Ch. Snowfire's Avatar Yvar, Ch. Snowfire's First Day of Summer, Ch. Neechee's Snowfire Dark Shadow, Winners Dog at the 1988 National Specialty and an area Specialty winner, and Ch. Snowfire's Sans Souci, one of the top-winning bitches in the breed today.

Snowfire stock is predominantly Alakazan and Monadnock with a smattering of Innisfree and shows how a kennel can stay very small and still be highly successful. At this writing, the Lehmans have only seven animals, all of them bitches, and all of them kept collectively in a single dog yard—a testament to good temperament.

Talocon

Established in 1970, John and Gail O'Connell's Talocon Kennels is based very solidly on Monadnock lines, and it is their aim to keep that emphasis, both in terms of type and temperament (which includes the desire to work).

Ch. Talocon's Flash was the O'Connell's first homebred champion, and he enjoyed not only a very successful, individual show career, but along with son Ch. Talocon's Arctic Echo was undefeated in Group in Brace competition, achieving seventeen Best in Show wins, making them a top winning brace in the nation, both among all breeds and in the history of the Siberian.

Flash offspring include Specialty winners Ch. Talocon's Arctic Aleta, Am. & Can. Ch. Talocon's Arctic Flair O'Kunuk, Ch. Talocon's Arctic Thunder, Ch. Cossack's Tavda and a number of Canadian champions, as well as team runners, lead dogs and registered Therapy Dogs.

Tawny Hill

In the glitz and hype of the contemporary show world, Adele Gray is a refreshingly low key but highly consistent force. Establishing her Tawny Hill Kennels in 1968 based on three Monadnock animals, Ch. Tawny Hill Baikal O'Monadnock, Ch. Tawny Hill Tanja of Monadnock and Ch. Tawny Hill Larna of Monadnock, she kept almost all the puppies from breedings to Ch. Monadnock's Akela, Ch. Savdajaure's Cognac and Ch. Alakazan's Nikolai, and was quickly on her way to achieving the 30-40 dog kennel she maintains today, trying, as she says, "to stick as closely to

Am., Can. Ch. Snoking's Gold Rush (Ch. Innisfree's Red Roadster ex Telemark's Chandelle), bred and owned by Richard and Jan MacWhade. *Stephen Klein*

Snoking's Action Jackson (Ch. Innisfree's Bring Me Luck ex Ch. Snoking's Cotton Candy), bred by Richard and Jan MacWhade. *Booth*

Ch. Snowfire's Viva, owned by Linda Leham, was the first home-bred champion for Snowfire Kennels. *William Gilbert*

135

A decade Later, Ch. Snowfire's Sans Souci was writing her own chapter in the Siberian history book. She has brought home numerous good wins including Group and Specialty honors. *Lloyd Seltzer*

Two sons of Ch. Talocon's Arctic Flash: Ch. Talocon's Arctic Thunder (left) and Ch. Talocon's Arctic Polaris.

Ch. Tawny Hill's Gaibryel (Ch. Alakazan's Nikolai ex Ch. Tawny Hill's Larna of Monadnock), owned by Adele Gray, was a significant early stud for this kennel. *Evelyn Shafer*

Ch. Tawny Hill's Gamyn (Ch. Savajaure's Cognac ex Ch. Tawny Hill's Molina) was an outstanding asset in the development of this family. *William Gilbert*

137

the breed Standard as God will allow and maintain the personality and type that was commonly known in the past as the 'Monadnock look'." In the process she has quietly finished some 25 homebred champions.

Teeco

Margaret Cook became involved with Siberians as house pets in 1967. But it was not until her children were more or less grown and independent that she formed Teeco Kennels in 1980, based on Marlytuk-Doonauk stock and some somewhat mixed Innisfree lines. Since then she has finished nineteen champions.

Her foundation bitch was a daughter of Ch. Doonauk's Jeuahnee of Keemah and Ch. Marlytuk's Elektra named Marmik's Toekee of Elektra, and her most significant foundation male was a son of Ch. Bundas Boston Moonshadow which she acquired from Dr. Gabriel Myers named Ch. Balcam's Teeco's S Taree Night, a grandson of Ch. Weldon's Beau Tukker and great grandson of Ch. Innisfree's Pegasus. From these and related dogs Teeco evolved. Perhaps the most notable is Ch. Teeco's Tallahasee Lassie, SD, number two winning Siberian bitch in 1988 and the first multiple Group winning bitch to earn a Sled Dog degree.

Margaret's greatest love is driving her dogs, competing in both sprint and mid-distance races, and she has served as Chairman of the Working Sled Dog Committee for the Siberian Husky Club of America.

Turick

Leonard and Carolyn Bain's Turick Kennels is undoubtedly heir apparent to Charlie and Carolyn Posey's Yeso Pac Kennel, not only because the vast majority of their stock comes from there, but because they perpetuate the same breeding philosophy that the same animal ought to be able to win in the ring and on the trail. They maintain both a six-dog and an eight-dog sprint team, finishing the 1989 season second and third respectively in their overall class season standings. They have twice won the coveted New England Sled Dog Club's Top Purebred All Siberian Team Award. And of the twenty-seven animals the Bains currently house, thirteen have SD (Sled Dog) Degrees, four are major pointed, one is SEPP rated, one is a champion, and several have won Best Sled Dog Awards at Specialties.

But the gem of their kennel to date is no doubt Leonard's coleader Ch. Kimlan's Leather N Lace, known as "Stevie," bred by the Hookers of Canada, who finished her championship in just nine shows including a National and two area Specialties, three majors, three Best of Breed Awards and a Group third—all from the Open bitch class.

She is also the first and, so far, the only bench show champion to receive an "Excellent" rating at a SEPP evaluation.

Marmik's Toekee of Elektra was the foundation matron for Margaret Cook's Teeco Siberians.

Am., Can. Ch. High Country's Hyper Holly, bred by the LaDukes, was Teeco's first champion.

Ch. Kimlan's Leather N' Lace, owned by Leonard and Carolyn Bain, has proven her exceptional ability as a lead dog and a show dog.

Turick's Devil in Disguise (Turick's Damien of Yeso Pac ex Ch. Kimlan's Leather N' Lace), owned by Leonard and Carolyn Bain.
Bernard Kernan

Ch. Valdea's Thor of Sundown, a winner of the Delaware Valley Specialty. *Earl Graham*

Ch. Valdeah's Valerie of Shenandoah (Ch. Valdeah's Samson of Desmar ex Valdeah's Medea). *Bruce Harkins*

Valdea

Duane and Lois Proctor's Valdea Kennels was founded in the early seventies based on Innisfree, Frosty Aire and Arctic lines in hopes of producing animals of the general type and soundness of Ch. Frosty Aire's Bannner Boy, CD. The Proctors' first bitch, Ch. Innisfree's Bona Dea of Viking, a daughter of Best in Show winner Ch. Dudley's Tavar of Innisfree, produced Best in Show winner Ch. Innisfree's Targhee, Delaware Specialty winner Ch. Valdea's Thor of Sundown and Ch. Valdea's Niki of Blue Igloo; while her daughters Valdea's Cassandra and Valdea's Medea went on to produce such animals as Ch. Valdea's Quasar of Blue Igloo, Ch. Valdea's Aurora, Chesapeake Specialty winner Ch. Valdea's Phantom Streak, Ch. Valdea's Valderie of Shenandoah, Ch. Valdea's Venture and Valdea's Vindicator Shenandoah, SD. They also finished Ch. Valdea's Samson of Des-Mar, sire of Ch. Pandi Valdea's Total Terra.

Veleah

Vel Leahy began in Siberians in 1972, establishing her Veleah Kennels on a Marlytuk-Doonauk foundation, with Innisfree crosses and recent introductions of Cudubhan, Demavand and Sno-Mate lines. Her most significant bitch, Ch. Highpoint Veleah Quicksilver, bred twice to Best in Show winner Ch. Innisfree's Pagan Sinner, produced Best in Show winner Ch. Veleah's Silver Patriot, Group winner Ch. Veleah's IBN Pagan, Group placer Ch. Veleah's Knight Rider, multi Brace Best in Show Ch. Veleah's Scarlet Fever and Ch. Veleah's Love Potion, Group placer Ch. Veleah's Satin Sinner and Specialty Best of Winners Ch. Veleah's Justin Thyme, CD, and Veleah's Smokin Joe, CDX. Ch. Veleah's Silver Patriot has himself gone on to produce the multi Best in Show winner Ch. Satarin's Pride N Joy, the top Siberian for 1989.

With two pups descending from these and similar combinations of Marlytuk, Doonauk and Innisfree, Veleah introduced Ch. Cudubhan's Sanity Claus, Demavand's Akela and Ch. Sno-Mates Rythem N Blue to the breeding program.

Yeti

Established in 1968, Joy and Robert Messinger's Yeti Siberians consist primarily of Savdajaure, Marlytuk and Baltic lines. Am., Can. & Bda. Ch. Snoridge's Rusty Nail of Yeti, Am., Can., & Bda., CD, provided a solid Savdajaure foundation, and when bred to Ch. Marlytuk's Georgie Girl produced an all-champion litter of four that included Ch. Yeti's Red Chili of Snoridge, winner of the 1975 National Specialty. Also a lead dog, Nail went on to sire his successor on Bob's team Ch. Yeti's Sorrel, as well as a number of other leaders.

Ch. Veleah's Silver Patriot, a BIS winning son of the celebrated brood matron Ch. High-point Veleah Quicksilver, shown here with owner Vel Leahy.

Ch. Snoridge's Rusty Nail of Yeti, CD, owned by Joy Graeme Messinger, holds the same conformation and obedience titles in the US, Canada and Bermuda.   *John Ashbey*

Ch. Yeti's Baltic Vin, owned by Joy Graeme Messinger.   *Ashbey II*

On the other side of the family, Am. & Can. Ch. Yeti's Chardonnay of Selito, a granddaughter of Ch. Arctic Flame of Long's Peak, was bred to Ch. Baltic Pacesetter to reinforce the Baltic strain, producing Ch. Yeti's Baltic Vin, multi Specialty winner and sire of such animals as Canadian Best in Show winner Can. Ch. Yeti's Takk of Telaka, Ch. Yeti's English Thanks and Am. & Can. Ch. Yeti's Pila Maye Nikki, CD—all out of Am. & Can. Ch. Yeti's Serendipity of Sundana, a homebred bitch also part Baltic. And today the Baltic part of the kennel continues with offspring of Ch. Yeti's English Thanks—Ch. Yeti's Blue Tango, CD, Can. Ch. Yeti's Bolero and Yeti's Cha-Cha.

THE SIBERIAN IN CANADA

The breed we know as the Siberian Husky was for many years the Siberian Huskie in Canada, and was not recognized by the Canadian Kennel Club until 1939, in large part because Harry Wheeler, the only breeder of these animals for many, many years, was reluctant to see them registered at all. Whether this reluctance was due to a desire to corner the market on the breed or a more probable desire to protect the working capabilities of the dogs which is almost inevitably compromised with registration is uncertain. But the dogs themselves were virtually the same as those that formed the foundation of the Siberian Husky recognized by the American Kennel Club—the Ricker-Seppala teams that were originally quartered at Poland Spring, Maine, and later moved to Wheeler's Gray Rocks Inn in St. Jovite—dogs such as Tserko, Kreevanka (registered in Canada as Kree Vanka), Toska (bred at least five times to Kreevanka), Bonzo (Wheeler's famous leader, though never producing any CKC stock), Dushka, Molinka, and Kingeak and Pearl (bred by Elizabeth Ricker but never AKC registered).

In October of 1939 Wheeler did finally register thirty-eight of these dogs, many of them posthumously, using the "of Seppala" suffix on many. His involvement in the breed continued until 1947 when Don McFaul (who had already been working with Wheeler stock registered with the Gatineau prefix) took over the strain and continued the "of Seppala" suffix until 1964. Though many of today's Siberians in Canada come fairly directly from United States kennels, there is still a remnant of these original dogs permeating Canadian pedigrees if one is willing to look back far enough, particularly in pedigrees that go back to Tony Landry's White Water Lake, Austin Moorcroft's Huskie-Haven, J. Malcolm McDougal's Malamak and Jeff Bragg's Markova Kennels.

Am., Can., Berm. Ch. Arcticlight's Number One Son was sired by Silver Shadrin and, like
his father, is a BIS winner. *Alverson*

Am., Can. Ch. Arcticlight's Silver Shadrin, Am.,
Can. CD, owned by Eric Van Loo, is a BIS winner.

Bain's Northern Kymric, outstanding, influential,
all-white racing dog from the earlier history of
this kennel.

144

Arcticlight

Arcticlight Kennels was established by Eric Van Loo in 1975 with dogs from Yeso Pac and Calivali lines which were later combined with Innisfree and Karnovanda to produce many champions in North America and Europe. The most renowned are the father and son Best in Show winners Am. & Can. Ch. Arcticlight's Silver Shadrin, Am. & Can. CD and Am., Can. & Bda. Ch. Arcticlight's Number One Son.

Other distinctions for this prefix include four international championships and Best in Show winners in France, Belgium, Japan and Australia. Out of all the good things that have come to Eric Van Loo through his Siberians, his greatest thrill was winning the all-breed "Breeder of the Year" tournament in 1989.

Bain's Northern

Steve and Sue Bain established Bain's Northern Siberians in 1970 based on indigenous lines, Wobiska and White Water Lake, to which they have added Igloo Pak and Nekanesu stock to produce some topflight and very influential racing dogs, and Innisfree and Midnight Sun lines to produce a very significant strain of show dogs.

From their very first litter, an inbreeding on their foundation bitch Rix's Blue Maze, they produced the highly influential white racing dog Bain's Northern Kymric; while from their second, out of the same bitch (bred this time for a bit more substance), they produced a litter containing six champions. Three of these were part of Sue's undefeated show team, and all competed on successful purebred racing teams.

Among the Bains' significant animals (all champions carrying the Bain's Northern prefix) have been Chs. Bain's Northern Rebel, Roblyn, Ryan, Cognac, Pride, Storm, Fleur de Lis, Foxy Lady, Firebrand, Forever Amber (a multiple Group placer), Red Mahogany (a Best in Show bitch), Summer Sunrise, Leather 'N Lace, Born to Win, Joint Venture, No Jakets Reg'd, Somethn Magica, Pay the Butler, Hasta B Shasta, Entrprise Road, Grand Prix, Tiffany Star, Winter Shadow, Bad Habits, Jessica Lange and Nordique.

CZYZ

RCMP Constable Richard Smith found an ideal "hobby" in the late 1970s when he became involved with sled dogs. While stationed in the Northwest Territories, Smith used his team of Siberians on official Royal Canadian Mounted Police winter back country patrols. This use earned

Ch. Bain's Northern Joint Venture, owned by Sue Bain, shown scoring a Group second at Perth County (Canada). *Alex Smith*

RCMP Constable Richard Smith and his daughter Alexandra with the lead dog Kortar's Pax. In the background is Kortar's Kiev.

Am., Can Ch. Yeso Pac's Grey Wolf, owned by Donald and Rosemary Hooker, continues the proud tradition of Siberians that can take their place before a sled or in the winners' circle at a dog show.   *John Ashbey*

Can. Ch. Kimlan's Koryna (by Grey Wolf), is yet another dual-purpose Siberian from the Hookers' successful kennel.   *Alex Smith*

Ch. Naakeah's against All Odds, SDU, a highly successful show dog is the first champion Siberian to earn the Sled Dog Unlimited title. Owner is Jane Burrell.

Ch. Naakeah's Catch T'Spirit O'Kabu, SDX, owned by Jane Burrell, has won four BIS, and was Canada's breed leader for 1988. He was the first and remains the only Siberian to hold the Sled Dog Excellent title.   *Alex Smith*

Ch. Shisaido's Frostkist Footman, owned by Sandy Cairns, a multiple BIS winner, was Canada's top show dog for 1985.

him and his Huskies the respect of local trappers, hunters and natives. Although Smith entered local races, his main interest was long-distance sledding in remote areas where, even today, snowmobiles rarely venture. In 1980, he undertook the formidable task of retracing the 2600-kilometer historic Northwest Mounted Police dog sled patrol routes from Fort Edmonton to Old Crow in the Yukon Territories. Every year since, Smith completed a segment of this remote route adhering as much as possible to old methods.

Under the auspices of Canada Post, CZYZ Kennels helped commemorate the 1988 bicentennial of Fort Chipewyan, Alberta, by retracing the old mail route from Fort Smith, in the Northwest Territories to Fort Chipewyan, Alberta, carrying 150 commemorative envelopes. This 150-mile trip along the trackless Slave River was timed to coincide with the release of the Explorer series of stamps. It was also the longest reenactment of an historic mail run in Canadian history.

CZYZ Siberians also appeared in the movie *Stonefox* in 1987. Other credits include commercials and print advertising. These dogs appear in school programs, winter festivals and media events. The primary concern of Richard Smith and wife, Diane, is to produce sound, working dogs without sacrificing temperament, attitude or intelligence.

Kimlan

Donald and Rosemary Hooker acquired their first Siberian in 1970 and established their Kimlan Kennels in 1976 based extensively on Yeso Pac lines. Out of Yeso Pac's Southern Comfort and Tadluck's Balashika came three champions, Ch. Kimlan's Koryak, CD, Ch. Kimlan's Kara, CD, and Ch. Kimlan's Kosima of Arcticlight, dam of Am. & Can. Ch. Arcticlight's Silver Shadrin, Am. & Can. CD, the top show Siberian in Canada in 1982.

In 1977 what would become Am. & Can. Ch. Yeso Pac's Grey Wolf came to Kimlan at five and one-half years of age after running on Yeso Pac's top New England purebred team. At six he began his show career, finishing in Canada within the year and in the United States just short of his ninth birthday. A notable mover in the show ring and performer on the trail, he is the source from which most subsequent Kimlan stock descends.

In 1981 at the Central Ontario booster, Grey Wolf took Best of Breed while his daughter won Winners Bitch and Best of Winners. Another Grey Wolf daughter, Ch. Snowmist's Satin Kimlan, was Best of Winners at the Ontario booster in 1983, and another, Ch. Kimlan's Koryna duplicated the feat in 1985; while her daughter, Am. Ch. Kimlan's Leather N Lace, shown only nine times in the States, finished with a Group third.

Ch. Snomist Disco, owned by Beryl Ramey, was first in the Stud Dog class at the SHC of Canada 1987 Specialty. This noteworthy producer takes the head of the line followed by his son, Ch. Snowmist's Mai Tai, and daughter, Ch. Caijunvale's Echo of Naakeah. Tai was BB at this Specialty and with his sister took Best Brace.   *Alex Smith*

Tom LeBlanc driving an eight-dog Snomist team, six of which were SEPP-rated: two Superiors, a Superior Excellent, A Good Superior and two Goods.

Naakeah

Jane and Bob Burrell established their Naakeah Kennels in 1972 based on a foundation bitch, Ch. Julu of Bluespruce (a mixture of Allerellie and Race Crest lines) and the males Bain's Northern F Deputy Dawg (a mixture of Bastion, S-K-Mo and Midnight Sun breeding), Am. & Can. Ch. Karlad's Foxfire of Naakeah (Midnight Sun breeding) and Ch. Sekene's Genesis (from Innisfree lines).

Usually outcrossing phenotypically similar animals, the Burrells believe strongly in the dual-purpose Siberian, have one of the top four mid-distance teams in Ontario, the only one composed of predominantly show dogs, and have made Canadian breed history on at least three occasions: Ch. Naakeah's Afternoon Delight, SDX, becoming the first Canadian champion to obtain her Sled Dog Excellent title, her daughter Ch. Naakeah's Against All Odds, SDU, becoming the first Canadian champion to earn her Sled Dog Unlimited title and Ch. Naakeah's Catch T'Spirit O'Kubu, SDX, the first number one ranked Siberian to earn a Sled Dog degree.

Shisaido

Sandy Cairns' established Shisaido Kennels in 1978 with Barry Thuen, later becoming Shisaido-Frostfyre with Mark Dakin and Jacalyn Bryant. Their stock is essentially Innisfree, founded on Ch. Shisaido's Butler O'Innisfree, a Group winner and multi Group placer, Ch. Innisfree's Agility Blu and Ch. Innisfree's Shisaido Sinkist, a Best in Show winner and multi Group placer.

In 1985 Ch. Shisaido's Frostkist Footman became Canada's Top Show Dog for All Breeds and is Canada's number three Top Winning Show Dog of all time. Breeding only eight litters by 1989, Sandy has managed to own ten Best in Show winners with an accumulation of sixty-two top awards.

Snomist

Beryl Ramey established Snomist Kennels with daughters Sue and Kim (now Leblanc) in 1973 based on Innisfree lines (for show purposes) and Anadyr and Calivali lines (for racing purposes), intermingling the different strains but tending to show different animals than those they race.

Thus, on the one hand, the Rameys have owned or produced over fifty Canadian champions, including such notables as Am. & Can. Ch. Snowmist's Mai Tai (number one Siberian in 1986 and 1987), while on the other, they have earned twenty-five Sled Dog degrees, nineteen Sled Dog Excellent titles, and one Sled Dog Unlimited degree. They have also participated in two SEPP evaluations, with seven of eight dogs passing, and were ISDRA Regional Silver Certificate winners in both the seven- and three-dog classes in 1981.

Ch. Bonzana of Anadyr, a remarkable racing dog, led a team in Europe at age 12 on loan from Alaskan Kennels to Manfred Molkmaus. Note the dog's beautiful head type.

Ethan Russell, age 7, and Ch. Baron of Karnovanda, CD racing in the 100-yard dash. Up to age 12, juniors race in the one-dog division. From 12 to 16, they use three dogs. At 16, they automatically enter the five-dog division, often winning over the adult five-doggers!

6

History of the Racing Siberian

by Ann Cook

SLED DOGS HAVE BEEN USED FOR TRANSPORT-
ation of freight for centuries, but the sport of sled dog racing began as an
outgrowth of the Alaskan gold rush. At the time, the atmosphere was right
for the spawning of a new sport. Prospectors, gamblers and adventure
seekers populated the small outposts of the territory. They encouraged
informal competition between local "dog punchers" who brought mail,
passengers and supplies from town to town. Eventually, more formal races
resulted, culminating in the first running of the All Alaska Sweepstakes in
Nome in 1908.

Sled dogs imported from Siberia made their racing debut the following
year in the 1909 All Alaska Sweepstakes. Initially, their smaller size and
tractability made onlookers skeptical of their ability to win races, but it
didn't take very long before the Siberian Huskies proved the skeptics
wrong. Demand for the breed increased in the next decade when John
Johnson and Leonhard Seppala won the sweepstakes with their Siberian
teams. Then, in 1925, the Serum Run, the great race for life, focused public
attention on sled dog teams and introduced both racing and the Siberian
Husky to the entirety of North America.

During the 1920s, the sport of sled dog racing spread across Alaska,
reached both northwestern and eastern Canada and took hold in the eastern, western and north central states of the U.S. Maine, New Hampshire
and New York joined the growing list of states holding races. While Arthur

Walden and his team of Chinook dogs dominated New England races held between 1922 and 1926, in 1927, Leonhard Seppala, on tour with forty-four Siberian Huskies (as a result of Serum Run publicity) accepted Walden's challenge to race at Poland Spring, Maine. Seppala defeated Walden, and this upset created interest in Siberian Huskies on the part of eastern team owners.

One such team owner was Elizabeth Ricker (later Nansen), who quickly gave up her Chinook dogs and went into partnership with Seppala, raising Siberian Huskies at her Poland Spring kennel. This kennel was only in operation from 1927 to 1932, but in that relatively short time span, Ricker produced the foundation stock behind nearly all modern Siberian Huskies, for while the breed increased in popularity in the east, it all but disappeared in Alaska, as Siberian dogs were once again bred into the native strains.

Many early Alaskan teams were owned by explorers, mining companies, and other commercial concerns. The dogs were trained and worked by hired drivers. Freighting, not racing, was the reason for keeping dogs. When entered in a race, teams were sponsored by their owners. Perhaps a high placing in a race had some favorable reflection on the company, but racing was simply a pastime, something to gamble on. In the eastern U.S. and Canada, team owners were often innkeepers, like Mrs. Ricker, and teams were used to give tourists rides. The beautiful and exotic Siberian Huskies were a better lure for tourists' dollars than mixed-breed dogs. In addition, the Siberians were faster than the larger freight-type dogs common to the east at the time and so were an ideal breed to race. It wasn't long before sled dog races became a part of many winter carnivals and spectators bought up pups from team owners, only to find themselves becoming involved in the sport.

Where, in the early 1920s, a sled dog race often consisted of only a few teams putting on what amounted to an exhibition, the close of the decade saw numbers of teams competing. Many of the teams were owner-driven, and rules for races became somewhat standardized in certain regions.

In 1925, the New England Sled Dog Club began its first season of organized competition and by the early 1930s boasted a schedule of five to seven races held throughout New Hampshire, Maine and Vermont. This schedule included well-attended events for young, or "junior" sled dog drivers. While some races were twenty or thirty-mile courses that began and ended with a dash down the main street of a small town, a few races were point-to-point courses, covering distances of over a hundred miles. Teams would travel from one town to the next, often stopping overnight before undertaking the next leg of the journey. Trail conditions varied greatly. Shorter courses were sometimes packed by horse-drawn snow rollers or by volunteers on snowshoes, or sometimes not packed at all.

Between 1929 and 1944, several important Siberian Husky kennels

154

Best wishes Lorna
Roger & Ch. Tucker

Roger Peitano, twice winner of the SHCA racing trophy, with his outstanding lead dog, Ch. Tucker, after winning at Tok, Alaska, 1969.

Dr. Roland Lombard, one of the greatest dog drivers of all time.

Discipline, dedication and the desire to win—Dr. Lombard in action with Ch. Helen of Cold River on lead.

155

emerged that form the "backbone" of modern Siberian racing pedigrees. Alex Belford's kennel, known by the prefix "Belford's," began operation in 1929 in Laconia, New Hampshire. Belford's Wolf and a bitch named Mona were purchased as a breeding pair from the Ricker-Seppala kennel. Ultimately, Alex Belford's son, Dr. Charles Belford, joined the enterprise. The younger Belford's outstanding racing record includes several New England championships, victories in races in New York and Quebec, and multiple wins at the World Championship Sled Dog Derby in Laconia. His wins prior to 1960 were accomplished with an all-Siberian team.

Also in 1929, Milton and Eva Seeley, then partners in Arthur Walden's Chinook Kennels at Wonalancet, New Hampshire, bred their first litter of Siberian Huskies out of a bitch from Seppala's stock by a dog owned by Mike Cooney of Fairbanks, Alaska. In 1931, Lorna Taylor (later Demidoff) acquired some of the offspring of Seeley's breeding, and began racing the dogs in New England.

Harry Wheeler of St. Jovite, Quebec, began his very successful racing kennel in 1930 with dogs purchased from the Ricker-Seppala kennel and a bitch from Belford's foundation litter named Nanna. By the latter half of the 1930s, William Shearer III had also purchased stock from the Ricker-Seppala kennel and added dogs from Wheeler's stock to create his famous Foxstand Kennels. Shearer, a talented and respected racer, was active in eastern competitions until the mid 1950s.

Marie Lee Frothingham's Cold River Kennels was established in 1936 and was based on Wheeler stock. For twenty years, the multiple teams fielded by Cold River were a formidable force in racing circles. When Cold River sold out to trainers Lyle and Marguerite Grant, their dogs went on to become foundation stock for the Grant's Marlytuk Kennels.

One of the highlights of sled dog racing of this era was the demonstration race held at the 1932 Winter Olympics in Lake Placid, New York. Though sled dog racing was not an official Olympic sport, the International Olympic Committee permitted a dozen drivers to compete in a fifty-mile, two-heat race. The New England Sled Dog Club garnered about twenty teams for tryouts at Wonalancet, New Hampshire. Several drivers were winners of championship races. The final selection included five Canadian teams and seven American teams. Chinook Kennels was represented by two teams, the first driven by Norman Vaughan, and the second by Eva Seeley, the only woman in the race. Leonhard Seppala, Harry Wheeler, Emile St. Godard, Shorty Russick and Earl Brydges were all present for the race. St. Godard won and Seppala finished second, continuing the rivalry between the Husky/Malamute/hound cross dogs favored by many Canadians, and the ever-popular Siberian Huskies.

IN THE WEST AND MIDWEST

Ashton, Idaho, was the site of the first recorded race in the western United States. A small group of drivers who kept teams for mail carrying and winter transportation formed the American Dog Mushers Association. On March 4, 1917, they held their first American Dog Derby during a tremendous blizzard which, however hazardous, did not dampen local enthusiasm for the sport. With only a brief recess during the war years, the derby continued to be run until 1948. Though Siberian Huskies were known in this region, most racers preferred sporting dog crosses or hounds. This became increasingly so in the early 1920s, when the original course, which ran from Yellowstone, Montana, to Ashton, a distance of about fifty-five miles, was abandoned in favor of an eight-and-a-half-mile circular track, which teams were to run around three times. This departure from the Alaskan style of trail racing was largely done to accommodate the plans of then-fledgling Fox and Pathé film companies that had arrived from California to film the race. Huskies, by nature, resent repeating any stretch of trail, so the more cooperative crossbreds won out.

As a result of the Ashton event, a circuit of races began in Idaho, Wyoming, Utah, Montana and California. The Truckee, California, race was a popular spectator event. Four film companies were attracted to film on location there, and many a dogsledding production made there included famous stars in the footage.

IN WESTERN CANADA

Racing in western Canada began before 1900 with informal events. The first Dog Derby at The Pas was held on March 17, 1916. The race featured something that The Pas became famous for: a mass start, that is, one in which all the teams depart from the starting line at the same time, instead of at timed intervals. The Pas also offered a thousand-dollar purse, or prize money, to the winner. (By contrast, the frugal New England Sled Dog Club did not offer prize money until the 1940s.) In the following years, many races in western Canada were modeled after The Pas, and involved long trails on which Huskies could excel. Along with some purebreds, local teams favored hound/Husky/Collie crossbreds.

ALASKA

Earl and Natalie Norris founded their Alaskan Kennels in Anchorage with AKC-registered Siberians that Mrs. Norris (then Natalie Jubin) brought north from Chinook Kennels. At the time, there seemed to be no registered Siberian Huskies in Alaska, although undoubtedly some unregistered strains existed, and dogs of part-Siberian lineage were common.

During the 1940s and 1950s, the Norrises were instrumental in rebuilding the sport of sled dog racing and the Siberian Husky breed in Alaska. In 1946, Earl raced in a seventeen-and-one-half-mile exhibition race with an all-registered team. Although he did not win the race, he succeeded in convincing local residents to hold the event on an annual basis. That race grew into the prestigious Fur Rendezvous World Championship at Anchorage, which, incidentally, Earl won in its second and third running. As a result of the "Rondy," as it is known, the Alaska Sled Dog Racing Association was formed in 1949. Other sled dog clubs, such as the Alaska Dog Mushers Association, based in Fairbanks, and the Tok Dog Mushers' Organization were to follow. In 1952, Natalie served as president of ASDRA. That year, she placed fourth in the World Championship, while Earl placed second. In 1954, Natalie won the Women's Rondy. She also won the Women's North American Championship at Fairbanks in 1970.

The Norris name has been associated with many excellent performances in a wide variety of races and sled dog events. In 1970, when Norris's son J. P. placed second at the Rondy to Alaska's perennial champion George Attla, Earl and his leader won the lead dog contest at that event. Still actively breeding and racing Siberians today, the Norrises have produced generation after generation of top-caliber working dogs. Their dedication to the breed has inspired legions of Siberian drivers worldwide, and their breeding stock is consistently chosen by both novice and professional racers throughout the U.S., Canada and Europe who wish to found or improve teams of purebred Siberian Huskies.

While dogs with the Norris prefix "Alaskan's" and suffix "of Anadyr" can be found in the pedigrees of practically all racing Siberians in the state of Alaska, a large concentration of these dogs also occurs on the west coast of the United States, due to either direct importation of dogs from the Norrises' kennel or indirectly through interbreeding of imported dogs. For example, Charles and Kit McInnes' outstanding "Tyndrum" kennel was founded in part on Norris bloodlines and from various McInnes dogs came the S-K-Mo kennel of Bob and Lou Richardson. The Richardsons also bred to Dichoda's Ch. Noho of Anadyr, a direct Norris import, thereby increasing Alaskan influence in their lines. Many western kennels show this pattern of acquisition.

WORLD WAR II AND THE POSTWAR LEGACY

At the onset of World War II, the New England Sled Dog Club adjourned their meetings with the intention of ceasing races until the war was over. Gas rationing and other "war effort" activities ended the travel and leisure time that had, in some years, bolstered as many as sixty winter

Ch. Tyndrum's Oslo, CDX (Pando of Monadnock ex Ch. U'Chee of Anadyr), lead dog for Charles and Kit MacInnes.

Igloo Pak's Tok (Alyeska's Sugrut of Chinook ex Igloo Pak's Misty), a product of Dr. Lombard's successful kennel, was a strong, positive influence on the breed.

carnivals in the state of New Hampshire alone. Skilled sled dog drivers joined search and rescue units of the armed forces. Kennels and pet owners alike gave their dogs to the War Department to be trained for arctic missions. For a while, hometown trails lay unbroken.

Siberian kennels continuing through the war, or building up just after the war, used a variety of stock from kennels of the 1930s, mixing what by then had become established bloodlines. Dr. Roland ("Doc") Lombard, already a handicap winner of the 1929 Laconia Sled Dog Derby, began registering his Siberian Huskies with the prefix "Igloo Pak" in the early 1940s. With his wife, Louise, Lombard chose stock from Chinook, Monadnock, Foxstand, Belford and Cold River lines. Some of his dogs were interbred with dogs from Roland Bowles's Calivali Kennel. Bowles, at one time a driver for Chinook Kennels, and race manager for the New England Sled Dog Club, owned a number of purebred Siberians in the pre- and postwar years, and dogs with his kennel name appear in most eastern and some western racing pedigrees. Bowles acquired dogs from many sources, among them New England racers Dick Moulton, Steve Tassey and Lester Moody. His dogs descended from sources such as McFaul, Gatineau, Chinook and White Water Lake.

Another rising postwar kennel, that of Jean and Keith Bryar, initially used Monadnock dogs (some purchased through J. August "Tat" Duval), and then a wide range of sources to amass excellent teams of Siberian Huskies. These dogs were variously registered with the prefixes "Mulpus Brook's," "Bryar's" and "Norvik" and, along with the teams fielded by the Lombards and Dr. Charles Belford, became an unbeatable force in eastern races of the forties, fifties, and early sixties.

Don McFaul, a racer from Quebec, purchased the remaining Wheeler dogs in 1950, when Wheeler's kennel ceased operation. In turn, Canadian J. Malcolm McDougall (Malamak) and Harold Frendt (Little Alaska) purchased stock from McFaul to create their teams. Prior to 1950, McFaul had registered his Siberians with the prefix "Gatineau." Gatineau dogs originated from Northern Light, Wheeler and Alyeska lines, and it was these dogs that formed the basis of the Little Alaska breeding program. Leonhard Seppala, in partnership with Earl Snodie at Bow Lake Kennels in Washington State used some Gatineau dogs as breeding stock during these years, along with a single dog of Igloo Pak origin. Some of these dogs were ultimately owned by Harold Frendt.

J. Malcolm McDougall's kennel's very successful team of Siberian Huskies began racing in the late 1940s. Although his dogs came from several sources, the core of his team was based on later McFaul ("Seppala") dogs. McDougall, a Canadian from Quebec, raced in the eastern United States and Canada until the late 1970s. Tony Landry's White Water Lake Kennel was also established in the late 1940s and remained active until 1968. Landry's dogs were based on stock from McFaul's Gatineau lines. Landry preferred close linebreeding, and his strain produced the sound basis behind many modern eastern and central Canadian racing kennels.

Frank and Phyllis Brayton's Dichoda kennels, based on Kabkol dogs of Monadnock origin, has been located in California since 1948. The purchase of Ch. Noho of Anadyr from Earl and Natalie Norris added Alaskan influence to their breeding program. While the Brayton's primary interest was in showing Siberians, some of their dogs were used by budding western racing kennels and figure in racing pedigrees today.

Jack and Donna Foster's Frosty Aire line, founded in 1955 on Tyndrum, and later Monadnock and eastern derivatives, also has limited influence on some racing pedigrees, particularly those in the midwest.

Some foundation dogs of this era come from less traceable sources. Teams of registered and unregistered dogs that were sold to the War Department or to private concerns when their owners were called to serve resurfaced after the war in new places. Ed Moody, former handler for Antarctic expeditions and the army, recalls selling his team of purebred Siberians (some unregistered) and crossbreds to the Union Pacific Railroad when he left Sun Valley, California, and was recalled to war. Some of those dogs appear to have run on the postwar team of Lowell Fields. Another team that helped introduce purebred Siberian Huskies to the West was that of Major John Rodman of Yellowstone, Montana. His dogs, obtained from the army, were of New England origin.

IMPACT OF THE CROSSBREDS

North America became a smaller place in the postwar decade. Transportation improved, and so did communication. Alaska seemed closer to the eastern U.S. than ever before, and eastern mushers felt the pull to compete in Alaskan races. In 1958, "Doc" Lombard upset tradition at the North American Championship in Fairbanks by becoming the first man from the "lower forty-eight" states to win the race. His all-registered Siberian Husky team also won the race at The Pas, Manitoba, that year. Two Siberian teams owned by Keith Bryar placed second and third at that race. Nevertheless, when "Doc" Lombard again won the North American in 1962, he purchased an exceptional native Alaskan dog named Nellie from competitor George Attla. In subsequent years, Lombard raised both crossbred dogs he acquired from Alaskan teams and registered Siberian Huskies. Over the next two decades, many drivers of Siberian Huskies followed Lombard's lead, and slowly, all-Siberian teams began disappearing from the winning ranks.

A combination of factors contributed to this decline. Foundation dogs of the 1920s and 1930s had come entirely from working stock, for at the time, the Siberian Husky was synonymous with working. Even after the

Naakeah Kennels' racing team, one of the top mid-distance teams in Ontario. Five of its members are also bench champions.

Earl Norris with the team that held the 25-mile track record in what was, at the time, the Alaskan championship. This record stood for several years and was finally broken by a team driven by George Attla. "Alladin" is in the lead position here.

American Kennel Club recognized the breed in 1930 and accepted its Standard in 1932 Siberian Huskies remained primarily in the hands of competing racers. Eventually, a generation or two of Siberians were selected for exhibition purposes only, without regard for their working ability, thereby beginning a dichotomy in the breed in terms of both physical structure and mental aptitude for working—what racers called "attitude." Numbers of good, fast, work-proven Siberians became harder to acquire.

Increased organization in the sled dog world, wider travel to competitions, and the rise of sled dog related periodicals exposed racers to many excellent hybrid dogs, bred especially for racing. These dogs were purchased, bred and traded around the United States and Canada, raising the general quality of racing dogs everywhere. In the east, the stronghold of Siberian Husky teams, racers began to feel constrained by having to work within a breed Standard, knowing that by increasing their kennel's gene pool with crossbreds, they were free to develop specialized animals, using any dog that exhibited speed and the desire to work.

At the same time, due to increases in population, particularly in the east and far west, open land on which races could be held was becoming scarce. Roads that in prewar days were left unplowed were now open in winter for vehicle travel. Race committees reacted to these changes by shortening courses. Even the famous World Championship Sled Dog Derby in Laconia, New Hampshire, curtailed its original thirty-mile trail (open class), eventually offering a trail only fourteen miles in length. Shorter trails favored sprinting dogs. Endurance, one of the qualities for which the Siberian was prized, became a less important factor in the outcome of races.

Some Siberian racers persevered and maintained winning teams throughout the 1960s and 1970s. Art and Judy Allen's Natomah kennels and the Kainino kennels of Doug Bard preserved the Little Alaska strain. Jim Keller's Igluk kennel maintained an excellent racing record in the Northwest using Norris bloodlines. In the east, kennels based at least in part on Lombard Siberians or kennels derived from Cold River stock continued to field some solid teams. Lloyd Slocum's early Arctic Trail team was made up entirely of purebred Siberians from Igloo Pak and Marlytuk kennels. In 1972, he won the Laconia Championship with a team composed largely of purebreds, and for several years he and his wife, Winnie, were winning New England races with teams of this makeup (some of Slocum's Siberians were eventually sold to Earl Kellet, and appear in Midwestern pedigrees). Charlie Posey (Yeso Pac), the "Rebel" from Virginia, became a racer known not only for his achievement on the trail but also for his sportsmanship. Toward the latter half of the seventies, teams such as that of Lee and Babe Muller (Smo-Ki-Luk), Fred and Barbara Jacobi (Kuscama), Darrell and Diane Stewart (Shanovok), Richard and Barbara Petura (Heritage North), Ric and Dorothy Siewert (Riv'n'dell), Steve and Debbie Elliff (Windigo), Bill and Mimsy Brisbois (Sinuvoda), Judy Russell

(Karnovanda), Tom and Rosemarie Weir (Kaila), Al Stead and Ann Slocum-Stead (Northome), Bob and Chris Landers (Krisland), Rob and Susan Tucker (Tshabet), Terry and Susan Quesnel (Atim) and Bob and Roberta McDonald (Snowy Mt.) created stock for racing kennels to grow on. Harris Dunlap, Terri Killiam, Bob Schirone and many other breeders of Alaskan Huskies also had a small stock of purebred Siberians that were added in to racing pedigrees. At the end of the decade, the Canadian kennels of Dennis and Wendy Fitzgerald, Leigh and Susan Gilchrist, and Debra Ryan (now Fogarty) supplied dogs to many fast all-registered teams including some of the winning limited class teams in the eastern United States.

Nevertheless, it seemed for a time that the Siberian Husky that had so easily eclipsed Arthur Walden's Chinook dogs and other early mixed breeds was itself being eclipsed by hounds, setter crosses and Alaskan village dogs which, ironically, carried a portion of Siberian blood in their veins.

ISDRA

In 1966, sled dog racing entered the modern age with the formation of the International Sled Dog Racing Association (ISDRA). New England Sled Dog Club member J. Malcolm McDougall suggested at the club's annual meeting that an association of sled dog clubs be created to bring about the standardization of the sport. Maine racer Bill Wilson expressed similar thoughts and agreed to chair a committee which included Kenneth "Stubby" Saxton, "Doc" Lombard, Keith Bryar, and Julian Beale. Perhaps a hundred sled dog clubs existed throughout the United States and Canada at this time, but Wilson found that few of the clubs maintained formal records, such as mailing lists, so the task of contacting members seemed difficult and organizing them insurmountable. Eventually, Can-Am Sledders, through the efforts of member David Deahn, helped Wilson arrange a meeting at Niagara Falls. About fifteen clubs were represented at the meeting. ISDRA elected "Doc" Lombard as its first president, an office he held from 1966 to 1970.

Membership in ISDRA grew rapidly as more and more racers saw the wisdom of ISDRA's policies to promote public interest in the sport of sled dog racing, provide information for proper management of races, create a uniform set of rules for racers everywhere, and enforce regulations concerning the humane treatment of sled dogs. Today ISDRA is a truly international organization with elected officials representing not only sled dog clubs in the U.S. and Canada but also in Europe. ISDRA has developed a championship point system, which allows racers from different regions to compare their skills by competing in ISDRA "sanctioned" races, that is, races that meet ISDRA's strict criteria for length and width of trail, course layout, purse distribution, and safety regulations. Medals are

Some legendary drivers in action (from top): Jean Bryar, Keith Bryar, Jim Briggs.

awarded to the top three racers in several categories, divided by team size.

While many race organizations do not seek official ISDRA sanctioning, ISDRA's racing rules are used at nearly all sled dog events worldwide. Based on New England Sled Dog Club Rules, which, in turn, trace back to the Nome Kennel Club rules that governed the All Alaska Sweepstakes, ISDRA's regulations are the greatest joining force in the sled dog world today.

GROWTH OF THE SPORT

In the last thirty years, the sport of sled dog racing has continued to grow. There are over two hundred sled dog clubs and race-giving organizations throughout the world. Some organizations such as the New England Sled Dog Club or the Mid Atlantic Sled Dog Racing Association (MASDRA) offer a full slate of races throughout the fall and winter seasons. Other organizations hold only one race, such as the Lakes Region Sled Dog Club whose famous World Championship Sled Dog Derby has provided world-class racers with seven decades of competition.

Small clubs offer races with classes limited to two or three dogs, four dogs, six dogs, and eight dogs. These races attract novice and recreational drivers. Anyone who can manage a team of dogs is welcome, and there are often "how-to-sled" clinics and "junior" events for children so a family can have a full day of fun.

In regions where snow is scarce, many enthusiasts race their teams on sandy trails using a three- or four-wheeled cart known as a "rig." In Oregon, sand dunes provide a year-round surface on which to run.

Some clubs divide certain popular classes, particularly the six-dog class, into a "sportman's" division, for those not interested in competing for prize money, and a professional class. Limited class races (eight dogs) and Open class races (more than eight dogs) are often dominated by professional teams. Open teams are allowed to depart from the starting line with as many dogs as the race's chief judge will permit, but few racers attempt to drive more than sixteen dogs since any team, however fast, that can't be maneuvered under strict control means trouble for the driver, the dogs and other teams sharing the trail.

SPEED RACING

Speed or "sprint" races are run over relatively short distances, usually five miles for teams of six dogs or less, eight to twelve miles for the limited class and twelve to thirty miles for the Open class. These races consist of two or, in the case of some Open class races, three heats, and a driver's finishing time is the sum of the times of the individual heats. In larger races, "day money" is paid to the top three finishers in each heat. Sometimes it is difficult to guess who will win the race, as a variable performance in successive heats can cost a team precious seconds of the total time.

While hundreds of speed races are held each winter throughout the United States and Canada, some of the classic races are held at Saranac Lake, New York, at Quebec City, Quebec, at Bemidji, Ely, Grand Rapids and Keliher-Shooks, Minnesota, at Priest Lake, Idaho, at Fort Nelson, British Columbia, at Kalkaska, Michigan, at Truckee, California and at Diamond Lake, Oregon.

THE IDITAROD AND DISTANCE RACING

Despite the increase in sled dog events in the "lower forty-eight," the advance of technology nearly ended the use of sled dogs in Alaska by 1970. Once used for hunting, trapping, guide work and general transportation, sled dogs were rapidly being replaced by snowmobiles and other all-terrain vehicles. History buff Dorothy Page and veteran musher Joe Redington, Sr., noted the decline and while planning an event to celebrate the hundredth anniversary of America's purchase of Alaska from Russia struck upon an exciting idea. The idea, a race over the old Iditarod supply trail that winds through villages and outposts from Anchorage to Nome, took six years to become a reality; but in 1973, thirty-four teams set out on the thousand-mile trek that promised a fifty-thousand-dollar purse, twelve thousand of which would be paid to the winner. Dick Wilmarth arrived in Nome after twenty days on the trail and became the first winner of the Iditarod Trail Race.

Interest in the Iditarod was immediate and widespread. As in the days of the Serum Run, media coverage spread the word that sled dogs were back on the trail. Alaskans revived breeding programs in hopes of producing teams that could run what has been termed "the last great race." Using the new science of sports medicine, trainers, dog team outfitters and dog food manufacturers began generating volumes of data on how to train, clothe and feed top-caliber running dogs and drivers.

In 1983, Iditarod organizers ruled that rookie drivers must have completed a two-hundred-mile race to be eligible to compete in the Iditarod Trail Race. This qualifier created a whole new race category. Known as "middle distance," it is composed of races 50 to 350 miles in length. Most middle distance races in Alaska are run with Open teams, but when the concept reached the "lower forty-eight," many clubs began offering limited class races of six dogs for sixty miles or ten dogs for a hundred miles. Today, several major long- and middle-distance races are offered on an annual basis. In addition to the Iditarod, the Yukon Quest runs a thousand miles from Whitehorse, Yukon Territory, to Fairbanks, Alaska, and requires a stop at U.S.-Canadian customs in the process. The John Beargrease Marathon is held each January in Grand Marais, Minnesota, and offers a five-hundred-mile Open class, a hundred-thirty-mile ten-dog class and a ninety-mile six-dog class. The Govenor's Cup race in Montana covers five hundred miles of territory, and Ontario's Marmora Cup Long Distance Sled Dog Challenge varies from one hundred fifty to two hundred miles in length, depending on the year. The mountainous Sandwich Notch Race winds along sixty miles of New Hampshire's early sled dog trails. The race is dedicated to the memory of local sled dog driver Eva "Short" Seeley.

Purebred Siberian teams have competed in all of these races and teams such as those of Canadian Don McEwen and American Doug Willet have won some of these challenges.

RACING SIBERIANS TODAY

While the number of registered Siberian Huskies currently competing in top-level races of all sorts is few, the attention of many racers, particularly those favoring endurance events or triathlons (three part races featuring speed, distance and freight-hauling heats) is again turning to the purebred Siberian. Many drivers are acknowledging the difficulty of maintaining consistency in breeding programs that use a wide variety of crossbred dogs. Kennels based on such large and variable gene pools cannot hope to predict type, structure or attitude in their upcoming pups. Therefore a winning team may fail to produce future winners. The Siberian, often thought to be limited due to the constraints of a Standard, now poses an attractive option for reducing variability in sled dog offspring. The Siberian possesses the traits of physical and mental toughness, a willing and cooperative attitude, and an ability to work long hours in harsh conditions. A number of top drivers are now noting that to be truly excellent, a racing dog must have some percentage of Siberian blood in its veins.

What of the dogs who are purebred Siberians? While most maintain a basic desire to work in harness, the 1980s saw many drivers of all-registered teams deeply concerned that examples of Siberians capable of world-class racing competition were rare. A program called Siberian Evaluation Performance Project (SEPP) was founded in 1982 and since its inception has endeavored to identify top-caliber Siberians through a testing program that involves a speed and endurance evaluation, skeletal measuring for comparison to the structure of world-class individuals, and a conformation evaluation conducted by an AKC-approved breed judge. The goal of SEPP is to make records of these superior dogs available for use in breeding programs that aim to reestablish the Siberian Husky as a competitive racing breed. SEPP's evaluators, Dr. Charles Belford, Dr. Roland Lombard, Richard Moulton, Harris Dunlap and Terri Killiam are no strangers to the winners circle at world-class events. SEPP evaluation tests are held annually. The location of the tests varies. To date, tests have been

Charles Belford (above) and Ronald Bowles (below) exemplify the style, persistence and courage required of an outstanding dog driver.

conducted coast to coast in the United States and in two locations in Canada. SEPP statisticians have recently noted that the offspring of early SEPP qualified dogs have been showing up for testing, and as predicted, they too are passing the evaluation.

Another program which recognizes the Siberian Husky as a racing dog was instituted in the 1980s by the Siberian Husky Club of America. The Sled Dog Degree Program awards Sled Dog (SD) certificates to Siberian Huskies who have completed five races within a minimum qualifying time, based on the finishing times of the winning teams. Higher degrees of Sled Dog Excellent and Sled Dog Outstanding are awarded to dogs who finish races within more stringent qualifying times. Sled dog degrees were created not only to recognize dogs who have worked in harness with proficiency, but also to provide incentive for the improvement of the performance of individual teams.

The International Siberian Husky Club offers annual awards to racing Siberian Huskies for outstanding performances in three-, six-, eight-, ten- and Open dog speed races and the long-distance class, as well. *The Racing Siberian Husky*, a magazine published by Heritage North Press, sponsors annual "Designated Regional Championships for Racing Siberian Huskies" by selecting certain key races and encouraging Siberian participation at these events.

In recent years, regional Siberian Husky Clubs have held an increasing number of events and "fun" races designed to raise Siberian owners' awareness of the unique qualities that must be preserved in the Siberian Husky if it is to continue as a working breed.

IN EUROPE AND BEYOND

Sled dog racing is becoming popular in foreign countries. While sledge breeds such as the Samoyed and the Greenland Husky were well-known to Europeans, it was the importation of the Siberian Husky from the United States to Switzerland, France, England, Holland, West Germany and the Scandinavian countries that influenced Europeans to begin racing. Initial importations began in the late 1950s and continue today.

In the 1960s, few countries recognized the Siberian Husky as a pure breed. Swiss fanciers began holding "Sled Dog Camps" where admirers and owners of Siberian Huskies and other sledding breeds could congregate to learn more about racing. At the time, European races were held exclusively by clubs attempting to promote purebred sled dogs, and so races did not permit crossbred dogs to enter. As a result, some countries were able to produce excellent strains of purebred working dogs. Influence from North American racing organizations caused European races to be opened to crossbred dogs in the late 1970s. Nevertheless, superior examples of purebred teams continue to compete in these races.

Europe's answer to the Iditarod is a series of races-within-a-race held in various Alpine locations called the Alpirod. This race premiered in 1988 and has had successful annual runnings, attracting entrants from a number of countries including the United States. Total trail mileage changes with each Alpirod. The longest trail to date has been 620 miles through France, Italy, Switzerland and West Germany.

The international nature of racing has been underscored by the formation of the International Federation of Sled Dog Sports which seeks to promote races that will draw teams from countries all over the globe. The Federation hopes to establish sled dog racing as an Olympic sport and will seek recognition as a demonstration sport at future winter games.

The Soviet Union, long silent on the state of its native breeds, has recently sent teams to compete in the Iditarod and the Alpirod. In addition, some Americans have been permitted to photograph sledge dogs in Siberia. Whether these dogs share lineage with the Siberian Huskies imported to Alaska at the dawn of organized sled dog racing may never be known, but it is just possible "Glasnost" may be good news for owners of racing Siberians worldwide.

Ch. Eumor's Kiev, UD, clearing the high jump in classic style.

7

The Siberian in Obedience

OBEDIENCE COMPETITION AS WE KNOW IT TO-
day did not exist in America prior to 1934. There did exist a few trials
geared to certain working breeds, but the emphasis was on aggressiveness
rather than companionship. All this changed in 1934 when Mrs. White-
house Walker, a Poodle breeder from Westchester County, New York,
grew tired of hearing that bench show dogs were beautiful but essentially
stupid and traveled to England to study their Obedience programs which,
she had heard, were oriented toward companionship rather than aggression. Upon her return, she set up an Obedience class in Bedford Village,
New York, with the idea of proving that not only could any breed be
trained in the rudiments of companionship, but that the training could be
done by the owner himself and did not require the special attention of a
professional dog trainer. After two years of hard work, she was rewarded
when the American Kennel Club accepted her program, and Obedience
trials received official sanction.

This was in 1936, two years before the organization of the Siberian
Husky Club of America and five years before a Siberian named King walked
into the ring and proved that even a strong-willed clown of a sled dog from
Siberia could earn a Companion Dog degree. It was another five years,
however, before his example was emulated. In fact, 1946 saw two Siberians
achieve their CDs. One was a dog named Ivan Alyeska Kolymski who,
like King before him, went no further in his training than the Companion

Dog degree. The other was Chornyi of Kabkol who, in the Siberian world, was to become to the Obedience ring what Togo had been to the trail or what Pando was to become to the conformation ring.

Whelped in 1945, Chornyi came to live with Richard and Virginia Garrett of Washington, DC, in April of 1946. Trained and handled exclusively by Mr. Garrett, Chornyi earned his Companion Dog (CD) title in December of that year, his Companion Dog Excellent (CDX) degree in September of 1947, his bench show championship in December of 1947, his Utility Dog (UD) title in April 1948, and his Tracking degree in April of 1949, making him the first Siberian to go beyond the CD and one of the few Siberians to this day to have earned the coveted UDT title. Chornyi lived until 1959, during which time his training was put to use by his entertaining children in hospitals and schools and by his aiding police on several occasions that required his remarkable tracking ability.

No doubt largely because of the example of Chornyi and the Garretts, other Siberian owners began working their dogs in Obedience. But enthusiasm did not catch on overnight. By 1950 there were only about ten Siberians with Companion Dog degrees, and through the 1950s only another sixteen entered the ranks. But in 1955 a Siberian owned by Beth Murphy and bred by Monadnock Kennels named Alaskan Twilight of Long's Peak did earn a perfect score of 200 points in a trial, and in 1960 Dr. Brillhart's Ice Chips of Marex earned the coveted "Dog World" award for outstanding performances in Obedience with scores of 197, 197 1/2 and 197, so that gradually the Siberian came to be considered a legitimate contender in the field.

Advanced titles, however, were still rare in the breed, and by 1960 only two dogs other than Chornyi had earned CDX degrees, and none had progressed further. In 1960, however, the Garretts again entered the scene, this time with a champion bitch they had acquired from Louise Foley and James Whitfield to replace Chornyi after his death. Her name was Ch. Chuchi of Tinker Mountain, and she proceeded to earn her CD in October of 1960, her CDX in October 1961, and in September of 1963 became the second Siberian to attain the UD. She then became the second Siberian to attain a UDT degree. This was in October 1965.

Although the Garretts never owned another Siberian, their contribution to the advancement of the breed in Obedience is probably unrivaled. Not only did their example serve as an inspiration to would-be Obedience contenders all over the country, but as active members of the All Breed Training Club at Rock Creek, Maryland, of which Mr. Garrett was president for many years, both maintained their interest in Siberians and helped many Siberian owners get started in this highly challenging and rewarding field. And it is no doubt largely due to their efforts and example that by the end of 1972 there were some four-hundred Siberians with Companion Dog Titles, almost fifty holding CDXs, over a dozen with Utility Dog

Ch. Chornyi of Kabkol, UDT

Chornyi in action

Ch. Chuchi of Tinker Mountain, UDT

degrees and three with Tracking degrees. Of these three, however, only Chornyi and Chuchi held the UDT title.

THE SIBERIAN'S APTITUDE FOR OBEDIENCE

Despite the Siberian's undeniable record in the field of Obedience, there has always been a certain reluctance on the part of many Siberian owners and breeders to enter the field. Some racing drivers argue that Obedience training suppresses some of the initiative and drive in their leaders. There have, however, been a number of excellent leaders who were also Obedience title holders. It is probably true that among the fastest teams in the world, there are few Obedience title holders, but then this elite group of dogs is so small that generalization is rendered ridiculous. It is also argued by some breeders that Obedience training may sufficiently suppress a dog's animation and hinder him in the conformation ring. This argument, however, is almost certainly unfounded, providing the training in both areas has been adequate and that the experience has been a happy one. In fact, Obedience training has often been employed to bring out the best in a young dog that, for one reason or other, has not had proper socialization in puppyhood, thus making him a better contender in the conformation ring.

With the possible exception, then, of the person interested in developing a very, very topflight racing team, in which case there is little time left for anything else, it is the general consensus that Obedience training is a great asset to any Siberian owner. For the owner of large numbers of Siberians, it is an excellent method of socialization and may be used as further preparation for the conformation ring. For the sled dog enthusiast, it has a number of advantages, ease in harnessing and reliability on the trail when unexpected situations arise being two of the more obvious. But it is the owner of the individual pet, or the owner of several dogs who values a close relationship with his animals who probably gains the most from Obedience. In the case of the unruly puppy who seems determined to run the household, it is a basic necessity. But even owners who have enjoyed long, comfortable, close relationships with their pet Siberians have been amazed to discover how much closer they felt to their animals after an Obedience course. For at its best, Obedience training is not merely a matter of learning a routine; it is an exercise in increasing communication, an exercise which is not over with a training class or the completion of a degree, but continues at home until the end of a dog's life as a constant process of renewing and refining the bonds of companionship between dog and master. A well-trained dog is a happy dog, a dog who has the security of knowing what is expected of him and who has the opportunity of partaking in the pleasure of pleasing his owners—an opportunity, strange as it may seem, that is not always afforded the average pet. For under even

176

The proper heeling position, demonstrated by Doncar's Snow Valley Flicka, UD, with owner Don Carlough handling.

John Holad with Ch. Savdajaure's Kunuk, CDX, show two of the heeling positions to avoid—at left, heeling in forging position and at right, heeling at lagging position.

the rowdiest, most strong-willed, stubborn exteriors, there lurks the inherent desire to please.

Tapping this desire, however, is not always an easy task, especially in a breed like the Siberian—renowned for his clownishness, his independence, and according to his detractors, his stubbornness. According to Don Carlough, one of the top Obedience trainers in the breed today, however, the Siberian is not so much stubborn as he is easily bored. The challenge in training him, then, becomes not so much a matter of getting the idea across as it is a matter of making the proposition interesting enough to merit the cooperation of this somewhat supercilious canine who is apt to find much of human behavior a little silly and of very fleeting interest. Getting a Siberian to perform a given exercise once is no great feat; getting him to perform the same exercise two or three times without adding his own comic variations, however, is quite another matter.

HINTS ON TRAINING THE SIBERIAN FOR OBEDIENCE

The purpose of this chapter is not to set forth a step-by-step guide to Obedience training. There are numerous books on the subject, and Obedience training classes are held by most all breed clubs across the country. These books and classes are invaluable to anyone interested because no matter how many dogs one has trained, one never learns everything there is to know about the field. The purpose of the following, then, is to set forth some guidelines that will be helpful in training your Siberian in Obedience, or even if you simply want to have a well-mannered house pet.

In the first place, one should acquire a good specimen of the breed. It is true that the Obedience ring allows dogs to compete who would be disqualified in the conformation ring, such as oversized dogs or those that have been altered. This should never be taken as an excuse, however, for either purchasing or breeding inferior specimens. One should seek a litter that exhibits the same conformation to the Standard one looks for if buying a show dog. The personality of a given puppy, however, may be of slightly greater importance in selecting a future Obedience contender than in selecting a potential bench show dog; for while the more dominant bowl-you-over puppy with proper handling can become a very flashy show dog, he is not the best bet for Obedience—especially if he is to be the first dog the family has owned. Having become accustomed to asserting his will over his littermates, he will be slower to subordinate his desires to those of his new owner and will always have a tendency to be more unruly. By the same token, one should avoid the shy, withdrawn puppy, as he will always have a tendency to find new places and situations frightening and distracting. By far the best puppy for the Obedience ring is the one who approaches a stranger in a cautious but friendly manner, who is affectionate but not

Stand for Examination—dog must stand-stay while judge examines dog. Modeled by Don Carlough with Doncar's Snow Valley Flicka, UD.

Dog sitting in front during the recall. Dog has come on first call, sits straight, within reaching distance.

Stay signal. Used when leaving dog for recall or group exercises.

overpowering. True, some people have had success in working with puppies with more extreme temperaments, but puppies exhibiting more moderate behavior are certainly the easiest to work with.

In naming a puppy, a certain amount of care should be taken in selecting both a fairly unique name and one that neither rhymes nor alliterates with any of the standard Obedience commands. The uniqueness of the name becomes important in that a dog performing in one ring is not distracted by having his name being called in another. And avoiding names like "Neal" which rhymes with "heel" or "Star," which begins like "stay," saves much confusion.

Although formal Obedience training does not usually take place until a puppy is five or six months old, there are a number of things that can be taught earlier. First, of course, is housebreaking. This is most effectively accomplished without the intermediate step of paper training. If a puppy is confined to a small area, such as his crate, and taken outside to the same spot after sleeping and eating and before and after playing, housebreaking can be accomplished very quickly. And gradually, as long as there are no accidents, he can be allowed greater and greater freedom in the house. Paper training simply serves to complicate the issue by first teaching the puppy to use the paper and then later discouraging him from doing what he has been taught.

It is also helpful during these early weeks to teach the puppy not to jump up on people, not to bite, not to steal food and to ride calmly in the car. Jumping up is always a difficult problem with Siberians, as they are by nature extremely exuberant. It is a habit that it is best to break early; do this by pushing your palms downward and kneeing the puppy in the chest while saying firmly, "No jumping!" and then playing with him and giving lots of praise. Do not say "Down." With the puppy who bites, even in play, one should grasp and shake the muzzle firmly while saying "No biting!" and then provide a great deal of praise. Discouraging food stealing can be effectively accomplished in a few sessions by deliberately placing food on the table and reprimanding the puppy whenever he takes it. Teaching a puppy to ride calmly in a car with you is most easily done by having a second person keep the puppy on a lead and, with praise and reprimand, encourage him to remain quiet.

By this point the puppy should also be learning to walk on a leash. This is most painlessly accomplished by fastening a buckle collar on him and allowing him to drag the lead around for a few minutes every day. Later, the other end of the lead can be picked up and, by way of gentle tugs and jerks and lots of praise, the puppy can then be taught to walk with his trainer.

It is at about this point that formal Obedience training can be initiated, for not only has the puppy become well-mannered enough to have around, he has also learned to pay attention. In other words, the channels of communication between dog and master have been established. Before

Figure Eight—Dog and handler heeling around two persons (posts) without sniffing or jumping on them. John Holad and Ch. Savdajaure's Kunuk, CDX. Posts: Peggy Grant and Anna Mae Forsberg.

Drop on Recall. In Open, the dog is left for recall. The handler calls dog and then must drop him on judge's command. Don Carlough and Doncar's Snow Valley Flicka, UD, demonstrate.

Retrieve over solid jump. Handler throws dumbbell over jump and sends dog after it; dog must jump hurdle, pick up dumbbell and return over hurdle.

181

Directed retrieve—signal to go out and retrieve glove.

Directed retrieve. Dog returning to handler with glove.

Directed retrieve. Dog sitting in front with glove after retrieve.

starting formal training, however, there are a few things one must always remember. First, such training requires a great deal of time and patience, and one should not undertake such a program without an honest self-assessment of one's capabilities. Second, never train when you are in a bad mood. Always give a lot of praise. And last, be creative: remember that the Siberian is more easily bored than most breeds and thus his trainer must always be adding new exercises and be on the lookout for different ways to capture the dog's interest.

Rewarding as Obedience work is, it is not without its harrowing moments. In fact, among those intrepid enough to enter a Siberian in the field, it is occasionally professed that there are few moments that are anything else. Dedication and determination are, of course, essential to the Obedience trainer; but of equal importance is that quality which, even among the most tight-lipped Obedience handlers, is always conspicuous— a sense of humor. Without this quality the Obedience enthusiast is lost, especially if his breed happens to be the Siberian Husky. The following article by Wes Meador gives a fairly vivid indication as to why this is so.

The Terror of Tanacross
by Wes Meador

In April of 1973, my wife, Debbie, and I entered a new and exciting phase of our careers as dog fanciers and Obedience enthusiasts—we purchased our first Siberian Husky. At the time, we were training for a local commercial school, plus being members of a training club, and so were exposed to 100 to 150 dogs a week in our capacity as instructors. We therefore felt that we had a pretty good notion of how to deal with any type of dog, even though we had never been actively involved in training a Siberian. As it turned out, we were sadly mistaken as Tosha developed into the most exasperating canine friend I have ever had!

The training techniques we were using at the time were really geared to Shepherds, Dobermans, etc., and as we found out, not truly effective on the dynamic Siberian Husky. I was training our only remaining Shepherd in Open work when we got Tosha, and as a result let her have free run of the place, so to speak, until she was about seven months of age. We felt, through past experience, that the best age to start a dog was between five and seven months old, with collar and leash breaking starting two weeks earlier. So we started Tosha in on this routine and everything went fine through puppy training until we hit formal training; then PFFFT!

It wasn't that she resisted the training—it was more that she thought it was a big bore. She'd look at me as if to say, "I've been running around the backyard for the last five months just having a great time, not bothering anybody, minding my own business, and then you have to go all masculine and dominant on me. I mean, *really!* I could abide it when you put that heavy thing on my neck, and did I complain when you made me drag that dumb piece of leather around, with it always hanging between my legs and me stepping on it and tripping and that sort of junk? But this business of jerking on me, and yelling at me, and making ugly faces . . . well, that really is a bit much, don't you think?"

Shortly after we started our daily tug-of-war (her going her way, and me going mine) she began a little psychological warfare of her own. Holes mysteriously started appearing in the backyard, at first in out-of-the-way places, then all over. Our backyard had a windbreak of young poplars which started disappearing—chewed off at the stump. You'd have thought she was a beaver the way she felled those trees. One of our daughter's rabbits turned up missing; then my wife's yews were chewed up, and at $12 a whack that was a low blow! By this time our erstwhile lovely backyard had begun to take on the appearance of a scene from Dante's Inferno, but when one of my beloved collection of science fiction classics, which I had indiscreetly left on the chaise lounge, turned up in pieces . . . well, brother, the battle was joined! The challenge had been issued! The gauntlet had been smacked in my face, not once, not twice, but over and over again!

I was just a little peeved by this time, so with my backbone stiffened, and my heart filled with firm resolve, I began training Tosha in earnest. It didn't take her very long to realize that I was deadly serious about this (in her mind) nonsense and that I was a lot bigger and stronger than she. So we came to an understanding—she would be a good little girl and not do all those naughty things she did so well, and I wouldn't dismember her, piece by piece.

When she was nine months old, or thereabouts, we got a little copper male, thinking it probably would help for Tosha to have a playmate to keep her out of mischief. Besides, he was so beautiful, and such a good pedigree, etc. Oh, brother! She didn't like this new addition one little bit. But she was smarter this time; no direct retaliation—just very subtle, insidious little things when we weren't looking. Like "accidently" knocking over the plaster horse we picked up in Mexico City, or . . . I can't go on. And, all this time, I had been taking her to fun matches and she was doing beautifully, the little stinker! So, we decided to start showing her, because if she was in a show, she couldn't be in the backyard at the same time, right?

By the time the first show came, I thought she was really ready—she had scored 199 1/2 in a fun match the week before and had been working very well with no backyard blitzkriegs for a week or so. I thought we were over the hump, but little did I realize.

In we went, our first show together, both of us excited and alert, tails wagging, ears up, and eyes bright. Everything went nicely until the Recall. When I called her, she just sat there—tail wagging, ears up, eyes bright, and disqualified. Well, it was her first show. . . .

The next shows were a weekend double-tailer in Kansas City. At the first one she was doing very well all through the preliminary exercises; then came the Recall. I had considered the possibility that I might have been a little harsh when I had called her before, so I was all prepared to call her in a happy, cheerful, and very probably silly tone of voice, so as to take no chances. Anyway, as I turned to await the judge's command, she sat there happy and alert again, the very picture of an obedient dog. My hopes were up. She looked so eager, I just knew she was going to come zooming when I called her! I looked at the judge and in a clear, resonant voice he said, "Call your dog." Tosha came flying in, perfect sit and everything—but the dummy had come when the *judge* had spoken, before I could call her. Disqualified!

The next show was the killer! She went through the exercises like a baby

184

Signal exercise. Left, hand signal to heel. Right, hand signal to stand dog.

Signal exercise. Hand signal to down dog from stand position.

185

Signal exercise. Hand signal to sit dog from a down position.

Scent discrimination—dog seeking out article which handler has touched. Dog must do this twice—once with leather article and once with metal article.

through a diaper. I was elated! I was ecstatic! I was happier than heck! If she had more than two points off in all the exercises, I was going to eat my leash. The group exercises were coming up and she had NEVER failed in them, never! The long sit went by without incident. On the long down she lay on her side and went to sleep, and I thought we had it made. Then it happened! A Miniature Poodle broke and went over to her. She started sniffing, and when the steward came over to get the Poodle, she broke and very jauntily followed him away. I was crushed! A near perfect score down the old drainola. But it could have happened to anybody, right? Yech!

After moping in my room for a week, I decided something had to be done— I didn't know what, but SOMETHING; my heart couldn't take much more (not to mention my liver, kidneys, and bladder, too). So I took Tosha up to my study, put her on my lap, and explained to her that if a little girl doggie wanted to grow up to be a big mamma doggie, then she shouldn't do things that gave her master coronary attacks, or apoplexy, or hissy-fits—it just didn't make sense! All right, I know this isn't the way a rational man is supposed to act, but I couldn't think of anything else to do. At least, nothing she would have survived. And would you believe, she qualified her next three shows, placing fifth, fourth, and first in Novice B!

All facetiousness aside, we have found that the Siberian Husky, as opposed to the "established" Obedience breeds (Doberman, Shepherd, Sheltie, Golden Retriever, etc.) must start training as a pup. They are of hardier constitution and temperament, and are much more difficult to train after they have begun to assert their independence. The male (he's no longer little) of Debbie's started his training at three and a half months and achieved his CD title at *seven months and two days*, placing in Group his last time out. He is the most lovable and gentle dog I have ever had the good fortune to be associated with and Tosha, despite all the trials and tribulations we have experienced, has become at sixteen months of age an exciting and (at times) brilliant performer. The big difference between the two is in the attitude with which they approach Obedience work. Tymber has never balked at anything we have tried to teach him, while Tosha's Obedience career has been marked by an almost terminal case of stubbornness. Even recently, while learning exercises for Open work, she would approach each one with an attitude of "Well, let's see if you *really* want me to do this stuff." My response to this attitude has been known to make strong men quake and send children screaming for their mothers. Tymber, on the other hand, reacts to a disapproving voice and has never had to be physically disciplined. I believe this difference is directly attributable to their ages when starting training.

Siberian Huskies are fantastic animals, both in conformation and Obedience, and the problems I had were my fault for using the wrong techniques and timetable. The Siberian is not the humble, devoted dog that the German Shepherd or Golden Retriever is, nor does he possess the high-strung and dependent nature of the Sheltie or Poodle. Siberians are unique unto themselves: proud, intelligent, independent, and gentle. I believe that the next decade will see the Siberian Husky established right alongside the German Shepherd, Doberman, Sheltie, etc., as a top Obedience breed, and I for one, plan to be right out there with the trembly knees and aching ulcers doing my best to see it happen.

So, if you're tired of the humdrum, uneventful, ordinary type of life, then start training your Siberian at, say, about twelve months; but if you have a history of coronary trouble, or are subject to gastrointestinal problems, then I wouldn't advise it.

Don Carlough, with Doncar's Snow Valley Flicka, UD, demonstrating action of a scent hurdle relay race at the Siberian Husky Club of America Specialty.

8

Showing Your Siberian

Today the Siberian Husky is more popular than ever. Because of his intelligence, beauty, tractability, and wonderfully gregarious nature, he is to be found in homes throughout the United States, Canada and Europe where he serves a house pet as well as in his original capacity as sled dog, both on pleasure teams and in active competition. In recent years, he has also made great inroads in the field of Obedience, a field he was not bred for but in which he has shown a great capacity to excel. But the area which, dog for dog, probably exerts the greatest influence on the progression of the breed is the conformation ring. Thus, it is helpful for even the most casual pet owner to have some idea of the basis and procedures of a dog show.

To many people who have never seen one, or who have attended one only briefly without fully understanding the procedures, a dog show may seem nothing more than a canine beauty contest—an absurd pageantry of displaced egos, painted toenails and coiffured pom-poms, the judging of which amounts to little more than the whim of the day.

As with most negative observations, there is at least a portion of truth in this picture. Today more and more people show their dogs purely as a sport, and many are not, themselves, breeders. Consequently, winning becomes the central object, an object which, without the basic notion of a breed's continuous improvement, is essentially meaningless. Also with competition greater today than it has ever been, there is an increased emphasis on showmanship, baiting, and, in some breeds, the kind of grooming designed to drastically alter the dog's natural appearance. Like all institutions, dog shows have their flaws, and these superficialities are what have made dog shows, like garden clubs, the object of facile and supercilious jibes by the uninformed.

On the other hand, at its basic level, the dog show is the very foundation of purebred dog breeding. It is there that the best specimens of a breed are brought together for comparison, where breeders meet and exchange information and make future breeding arrangements, where all that makes a breed a breed—namely type, temperament and soundness—is kept alive and where virtually the future of a breed is decided. So as long as breed clubs strive to maintain meaningful standards for their breeds, dog shows are good for dogs.

It might, of course, be questioned what, in this day and age, the value of maintaining purebred dogs in the first place is. By way of justification, it can only be pointed out that not only is the purebred dog one of man's most ingenious inventions, a link with the life and ingenuity of our historical past, he is, in a more radical sense, a link with that which is primal in all of us—the beauty, dignity, grace and simply proffered affection that, in an increasingly cold and mechanical age, acts as a touchstone to what, at heart, we still are. He is an integral part of our heritage and as such deserves preservation and protection.

WHAT MAKES A WINNER?

The basis upon which dogs are judged in the show ring is what is known as the *Standard*. The Standard of any breed is set forward by members of its breed club and represents an idealization of what that breed should look like—in terms of physical appearance and structure—and act like—in terms of temperament. In evolving this Standard, two factors are always kept in mind: 1) the original function of the dog, and 2) given the original function and natural tendency of the breed in terms of appearance, what is most pleasing to the eye.

Broadly speaking, *type* is what makes a breed a breed: those aspects of appearance such as coat, skull structure, ear type and set, and general physical proportions that differentiate one breed from another. *Soundness* refers to the basic skeletal and muscular structure of the dog and varies little from breed to breed. Cowhocks, for instance, are frowned upon in all breeds. *Temperament* is the third consideration in an assessment of a dog and, since it is really a subdivision of type, varies from breed to breed according to the function for which the dog was bred.

These are the aspects of a breed, then, that a judge must weigh and consider before choosing a winner. This is why to a novice the show ring can be such a confusing place. He may see a dog that he feels is obviously the most beautiful—meaning it fits his general idea of what the breed should look like—not even receive a ribbon. What he may not have noticed

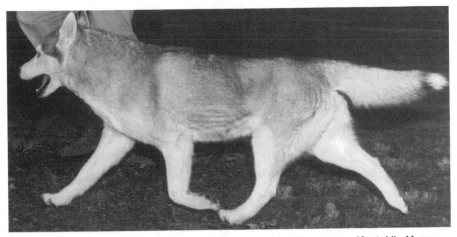

When fanciers talk about reach and drive, this is what they mean. Kontoki's Messy Bessie at 7½ years still able to cover ground.

Am., Can. Ch. Cudubhan's Choklat Moose, a favorite at John and Jan Linnehan's Cudubhan Kennels and "a Marlytuk bitch in all the good senses of the phrase."
John Ashbey

Ch. Teeco's Tallahasee Lassie, SD, owned and bred by Margaret Cook, was the #2 Siberian bitch in America for 1988.
Chuck Tatham

is that something in the dog's structure is unsound, having a bad front or rear, or he may be unsound in a place only the judge would notice, having a bad bite or insufficient muscle mass.

The next mistake made by the person at ringside is not usually made by the novice but by the person who has learned something about structure. He considers only the soundness of the dogs and is surprised or feels slightly superior if the judge picks a dog with some fairly obvious structural fault. What he has forgotten is that the judge must find what he feels is the best blend of type and soundness in the ring that day, and the dog that the viewer felt was the most faultless may have borne only a vague resemblance to the breed Standard as to type. Every dog, no matter how good, has some fault. The key to judging, however, is not the ability to ferret out a fault, but the ability to recognize aspects of a dog that are truly superior and weigh those against the superior aspects of his competitors. Negative judging, that is judging that is based solely upon eliminating a dog from consideration when a weakness in structure is discovered, will normally result in a sound but generally mediocre dog receiving the ribbon. It should be remembered that occasionally even a mongrel is sound, and that if you lose type, you've essentially lost a breed.

The process of viewing the judging from ringside is made more complicated by the fact each judge varies somewhat in the balance he seeks between type and soundness, that different dogs show differently on different days, and that evidences of temperament problems, such as growling or shying away when being examined, may go unnoticed by everyone except the judge. So it is best to be wary of experts at ringside, for although one can learn a great deal from people's comments, no one else sees what the judge sees. And even disregarding that fact, it is a rare spectator who actually knows more than the judge. Opinions come cheaply in the dog world, but the true acquisition of knowledge, as in any field, is a long and arduous process.

TRAINING FOR THE SHOW RING

Training a dog for the conformation ring, while not as difficult as training one for the Obedience ring, is not as easy as it might seem and requires a reasonable amount of time, energy and patience. Furthermore, since dog and handler operate as a team in the ring, a certain amount of time is necessarily spent in training oneself to adapt to the various peculiarities of a given animal, as each dog will react somewhat differently to different stimuli.

Basically training can be broken down into two phases: 1) familiarization or initiation, and 2) actual ring training. The first phase can start as early as six or eight weeks, although it is not absolutely essential that it begin this early. However, much of what makes a dog stand out in the ring is that extra spark of interest, the fact that he is enjoying what he is doing, and this quality is usually more easily instilled in puppyhood.

During the initiation period there are basically three things the puppy should be familiarized with: his crate, his collar and lead, and people. Often upon attending their first dog show, people are alarmed at the sight of hundreds of caged animals. Animals, however, do not seem to suffer the same kind or degree of claustrophobia as humans. In fact, left to their own devices, dogs, like other animals in the wild, will intentionally seek out small, secure places in which to rest or sleep. For this reason, if a puppy is encouraged to sleep in his crate if he is a house dog, or to spend a few hours each week in it if he is a kennel dog, the crate becomes home and the place he feels safest, especially among the clamor and bustle of a dog show.

Leash breaking is also a vital part of this early training for, although a dog can be readily trained to grudgingly move on a lead, he will not move with the freedom and assurance necessary for proper ring deportment unless he is thoroughly familiar with, and unintimidated by, the lead. For this reason a puppy should be encouraged to walk on the lead a few minutes a day at the earliest possible age. Tidbits are a helpful means of encouragement during these practice sessions which should be kept short and fun. It is also best to practice somewhere other than the puppy's backyard, since he will be likely to find the sessions more appealing in somewhat less familiar surroundings, it being only logical that if sessions are held in an environment where he normally experiences complete freedom, he will only find the lead an unpleasant infringement on that freedom.

Having the practice sessions outside of the puppy's normal domain also furthers his socialization, the third aspect of early training. From the time a puppy is three weeks of age, he should be exposed to as much human contact as possible, getting used to being touched and played with. And from the time that he can walk on a lead, he should be exposed to as many people and environments as possible. Shopping centers are excellent for familiarizing a puppy with the noise and hubbub of human behavior, especially if he has any tendency toward shyness.

After the puppy has been familiarized with his crate, his lead and people, it is time for more directed training. He should become accustomed to moving in the various patterns required in the show ring: the up and back, the "L," the triangle, and, although it is used less frequently, the "T." He should also get used to circling the ring counterclockwise. Although for the most part a dog is gaited on the left of the handler, ring decorum requires that the dog always be kept between the handler and the judge. Thus, it will be noted that in order to perform the "L" or the "T" patterns, it is necessary to change hands. Consequently it is useful to train a puppy to gait on either side of his handler, the lead always being held in the hand nearest the dog. "Honoring the judge" a formality that involves making a small circle in front of the judge before moving if the judge is standing on the handler's right, should also be practiced. This formality also offers the judge an unobstructed view of the dog from the time he begins a pattern until he finishes it. It should not, however, be overdone. One should always bear in mind that the judge is working to a strict timetable and cannot afford to have his time wasted by handlers who insist on moving their dogs in large, leisurely circles while honoring the judge. And, of course, there is no reason to go through the formality when it is possible to move the dog in the prescribed pattern without obscuring the judge's view of him.

It is also at this point that the puppy should be learning to stand for examination, to be felt over by someone other than his handler from head to tail. This examination also includes checking the puppy's bite and, if it is a male, feeling for testicles. He should also be getting used to being set up, that is have his legs placed in a show pose. Since the Siberian is considered one of the "natural" breeds, it is preferable that a dog be trained to walk into a show pose, using bait if necessary, and not be set up by the handler. However, no matter how sound and how well trained the dog is, there will be times when one foot or another is out of position, and it will be necessary to reset it in a hurry. So since Siberians are more rambunctious than many breeds, it is helpful to have a puppy get used to having his legs placed as early as possible. In doing this, it is better to place a front leg by taking it just below the elbow and the back leg at the stifle joint or just below, as this affords greater control than if the leg is held further down. However, one should guard against overhandling for, as the judge William Kendrick once remarked, no handler can show a dog as well as the dog can show himself. The handler's job is merely to make sure that the dog shows himself to best advantage, and a handler who is constantly fussing with his dog only distracts the judge and draws attention to himself and away from the dog.

This second stage of training is made much easier by enrolling in one of the handling classes that are held periodically by local all-breed clubs. This not only is a useful place to get constructive criticism, it also exposes a puppy to many other dogs. Furthermore, it is one place to learn about upcoming fun matches and matches sanctioned by the American Kennel Club. These matches are run very much like a regular dog show, except that there are no championship points awarded and the entry fees are minimal. And they are by far the best places to give a puppy ring experience.

STRUCTURE OF THE DOG SHOW

During the time that one is training a puppy, it is useful to attend at least one all-breed point show to get some idea of ring procedure and to watch some of the better handlers. The structure of the classes is really

Ch. Kontoki's Hot Lips, owned by Marlene DePalma and Thomas Oelschlager, is an elegant, BIS-winning daughter of the celebrated Ch. Kontoki's One Mo' Time. *Booth*

Ch. Amchitka's Amie Valentina, owned by L. Stewart and Gloria Cochrane was one of the breed's top-winning bitches of the 1970s. In this photo she was 8½ years old. *Bernard Kernan*

Ch. Marlytuk's Sachem of Canaan, owned by Carol Nash, was a top winner during the late 1970s and early 1980s. He was also a significant stud force. *Dick Alverson*

quite simple and can be followed in the catalogue that is sold on the grounds. Briefly this is the procedure:

First, second, third and fourth prize ribbons are awarded in each of the following classes: Puppy Dogs, Novice Dogs, Bred by Exhibitor Dogs, American Bred Dogs and Open Dogs. The winners of all the classes then compete for the Winners Dog ribbon and the Reserve Winners Dog ribbon. The Winners Dog is the only one eligible to receive championship points, the number of which varies according to the number of entries.

The same procedure is then followed for bitches until a Winners Bitch and Reserve Winners Bitch are determined.

At this point the Winners Dog and Winners Bitch reenter the ring with any Specials, that is, dogs who have already completed their championships, to compete for the Best of Breed award. After this award is given the judge then awards the Best of Opposite Sex ribbon to the specimen he feels is the best from among those of the opposite sex from his Best of Breed winner. He then awards his Best of Winners ribbon to either the Winners Dog or Winners Bitch, depending on which he feels is better.

The winner of the Best of Breed award is then eligible to go on to compete in the Working Group, the winner of which then goes on to compete for Best in Show.

9

Official AKC Standard of the Siberian Husky—with Author's Commentary

W E HAVE ALREADY NOTED THAT THE STAND-
ard is the basis upon which dogs are judged in the conformation ring. In actual fact, of course, dogs in the breed ring are judged comparatively, one against the other, and the Standard merely sets the guidelines for this comparison. Assumably in a good class there will be a number of dogs that conform to the basic tenets set by the Standard. The judge then must resort to a comparison of the more indefinable areas of canine aesthetics such as carriage and bearing, perhaps looking for what the noted judge William Kendrick is fond of calling "the look of eagles." Or he may resort to the more technical areas of structure and pick, among a number of well-moving, well-balanced dogs, what he feels is the very best moving specimen.

This kind of latitude in choosing a winner is what makes a dog show, and it is precisely this latitude that is written into every breed Standard. They are written, after all, in words, which are necessarily open to interpretation, and they are written only to the level of technical knowledge available to its composers at a given time. Most breed clubs strive to keep their Standards as clear and up-to-date as possible. But this is a more difficult task then it might at first seem. For instance, most of the early Standards were written by horsemen who, when using a phrase like "a cleverly built hunter," had a precise idea of what this connoted. But to

SKULL medium size, in proportion to body; slightly rounded on top; tapering gradually from widest point to eyes

EYES almond-shaped; moderately spaced; set trifle oblique; expression keen, friendly, interested, mischievous. Color brown or blue—one of each or parti-color acceptable

STOP well defined

NOSE black in gray, tan or black dogs; liver in copper dogs; may be flesh-colored in white dogs; pink-streaked acceptable

MUZZLE medium long; from nose to stop about equal from stop to occiput; tapering gradually to nose; lips well-pigmented, close-fitting; scissors bite

CHEST deep, strong, not too broad

FORELEGS straight, well-muscled; substantial bone, but not heavy; strong pasterns

FEET oval, medium size, compact; well furred between toes and pads (trimming for neatness permitted); pads tough, thickly cushioned

SIZE: (At withers): Dogs, 21" to 23½"; Bitches, 20" to 22". Weight in proportion to height: Dogs, 45 to 60 lbs.; Bitches, 35 to 50 lbs.

APPEARANCE: Medium size, moderately compact well-furred dog of power and grace; body proportions reflect speed and endurance; firm, well-developed, never coarse.

EARS medium size, triangular, close-fitting, set high on head; thick, well-furred; erect, slightly arched, with slightly rounded tips straight up.

NECK medium length; arched; carried erect when standing, extended when moving

SHOULDERS powerful, well laid back, approximate 45° angle

BACK: Length medium; strong; topline level; loins taut, lean; croup slopes away from spine at angle

TAIL, well-furred brush, set on just below level of topline; when up, does not curl to either side of body, or snap flat against back; in repose, trailing tail is normal

HINDQUARTERS well-muscled, powerful. Stifles well-bent. Hind legs (rear view) parallel, moderately spaced. Dewclaws to be removed.

RIBS well-sprung, deep

DISQUALIFICATIONS: Dogs over 23½"; Bitches over 22".

DOUBLE COAT: Undercoat soft, dense, sufficiently long to support outercoat. Outercoat straight, smooth-lying, medium in length, well-furred appearance but not obscuring clean-cut outline

COLORS: All colors allowed

Visualization of the SIBERIAN HUSKY standard, reproduced courtesy of the publisher, from DOG STANDARDS ILLUSTRATED © Howell Book House.

generations who came after them who were not horsemen, a phrase like this might seem vague and not very useful. Another problem is simply that the connotations of certain phrases may be different in different parts of the world. Thus, many breed standards in England ask for a "straight front," meaning not a straight shoulder when viewed from the side as we would tend to interpret it, but a parallel positioning of the front legs when viewed from the front.

Added to these problems is the fact that initially a Standard evolves merely as a description of the few available specimens of that breed, without too much consideration for what is perhaps ideal. For instance, the Siberian Standard once asked for rather large "not too compact" feet and a "rather short" neck. Later it was decided that the somewhat splayed foot found in many of the early specimens was perhaps more coincidental than functional and that the more compact foot required by most breeds was more desirable. Also, when it was found how important the neck was for the proper maintenance of balance when moving, the phrase "rather short" was changed to "medium in length."

There are then two kinds of vagueness found in any given breed Standard. The first is simply the result of the ambiguity of language or the limits of knowledge and is, for the most part, unintentional. The second is the intentional leeway left for interpretation. Because the Siberian came to this country very recently as a still-functioning working dog, and because "naturalness" has always been an important quality to his fanciers, the emphasis in the Standard has always been on function. Consequently, the Siberian Husky Standard is what might be called a fairly loose Standard, its emphasis being placed upon soundness and the basic requisite of type, without undue emphasis on coat color, markings, eye color, or even the precise structure of the skull. However, there is a Standard, and although judging is necessarily comparative, and although any breed is subject to certain changes in fashion, it would be wrong to assume too much leeway in interpretation. The following analysis of the Standard is intended, then, to clarify some of the ambiguity and to define some of the limits of interpretation.

CURRENT AKC STANDARD FOR SIBERIAN HUSKIES

General Appearance

The Siberian Husky is a medium-sized working dog, quick and light on his feet and free and graceful in action. His moderately compact and well-furred body, erect ears and brush tail suggest his Northern heritage. His characteristic gait is smooth and seemingly effortless. He performs his original function in harness most capably, carrying a light load at a moderate speed over great distances. His body proportions and form reflect this basic balance of power, speed and endurance. The males of the Siberian

Husky breed are masculine but never coarse; the bitches are feminine but without weakness of structure. In proper condition, with muscle firm and well developed, the Siberian Husky does not carry excess weight.

Comment: The Siberian is, quite simply, a dog invented by an Indian, an extremely frugal animal bred for a harsh environment; so underlying this simple description is a prescription for moderation that would please even the staunchest Aristotelian. In the space of several sentences, we find that the Siberian is "medium-sized," "moderately compact," reflects a "balance of power, speed and endurance," that males are "masculine but not coarse" and bitches "feminine without weakness of structure," that both should be "dry": carrying no excess weight, not fleshy or loose. We find, also, the reason for this prescription: that the original function of the Siberian was to carry a "light load at moderate speed over great distances." This is a tremendously important phrase in coming to an understanding of the conformation of the Siberian, for although he has gained much recognition for his accomplishments in the area of Arctic and Antarctic exploration as well as in the field of sled dog racing, he was intended neither as a heavy draft animal nor as a sprinter. He was bred to pull light loads often as much as one hundred miles in a single day, a job that required a dog that was "quick and light on his feet and free and graceful in action." Anything clumsy or heavy in movement would be unable to maintain the pace required of these dogs; anything too refined would lack the necessary pulling power and stamina.

Size, Proportion, Substance

Height: Dogs, 21 to 23½ inches at the withers. Bitches, 20 to 22 inches at the withers. Weight: Dogs, 45 to 60 pounds. Bitches, 35 to 50 pounds. Weight is in proportion to height. The measurements mentioned above represent the extreme height and weight limits with no preference given to either extreme. Any appearance of excessive bone or weight should be penalized. In profile, the length of the body from the point of the shoulder to the rear point of the croup is slightly longer than the height of the body from the ground to the top of the withers. **Disqualification**: Dogs over 23½ inches and bitches over 22 inches.

Comment: Size is as integral a feature of the Siberian as coat texture or ear set and just as important to his functionality. A dog smaller than that called for by the Standard will lack the necessary strength to be a good sled dog, while one larger will lack the speed and endurance. So again it is the moderate that is required with absolutely no preference given to either extreme set by the Standard. This is important to realize even though in a large class it is often the larger specimens that stand out immediately simply because of their size. However, a dog standing 23½ inches at the shoulder is in no way preferable on a team to one who stands 22. It should be remembered that Togo weighed only 48 pounds. It is also interesting to note that as a possible by-product of this insistence upon the maintenance of medium size, Siberian fanciers have so far avoided many of the problems found in breeds where greater size is preferable, problems such as hip dysplasia and osteochondritis that remain relatively rare in this breed.

Head

Expression: Is keen, but friendly; interested and even mischievous.

Eyes: Almond shaped, moderately spaced and set a trifle obliquely. Eyes may be brown or blue in color; one of each or particolored are acceptable. **Faults**: Eyes set too obliquely; set too close together.

Ears: Of medium size, triangular in shape, close fitting and set high on the head. They are thick, well furred, slightly arched at the back, and strongly erect, with slightly rounded tips pointing straight up. **Faults**: Ears too large in proportion to the head; too wide set; not strongly erect.

Skull: Of medium size and in proportion to the body; slightly rounded on top and tapering from the widest point to the eyes. **Faults**: Head clumsy or heavy; head too finely chiseled.

Stop: The stop is well-defined and the bridge of the nose is straight from the stop to the tip. **Fault**: Insufficient stop.

Muzzle: Of medium length; that is, the distance from the tip of the nose to the stop is equal to the distance from the stop to the occiput. The muzzle is of medium width, tapering gradually to the nose, with the tip neither pointed nor square. **Faults**: Muzzle either too snipy or too coarse; muzzle too short or too long.

Nose: Black in gray, tan or black dogs; liver in copper dogs; may be flesh colored in pure white dogs. The pink-streaked "snow nose" is acceptable.

Lips: Are well pigmented and close fitting.

Teeth: Closing in a scissors bite. **Fault** Any bite other than scissors.

Comment: Along with coat type and the general size and proportion of the body, the head is the primary indicator of *type* in a breed and thus is an important factor in the assessment of any purebred dog. It has been argued that heads are basically a matter of aesthetic whim and have little to do with the actual functioning capability of a breed. This is, of course, not altogether true. A Siberian, for instance, would be hard-pressed to survive in an Arctic climate with anything but a well-furred ear, and an argument could probably be made that the smaller ear, as opposed to that

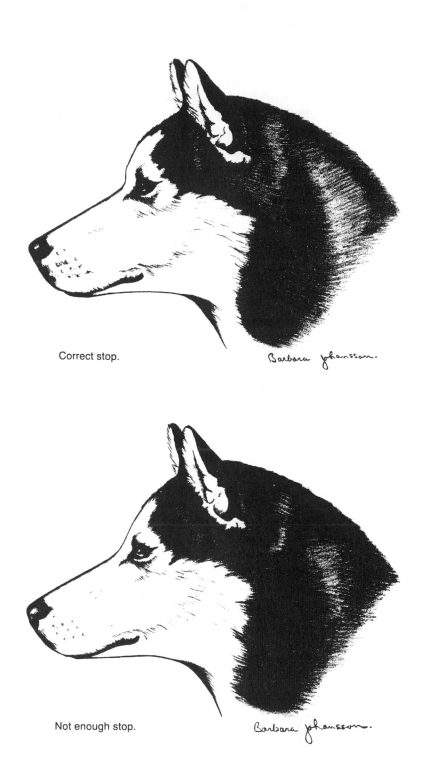

Correct stop.

Barbara Johansson.

Not enough stop.

Barbara Johansson.

of the German Shepherd, would be less vulnerable to cold. The erect ear is also more generally efficient than the lop ear and less prone to infection. It has further been hypothesized by Richard and Alice Fiennes in their book, *The Natural History of Dogs*, that the well-defined stop called for in the Siberian Standard allows for the maximum development of the frontal sinuses which trap exhaled warmed air, thereby forming a warm cushion over the delicate tissues of the eyes and forebrain and also helping warm the cold inhaled air as it passes along the nasal passages. It has been argued by veteran drivers like Roland Lombard that a muzzle shorter than that required by the Standard fails to warm the air sufficiently before entering the sinuses. The requirement for close-fitting lips would be necessary for survival in subzero temperatures, one of the things noted by the earliest fanciers of the breed being the dogs' ability to work with their mouths closed, thereby avoiding frostbite of the lungs. The scissors bite is the most efficient for tearing and eating and, perhaps more importantly, for severing the umbilical cord during whelping. The medium-sized head, like the medium length of neck that is called for later in the Standard, is optimal for endurance, the head and neck performing a vital function in the maintenance of balance and the movement of the front assembly. Since it can probably be further argued that the almond-shaped eye that is called for by the Standard is the one most easily protected between the frontal bones and zygomatic arch (cheekbone), it being the eye most frequently found among wild Canidae, this leaves only the slightly oblique eye set and very high ear set called for by the Standard in the realm of simple aesthetic preference. But since these characteristics were found on the majority of early specimens, and since they are among the characteristics distinguishing the Siberian from his cousins, the Malamute, Samoyed and the now no longer recognized Eskimo, requiring their maintenance seems eminently justifiable.

Neck, Topline, Body

Neck: Medium in length, arched and carried proudly erect when dog is standing. When moving at a trot, the neck is extended so that the head is carried slightly forward. **Faults**: Neck too short and thick; neck too long.

Chest: Deep and strong, but not too broad, with the deepest point being just behind and level with the elbows. The ribs are well-sprung from the spine but flattened on the sides to allow for freedom of action. **Faults**: Chest too broad; "barrel ribs"; ribs too flat or weak.

Back: The back is straight and strong, with a level topline from withers to croup. It is of medium length, neither cobby nor slack from excessive length. The loin is taut and lean, narrower than the rib cage, and with a slight tuck-up. The croup slopes away from the spine at an angle, but never

Correct ear set.

Ears set too wide.

so steeply as to restrict the rearward thrust of the hind legs. **Faults**: Weak or slack back; roached back; sloping topline.

Comment: The neck is primarily what keeps a dog from falling on its face as the rear drives it forward. Muscles attached just below the base of the skull lift the forelimbs and propel them forward and back. The strength of these muscles is evident in the arched neck when the dog is alert and standing. But as they come into play in the moving dog, it becomes necessary for the head and neck to extend forward for maximum effectiveness. In the Siberian, we ask that the neck be medium in length simply because, like the medium skull, bone, etc., this is the most effective size where both speed and stamina are desirable.

The chest houses heart and lungs and so should be of sufficient depth to provide ample room. But in a breed designed for maximum suppleness at a lope, the chest cannot be too wide, and must be flattened on the sides. Otherwise it will impede the free movement of the front legs. So, too, with depth of chest. According to Roland Lombard, there has probably never been an effective sled dog with a chest deeper than its elbows. In fact, in the well-built Siberian, it is probably only the hair of the chest that brings it to the level of the elbows, the chest itself being just higher and out of the way.

The topline of the back of a dog from the base of the neck to the end of the croup forms a sort of lazy "S" which, when the dog moves, allows energy to flow forward as a sort of ascending double wave through the croup and loin, the midback, and on into the neck. So, although the Standard asks for a "level topline," what is meant is the appearance of a level topline since, in fact, the spine dips downward from the withers above the shoulders before rising into the arch of the spine that creates the "tuck-up" in the loin. That arch is the main point of energy transference from the rear to the front, and in the effective galloper those muscles will be extremely powerful.

Tail

The well-furred tail of fox-brush shape is set on just below the level of the topline, and is usually carried over the back in a graceful sickle curve when the dog is at attention. When carried up, the tail does not curl to either side of the body, nor does it snap flat against the back. A trailing tail is normal for the dog when in repose. Hair on the tail is of medium length and approximately the same length on top, sides and bottom, giving the appearance of a round brush. **Faults**: A snapped or tightly curled tail; highly plumed tail; tail set too low or too high.

Comment: The comment is occasionally heard at ringside, "A dog doesn't run on his tail." Overlooking the tail set and carriage in one's assessment

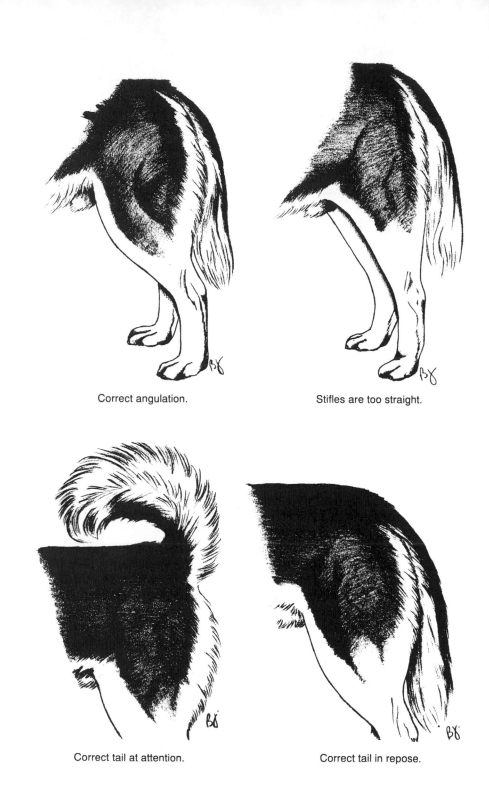

Correct angulation.

Stifles are too straight.

Correct tail at attention.

Correct tail in repose.

Incorrect tail—excessive plumage.

Incorrect tail—curled to one side of body.

Incorrect tail—snapped flat to back.

of a dog, however, is rather like overlooking the last chapter of a novel. Few good novels have bad last chapters and few mediocre ones have particularly good endings. This is because the success or failure of a last chapter is largely dependent on what has come before. And, if anything, this is truer of dogs than of novels, for the novelist might just be lucky enough to come up with a brilliant enough finale to momentarily transform in the reader's mind the mediocrity that has come before. Such sleight-of-hand, however, rarely takes place in nature, as the bones and muscles of the body are intimately interrelated and not subject to good days and bad days, as are the workings of a writer's mind.

The demands made for the tail, then, are intimately related to the demands made for the more obviously functional parts of the body. The set of the tail, for instance, is dependent on the angle of the croup, a slightly sloping croup placing the base of the tail just below the level of the topline. The tail carriage, on the other hand, indicates a great deal about the condition of the muscles along the spine, a tightly snapped tail or tail deviating to one side or the other being caused by poor muscling. And since these muscles that control the tail carriage are also influential in propelling the dog, it is unlikely that muscles that are inefficient for the one job will be any more efficient for the other.

The tail is thus much more than decoration. Rather it is a kind of critique on what has come before. So, although it is true that a dog does not run on his tail, it is equally true that a dog who runs well will normally exhibit a good tail set and carriage.

The distinctive tail shape and carriage of the Siberian also has its basis in function, for we are told that not only was this thick brush necessary for covering the dogs' noses while sleeping in subzero temperatures, but that the distinctive over-the-back or straight-trailing carriage was less apt to get tangled in the harnesses, and that many dogs of crossbreeding had to have their tails docked to avoid this problem. The request for the even brush shape rather than a heavily plumed tail is simply consistent with the medium-length coat that is requested later in the Standard.

Forequarters

Shoulders: The shoulder blade is well laid back. The upper arm angles slightly backward from point of shoulder to elbow, and is never perpendicular to the ground. The muscles and ligaments holding the shoulder to the rib cage are firm and well developed. **Faults**: Straight shoulders; loose shoulders.

Forelegs: When standing and viewed from the front, the legs are moderately spaced, parallel and straight, with the elbows close to the body and turned neither in nor out. Viewed from the side, pasterns are slightly slanted, with the pastern joint strong, but flexible. Bone is substantial but

Correct front

Front too narrow

Front too wide

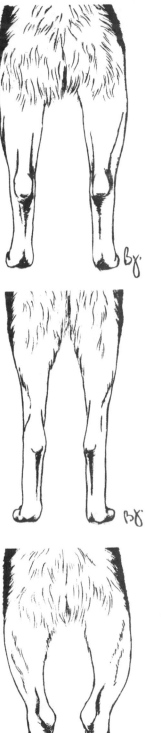

Correct rear

Rear too narrow

Cow hocked

209

never heavy. Length of the leg from elbow to ground is slightly more than the distance from the elbow to the top of withers. Dewclaws on forelegs may be removed. **Faults**: Weak pasterns; too heavy bone; too narrow or too wide in the front; out at the elbows.

Feet: Oval in shape but not long. The paws are medium in size, compact and well furred between the toes and pads. The pads are tough and thickly cushioned. The paws neither turn in nor out when the dog is in natural stance. **Faults**: Soft or splayed toes; paws too large and clumsy; paws too small and delicate; toeing in or out.

Comment: In asking for a well laid back shoulder, we take the Standard to mean a shoulder blade that is angled approximately 30 to 40 degrees from the perpendicular, with 35 degrees being perhaps ideal. This, at least, is what studies of the racing sled dog have indicated. And though the benefits of extreme shoulder layback have long been touted by reach and drive enthusiasts of the show ring, Curtis Brown is probably right in his book *Dog Locomotion and Gait Analysis* when he suggests that extreme shoulder layback is probably only highly desirable in dogs who were made to dig. For the endurance galloper, he favors a 30-degree layback with a long upper arm.

This optimal angle of 30 to 35 degrees, then, is established when the heel pad is set directly under the center of the shoulder blade and not when the feet are any further forward, as is sometimes the case in the show ring when the front is "dropped" into position by the handler. This is why it is also asked that the upper arm angle backward to the elbow and not be perpendicular to the ground, since a straight-shouldered dog can be made to give the appearance of having more shoulder layback by bringing the front legs forward, thus rotating the shoulder blade backward. The result, however, will be to bring the upper arm perpendicular to the ground.

But it is the muscles, tendons and ligaments, and how they function, that are of paramount importance. A front assembly is only as good as it functions, and it is while gaiting that a shoulder can be best appraised, according to its fluency, rotation of the blade, shock absorbancy and smoothness of topline. To the feel, good shoulders allow good muscling—the larger the blade, the larger the area for muscle adherence. And the smoother the blend of neck into topline, whether standing or gaiting, the better.

The front leg bones of the Siberian should be what is sometimes referred to as "bladed," that is to say, oval in shape (like the feet) and a bit sharp at the front edge. They are moderately (maybe a palm's breadth) spaced for maximum efficiency. Pasterns are slanted slightly for maximum resiliency and flex, and the bone is moderate.

The feet of the Siberian are his livelihood, and must be oval, strong, and definitely neither small nor round, however attractive judges sometimes find small cat feet. Small feet injure easily, and round feet with their shorter digits offer less flex and resiliency, and usually prefigure short, straight pasterns. And, of course, though dogs can certainly be set up in the show ring with their front toes pointing straight ahead, the more natural position for the feet on a well-built Siberian is with an approximate 10-degree toeing out. Otherwise, when the feet converge when moving, the strong middle toes do not land pointing straight ahead and taking the bulk of the stress.

Hindquarters

When standing and viewed from the rear, the hind legs are moderately spaced and parallel. The upper thighs are well muscled and powerful, the stifles well bent, the hock joint well defined and set low to the ground. Dewclaws, if any, are to be removed. **Faults**: Straight stifles, cowhocks, too narrow or too wide in the rear.

Comment: This description of hindquarters is again in the interest of speed and endurance. The highest-hocked animals, like rabbits, run fastest but tire quickly. Short pasterns mean endurance. But though the Standard calls for a low hock joint, it is worth noting that Doc Lombard warns against a rear pastern that is too short, a hock joint that is too low, because too much speed is lost.

Coat

The coat of the Siberian Husky is double and medium in length, giving a well-furred appearance, but is never so long as to obscure the clean-cut outline of the dog. The undercoat is soft and dense and of sufficient length to support the outer coat. The guard hairs of the outer coat are straight and somewhat smooth lying, never harsh nor standing straight off from the body. It should be noted that the absence of the undercoat during the shedding season is normal. Trimming of whiskers and fur between the toes and around the feet to present a neater appearance is permissible. Trimming the fur on any other part of the dog is not be condoned and should be severly penalized. **Faults**: Long, rough, or shaggy coat; texture too harsh or too silky; trimming of the coat, except as permitted above.

Comment: The Siberian coat is unique among Arctic breeds because of its medium length, both the Malamute and the Samoyed having a somewhat longer, shaggier coat. The reason for this difference lies primarily in the difference in the climates in which these dogs were originally bred. In the case of the Siberian, the specific conditions of climate and terrain found in his homeland made the formation of ice balls in a long coat an ever-present danger. Thus, consciously or unconsciously, the Chukchi developed a coat on their dogs that could both withstand the Arctic cold and prevent the formation of ice balls. And it is for this reason that the long, shaggy, or coarse coat is specifically faulted by the Standard. Nevertheless, there does exist a certain range of coat length, probably from about one inch to three inches, that is considered typically Siberian so long as the outline of the dog remains unobscured and the texture is correct. The love of profuse coat in the show Fancy has led some breeders to produce coats so profuse as to require trimming of the underline to maintain a clean-cut outline. This is specifically prohibited by the Standard.

Color

All colors from black to pure white are allowed. A variety of markings on the head is common, including many striking patterns not found in other breeds.

Comment: One of the great delights of Siberians is their variability of color as well as markings—everything from all black to all white being both permissible and desirable. Usually symmetry is more aesthetically pleasing than asymmetry, but even so-called piebalds or pintos (though apparently not desirable to the Chukchi nor many of the early breeders) are acceptable and occasionally even exquisite.

Gait

The Siberian Husky's characteristic gait is smooth and seemingly effortless. He is quick and light on his feet, and when in the show ring should be gaited on a loose lead at a moderately fast trot, exhibiting good reach in the forequarters and good drive in the hindquarters. When viewed from the front to rear while moving at a walk the Siberian Husky does not single-track, but as the speed increases the legs gradually angle inward until the pads are falling on a line directly under the longitudinal center of the body. As the pad marks converge, the forelegs and hind legs are carried straight forward, with neither elbows nor stifles turned in or out. Each hind leg moves in the path of the foreleg on the same side. While the dog is gaiting, the topline remains firm and level. **Faults**: Short, prancing or choppy gait, lumbering or rolling gait; crossing or crabbing.

Comment: With the exception of a few stipulations made in the interest of type and refinement, everything in the Standard so far has led up to this demand for "smooth and seemingly effortless" movement. In other words, this is where the phrase "the whole equals the sum of the parts" is particularly relevant, since, basically, the moving dog is the whole dog. Consequently, a dog who has exhibited a well-bent stifle but a somewhat

212

steep shoulder will likely show this discrepancy when moving. Balance is the key to movement, in other words, and a dog who is slightly under-angulated, but balanced, front and rear, will likely move better than, and is thus preferable to, a dog who is extreme in one quarter or another. The request for single-tracking and for the rear legs to follow in the line of the front is in the interest of efficiency. A dog who is more angulated in the rear than in the front, for instance, is likely to crab, especially if he has a short, stiff back. In other words, he will tend to move diagonally to the line of travel, placing his rear feet to one side or the other of his forefeet in order to avoid having his rear feet actually hit his front feet. Short, prancing, or choppy gaits are usually caused by insufficient angulation or straight pasterns, and since this causes the dog to bob up and down rather than move directly in the line of travel, he is apt to be slower and tire more quickly. A lumbering or rolling gait is caused by a dog's inability to single-track properly, either because of an inherited weakness in structure or poor muscle tone. Often overweight dogs exhibit this tendency, and puppies often tend to roll somewhat before they develop adequate muscles and coordination. Since this type of movement also produces motion in a direction outside the line of travel, it is less than efficient. The same is true of any movement of the legs other than directly forward to a point directly under the longitudinal center of the body.

Occasionally the comment is heard at ringside, "That dog looks like he could pull a sled." Too often this comment is made in reference to a heavily boned, heavily muscled dog who, when simply being gaited, already looks like he is pulling a two-hundred-pound load. Remember that the Standard asks for a balance of power, speed and endurance and that this balance will be reflected in a dog who is "light and quick on his feet" and whose "gait is smooth and seemingly effortless."

Temperament

The characteristic temperament of the Siberian Husky is friendly and gentle, but also alert and outgoing. He does not display the possessive qualities of the guard dog, nor is he overly suspicious of strangers or aggressive with other dogs. Some measure of reserve and dignity may be expected in the mature dog. His intelligence, tractability, and eager disposition make him an agreeable companion and willing worker.

Comment: Temperament is of utmost importance in a Siberian Husky. An aggressive dog is not a team dog, and since the Siberian is a sled dog, any sign of aggression toward other dogs should be severely penalized. It has been pointed out in defense of more aggressive dogs that the majority of the early Chukchi teams were neutered, except for the lead dog. Evidence, however, points strongly to the viewpoint that these dogs were neutered not to avoid fighting but because a neutered dog, having a more retarded metabolism, requires relatively less food. It also insured that only the best dogs were active in breeding.

Summary

The most important breed characteristics of the Siberian Husky are medium size, moderate bone, well-balanced proportions, ease and freedom of movement, proper coat, pleasing head and ears, correct tail, and good disposition. Any appearance of excessive bone or weight, constricted or clumsy gait, or long, rough coat should be penalized. The Siberian Husky never appears so heavy or coarse as to suggest a freighting animal; nor is he so light and fragile as to suggest a sprint-racing animal. In both sexes the Siberian Husky gives the appearance of being capable of great endurance. In addition to the faults already noted, the obvious structural faults common to all breeds are as undesirable in the Siberian Husky as in any other breed, even though they are not specifically mentioned herein.

10

Dialectics of the Breed: The New and the Old, the Show Ring and the Harness

---

FROM THE BEGINNING THERE WERE THOSE who were drawn to the Siberian for his looks, and those drawn by his worth as a working sled dog. But most pioneer breeders were interested in both, and as a consequence the probable peak of the breed as a truly dual-purpose animal happened, in very general terms, during the late 1940s and 1950s. After that point, the demands of specialization created divergence: the show people going in one direction, the racing enthusiasts in another.

The show people concentrated on developing animals to be exhibited at a trot, while racers were interested in gallopers. Dog show exhibitors tended to want a profuse coat; racers, particularly sprint racers in the continental United States increasingly wanted less coat so that the dogs would not overheat. Dog show judges were often lured by animals excessively bulky and/or dumpy (often claiming, "It looked like it could pull a sled"), while racers often gravitated toward animals so refined and/or rangy as to exhibit almost no breed type.

By 1960 the Siberian had just completed its most successful decade as a racing sled dog. Earl Norris had won the Fur Rendezvous World

A group of imports from Siberia, circa 1930: Kreevanka is shown at far left and Tserko is at far right. Note the beautiful head type and body proportions on both dogs.

Siberians from Alaskan Kennels with Rita Norris during the early 1950s.

Championship in 1947 and 1948 with all-Siberian teams; Natalie Norris had won the Fur Rendezvous Women's World Championship in 1954; Kit MacInnes had won the Fur Rendezvous Women's Championship in 1955 along with the Women's North American Championship in 1955 and 1956; Roland Lombard had won both The Pas and the North American Championship in 1958; and in races in New England and Canada, Charlie Belford had won fifty-four of sixty-seven races, spanning the years 1951 to 1958 and culminating with a win at Laconia—his team containing not only purebred Siberians, but four white ones. Out of this era came such famous leaders as Ch. Igloo Pak's (pronounced pake) Chuckchee, Ch. Helen of Cold River (both Lombard leaders), Timmy of Gatineau (Belford's), Foxstand's Shango (Bill Shearer's), and Ch. Bonzo of Anadyr (Norris's). These in turn were followed in later decades by such dogs as Igloo Pak's Tok, Alaskan's Asto of Anadyr, and even later, Igloo Pak's Wing A. Most were still animals that could, and sometimes did, excel in the show ring. Bonzo was, in fact, the first Siberian to win a Best in Show.

The breed was also entering its most successful period as a show dog, with increased numbers of Group wins and several Bests in Show during the 1960s, largely thanks to the genetic influence of Ch. Monadnock's Pando, followed by a flurry of success in the 1970s and 1980s: with Ch. Innisfree's Sierra Cinnar winning a record thirty Bests in Show, including the 1980 Westminster event; his son Ch. Kontoki's Natural Sinner winning a record sixteen Specialty shows; a granddaughter Ch. Indigo's Intity winning twenty Bests in Show (a record for a bitch); and a great-grandson Ch. Kontoki's One Mo' Time breaking all records with thirty-five Best in Show wins. Cinnar supplanted Ch. Marlytuk's Red Sun of Kiska as the most sought-after red stud of the period, his daughter, Ch. Innisfree's Newscents Niavar, eventually supplanting Sunny's daughter, Innisfree's Kismet, as the number one producing brood bitch with sixteen champion get to Kismet's thirteen. Sixty-one Siberians have now won all-breed Best in Show honors. These dogs represent over fifty distinct prefixes.

But the show ring is a limited arena in which to appraise the full merits of an animal, and certainly provides no adequate means of gauging the essential athleticism of a contestant. As Curtis Brown writes in his *Dog Locomotion and Gait Analysis*, "Appraising the performance capability of an animal in the ring is rather like trying to assess an athlete as he walks to the refrigerator to get a glass of milk."

Moreover, show ring success, however exhilarating, often has its darker side. Attention to superficialities and excessive emphasis on grooming may work to distract many judges from important distinctions of type and body proportions.

In regard to body proportions, some distinction needs to be made between the sprint animal and the distance animal, though there is perhaps less distinction than was once thought. At a recent seminar in Wisconsin, Earl Norris was asked the difference between his best sprint animals and his best distance animals. "Nothing," he replied. Fast dogs, it has been found, tend to be fast, whatever the distance, and Iditarod racers, for instance, have over the years relied less on the bigger, heavier animals that were once supposed more suitable for long, grueling distances, and more on lighter, sleeker, leggier animals.

But it is probably safe to assume that the distance animal will likely be just a little closer to square than the sprint animal needs to be, a little better balanced, and probably have *slightly* more chest and *very slightly* less leg.

The show ring, on the other hand, has tended to reward dogs lower on leg and/or longer in back (the two being somewhat difficult to differentiate) than is functionally ideal. This is largely because short-legged animals often appear in the context of the show ring to be better movers, the shorter legs giving the impression of greater reach and drive, and the longer back making it easier for the dog to avoid crabbing and other irregularities of movement. This kind of lower-to-the-ground animal will often exhibit more depth and breadth of chest, and will sometimes even give the impression of more shoulder layback than its leggier competitors. The upper arms on these dogs, however, are almost invariably shorter than ideal, the bone is usually too heavy to allow the dog to run very far very fast; and, in terms of soft tissue, they often seem fleshy, soft and loose. Accompanying these tendencies is often a round cat foot which, though neat and attractive, is not as effective as the oval foot called for by the Standard.

In fact, each of these functional issues is pretty clearly anticipated by our very well-written Standard, but it is always difficult to wean judges away from the attraction of bulk and/or slick presentation, and to get them to understand the advantages of the slightly leggier, narrower, more refined animals.

Related to this issue of bulk is the issue of the rate of maturation. Too many people have been too eager to finish their champions at a very young age, setting records for the youngest finished, the youngest Best in Show winner, etc. The upshot of this is that too often our Specials classes look like the livestock exhibit at a country fair—the steroid supplemented beef-on-the-hoof look that makes a mockery of the sleek athletic breed that originally came to this country. Slow maturity is generally best, no matter the kind of animal, but this is especially true of sled dogs—the best of whom can function effectively in harness until age nine or ten, sometimes older.

Recently, the apparent loss of athleticism in the breed has led to several thoughtful attempts to remedy the problem. The Siberian Husky Club of America has instituted a Sled Dog Degree Program, a number of mid-distance races have been established to better test the traditional performance strengths of the breed, and the Siberian Evaluation Performance

Ch. Marlytuk's Red Sun of Kiska (1966–1980), one of the breed's all-time greats in the show ring, in harness or as a producer. He is shown here at age 10 scoring a good BB win under judge H. M. Cresap at the Long Island KC. *William Gilbert*

Am., Can. Ch. Innisfree's Sierra Cinnar, bred by Michael Burnside and owned by Innisfree Kennels, was a true breed immortal. His BIS win at Westminster in 1980 was one of 30 that he scored during his highly successful career. He is the top producer in the history of the Siberian and is partly responsible for reintroducing a little more height on leg during the 1970s. Here he is being presented with first in the Working Group at the Trumbull County KC under judge Eileen Pimlott, handler Trish Kanzler. *Dick Alverson*

219

Program (SEPP) has become a yearly event to try to identify and encourage truly superior athletes within the breed.

Of these attempts at remedy, probably the SEPP evaluations are the most exciting, bringing together as they do not only the best of our performance animals, but the best of our longtime performance drivers as evaluators. Of these, Roland Lombard, Charles Belford and Richard Moulton are certainly the most experienced and successful, with memories that go back to the very first dogs Seppala brought to New England.

So it is very lucky that these three, along with coordinator Vincent Buoniello (himself a dog driver and AKC-approved judge), have produced a document representing their viewpoint on the breed, a viewpoint garnered over decades of close observation. It must be emphasized that this is *not* the Official Standard of the breed, but it is a significant document from both the historical and performance viewpoint.

SIBERIAN EVALUATION PERFORMANCE PROJECT (SEPP)

Revised Standard for the Siberian Husky (Not official SHCA Standard)

Written By: Roland "Doc" Lombard, DVM; Charles Belford, DVM; Richard Moulton

Co-ordinator: Vincent Buoniello

General Appearance

The Siberian Husky is a medium-sized working dog, quick and light on his feet and free and graceful in action. His well-balanced and well-furred body, erect ears and brush tail suggest his Northern heritage. His head presents a finely chiseled, foxlike appearance, and his eyes have a keen and friendly expression. His characteristic gait is tireless and almost effortless when free or on a loose leash, but showing great strength when pulling. The trot is brisk and smooth and quite fast. Generally bitches are smaller than dogs, averaging two inches in height less and ten pounds less in weight, but length of body may be longer than males. Siberians range in build from moderately compact (but never "cobby") to moderately rangy: in all builds the bone must be medium, the back powerful, never slack from excessive length.

Head

Skull: Of medium size and in proportion to the body; slightly rounded on top and tapering gradually from the widest point to the eyes.

Keith Bryar (handler) and Colonel Norman Vaughn (driver) loading the first entry from the lower 48 states for the Fairbanks North American Championship, 1953. Col. Vaughn was flown up by the Air Force from his station in Virginia. Bryar had been training the dogs in New Hampshire. One of the Siberians was raised in Virginia and had never been on snow before being selected for the team. *Air Force*

Ch. Bonzo of Anadyr, CD, the breed's first BIS winner, in the lead during a North American championship at Fairbanks, during the late 1950s.

Dr. Roland Lombard waiting to board a plane to Alaska in 1958. The dog on his right is Timmie of Gatineau, a great leader with excellent breed type. He was on loan from Dr. Charles Belford for this occasion.

Natalie Norris with Alaskan's Astro of Anadyr, the lead dog when Mrs. Norris and her team won the North American Womens' Championship in 1972. Again, note the beautiful head type on this accomplished sled dog.

Muzzle: Of medium length; that is the distance from the tip of the nose to the stop is equal to the distance from the stop to the occiput. The stop is well defined and the bridge of the nose is straight from the stop to the tip. The muzzle is of medium width, tapering gradually to the nose, with the tip neither pointed nor square. The lips are well pigmented and close-fitting, teeth closing in a scissors bite. **Faults:** Head clumsy or heavy, muzzle bulky (like Malamutes), skull too wide between ears, snipiness, coarseness, insufficient stop, any bite other than scissors. If muzzle is too short, cold air is not properly warmed before reaching the sinuses and lungs.

Ears: Of medium size, erect, close-fitting, set high on head and well covered with hair on the inside. There is an arch at the back of the ears. Ears are up to one-third taller than width at base, and moderately rounded at tips. When dog is at attention, ears are usually carried practically parallel on top of head. **Faults:** Ears too large in proportion to head, too wide-set; low-set; not strongly erect, too pointed or short like a Malamute.

Eyes: Almond shaped, moderately spaced and set a trifle obliquely. The expression is keen, but friendly; interested and even mischievous. Eyes may be brown or blue in color; one of each or particolored are acceptable. **Faults:** Eyes set too obliquely; set too close together.

Nose: Black in gray, tan or black dogs; liver in copper dogs; may be flesh colored in pure white dogs, but not pink. The pink-streaked ''snow nose'' is acceptable.

Body

Neck: Medium in length, moderately arched and carried proudly erect when dog is standing. When moving at a trot, the neck is extended so that the head is carried slightly forward. **Faults:** Neck too short and thick, neck too long, too well arched, causing dog to run with head up, this shortening the reach.

Shoulders: Scapula should be at an angle of 30 degrees to 40 degrees, the ideal being 35 degrees. There is a lower scapular forward and rear rotation of as much as 15 degrees. The scapula, humerus, and pelvis should be of equal length. Spacing between the shoulders at the withers should be at least two inches. The upper arm angles slightly backward from point of shoulder to elbow and is never perpendicular to the ground. The muscles and ligaments holding the shoulder to the rib cage are firm and well developed. **Faults:** Straight shoulders, loose shoulders.

Chest: The deepest point should be just behind and slightly above the elbows. **Faults:** Too narrow, barrel, too deep.

Back: The back is strong with a slight slope from the withers to the croup. There is a slight arch (wheelback) at the end of the rib cage—positioned above forward one-third part of loin. Length of back: keel bone (breastbone) to end of croup is approximately 10 to 15 percent longer than height (ground to withers). Back should not be cobby or slack from excessive length. The loin is taut and lean, narrower than the rib cage with a definite tuck-up. The croup slopes away from the spine at an angle of approximately 35 degrees. The correct slope of the pelvis is essential as the power from the foot, traveling through the limb to the femur, has to be transmitted through the pelvis to the spine in as direct a line as possible. Slope of pelvis should be 30 degrees to 35 degrees for best effects. **Faults:** Weak or slack back, roached back, cobby, flat croup.

Legs and Feet

Forelegs: When standing and viewed from the front, the legs are moderately spaced, parallel and straight, with elbows close to the body and turned neither in nor out. When standing, the front feet should be angled outward at about 10 degrees (toe out)—this is very important because when the dog moves and his feet swing inward under the center of gravity, the action will be off his center toes, with the small toes being used merely for balance on the turns. Feet that are straight ahead when standing cannot be rotated properly when swung inward, causing the action to come off one center toe and one small toe and providing less efficient action. Viewed from the side, pasterns are slightly slanted 10 degrees to 15 degrees with pastern joint strong but flexible. Bone is medium but never heavy (like a Malamute). Length of the leg from elbow to ground is slightly more than the distance from the elbow to the top of the withers. Dewclaws on forelegs may be removed. **Faults:** Weak pasterns, too heavy or too light bone, too narrow or too wide in the front, out at the elbows, feet straight ahead when standing (no toe out).

Hindquarters: When standing and viewed from the rear, the hind legs are moderately spaced and parallel. The upper thighs are well muscled and powerful, the stifles well bent, the hock joint well-defined, and hocks in balance with rest of hind legs. Dewclaws, if any, are to be removed. **Faults:** Straight stifles, cow hocks, too narrow or too wide in the rear, sickle hocks.

Feet: Oval in shape, but not long, toes well arched. The paws are medium in size, compact and well furred between the toes, and pads are tough and well cushioned. Pad color in order of preference; lemon, black, mottled (lemon and black), orange (pink not desirable). **Faults:** Flat or splayed toes, paws too large and clumsy, paws too small and delicate, cat foot, thin or pink-colored pads.

Tail

The well-furred tail of fox-brush shape is set on just below the level of the topline, and is usually carried over the back in a gracious sickle curve when the dog is at attention. When carried up, the tail does not curl to either side of the body, nor does it snap against the back. A tight or snapped tail usually indicates incorrect slope to the pelvis. A trailing tail is normal for the dog when working or in repose. Hair on the tail is of medium length and approximately the same length on top, sides and bottom, giving the appearance of a round brush. **Faults:** A snapped or tightly curled tail, tail set too high or too low.

Gait

The Siberian Husky's characteristic gait is smooth and seemingly effortless. The most efficient gait for the Siberian is the lope and the gallop. He is quick and light on his feet, and when in the show ring should be gaited on a loose lead at a moderately fast trot, exhibiting good reach in the forequarters and good drive in the hindquarters. When viewed from the front to rear while moving at a walk, the Siberian Husky does not single-track. But as the speed increases the legs gradually angle inward until the pads are falling on a line directly under the longitudinal center of the body. As the pad marks converge, the forelegs and hindlegs are carried straight forward with neither elbows or stifles turned in or out. Each hind leg moves in the path of the foreleg on the same side. While the dog is gaiting, the topline remains firm and level. **Faults:** Short, prancing or choppy gait, lumbering or rolling gait; crossing, crabbing.

Coat

The coat of the Siberian Husky is double and medium in length, giving a well-furred appearance, but is never so long as to obscure the clean-cut outline of the dog. The undercoat is soft and dense and of sufficient length to support the outer coat. The guard hairs of the outer coat are straight and somewhat smooth lying, never harsh nor standing straight out from the body. It should be noted that the absence of the undercoat during the shedding season is normal. Trimming of the whiskers and fur between the toes and around the feet to present a neater appearance is permissible. Trimming of the fur on any other part of the dog is not to be condoned and should be severely penalized. **Faults:** Long, rough or shaggy coat; texture too harsh or too silky; trimming of the coat, except as permitted above.

Color

All colors from black to pure white are allowed. A variety of markings on the head is common, including many striking patterns not found in other breeds.

Temperament

The characteristic temperament of the Siberian Husky is friendly and gentle, but also alert and outgoing. He does not display the possessive qualities of the guard dog, nor is he overly suspicious of strangers or aggressive with other dogs. Some measure of reserve and dignity may be expected in the mature dog. His intelligence, tractability, and eager disposition make him an agreeable companion and willing worker.

Size

Height: Dogs, 21 to 23½ inches at the withers. Bitches, 20 to 22 inches at the withers. *Weight:* Dogs, 40 to 55 pounds. Bitches, 35 to 45 pounds. Weight is in proportion to the whole dog. The measurements mentioned above represent the extreme height and weight limits, with no preference given to either extreme. Overweight dogs should be penalized. **Disqualification:** Dogs over 23 ½ inches; bitches over 22 inches.

Summary

The most important breed characteristics of the Siberian Husky are medium size, moderate bone, *well-balanced proportions*, ease and freedom of movement, proper coat, pleasing head and ears, correct tail, and good disposition. Any appearance of excessive bone or weight, constricted or clumsy gait, or long, rough coat should be penalized. The Siberian Husky never appears so heavy or coarse as to suggest a freighting animal. In both sexes the Siberian Husky gives the appearance of being capable of great endurance and speed. In addition to the faults already noted, obvious structural faults common to all breeds are as undesirable in the Siberian Husky as in any other breed, even though they are not specifically mentioned herein.

What is most immediately striking about the SEPP Standard is its similarity to the Official Standard, though some of the phrasing has been taken from earlier Standards. The important words "foxlike," for instance, along with references to the Malamute, were dropped from our current Standard because the AKC wished to drop all reference to other animals or breeds in all of their Standards. But foxlike is a very telling adjective

Two of the most famous and influential racing leaders of the past two decades were Bonzo of Calivali (Igloo Pak's Jan ex Yeso Pac's Anyia) and his contemporary, Igloo Pak's Wing A. Note the relatively narrow front on Wing A.

in reference to substance and type; a dog who is foxlike in appearance simply cannot be coarse. And because most of the pioneers in the breed were also familiar with and involved with the Alaskan Malamute, reference to that breed has long been a natural form of distinguishing the parameters of type and substance within the breed.

Like these shifts of phraseology, many of the variances from the current AKC Standard are simply in the interest of descriptive clarity. Ears are a bit more precisely described, for instance, and the description of the shoulders is more detailed and technical.

The front assembly, of course, is probably the most complex and controversial aspect of canine anatomy, and experts like Rachel Page Elliott distrust the use of angle measurement as simply too inaccurate. But the 35-degree angle called for here has been largely borne out among the better animals measured at SEPP evaluations and is taken by most racing enthusiasts to be ideal. Straighter-shouldered dogs can often run just as fast, but they are more injury-prone and tend to break down on the downhill. On the other hand, since canine shoulder blades are not fixed like equine shoulders, angulation can be seen to increase with age and exercise as muscles and tendons stretch and strengthen.

The 15-degree rotation of the lower scapula described here at the insistence of Dr. Lombard is a significant addition to the perception of fronts, as is the insistence on the slightly outward-pointing posture of the toes when the dog is standing. The demand for two inches (or three fingers) between shoulder blades was Seppala's dictum; any less, he said, and the dog loses efficiency.

The description of the back here, especially the reference to "wheelback," is quite apparently different from that of the Official Standard's request for a level topline but in fact is merely a more accurate description of what necessarily follows from the Standard's demand for "tuck-up"—though here, of course, the phrase is "definite tuck-up" rather than "slight tuck-up" (one of the differences perhaps between a long-distance galloper and a long-distance trotter).

Pad color also gets attention in this Standard, this time at the insistence of Dr. Belford who notes a correlation between pad toughness and color, listing lemon as the most preferred. While pads are of the utmost importance to a working dog, there seems to be no strict consensus on this point. Natalie Norris has asked numerous Iditarod drivers about their observations on pad color and performance, and so far none has found much correlation.

The only other major variation is the issue of weight: five pounds less for both dogs and bitches. This is not just a matter of performance necessity, but one of historical accuracy—the very biggest of the early Siberians being Belford's Wolf, weighing in at 55 pounds. On the other hand, whether a 48- or 50-pound bitch loses functionality may be a slightly different issue.

Alaskan Kennels' team with driver Chris Camping winning the freight race at Willow Winter Carnival with seven of the Siberians he raced in the 1975 Iditarod. These dogs exemplify speed, power and endurance and have the length of leg that help them cope with the rigors of the trail.

Alaskan's Speed of Anadyr and Alaskan's Kiev of Anadyr starting for Nome in the 1978 Iditarod in the team of Bob Chlupatch.   *Earl Norris*

The surprising omission from this Standard is any reference to leg length/chest depth proportions. But this is likely merely an oversight since it is pretty much agreed among performance enthusiasts that Curtis Brown is right in claiming a long-distance galloper must have an elbow-to-ground ratio of 1.1 to 1.25 in proportion to the body depth from withers to deepest point of chest. Of course, there have always been those who argue the Siberian is really a long-distance trotter, but it was Seppala himself who gave the advice to Alex Belford, "If you want to win races, you can't let these dogs trot. They're too slow at a trot." And when the first United States breeder of Siberians, Elizabeth Nansen (née Ricker), was asked many years ago to judge, she insisted the dogs be moved at a lope, not a trot. Needless to say, many people were upset, but her point was clear.

Indeed, the nearly square body proportions called for by the Official Standard clearly imply the galloper, but the SEPP Standard is more explicit in saying, "The most efficient gait for the Siberian is the lope and the gallop." Note too, that this Standard calls for bone to be "medium but never heavy" as opposed to the slightly more confusing "substantial but never heavy" phrasing of the Official Standard.

This Standard appears here not to start a revolution, necessarily, but as a document of historical and educational significance. For if our breed has had an edge in the past, it has been largely due to its underlying health, intelligence and overall athleticism, and if we let the breed dissolve into powder puffs and hairdressers' mannequins, then we will have lost the essential resilience of the breed and the noble past it evolved from.

Will we again see the Siberian Husky come to the forefront of racing sled dogs? Probably not in any large way. Courses and conditions have changed. Technology and scientific attitudes have turned many racing dog yards into Frankenstein laboratories where the dogs are considered mere machines to probe, alter and otherwise subject to the excesses of human vanity. But behind the freaks that emerge from such places, and world-class racing dogs are freaks in the way most world-class athletes are freaks of nature, there is always the steady, sturdy Siberian Husky providing lead-dog intelligence, good feet, good metabolism and a good many other virtues his detractors are often loath to admit.

These are the virtues that we as breeders and fanciers can strive to maintain. But it means we must pay strict attention to the tenets of our Standard as applied to the galloping sled dog. It means we must come to truly appreciate the fact that in a working sled dog, less is often more: less bulk, more speed and endurance. And it means we must continue to work these dogs, maintaining that wonderful working attitude and testing the soft tissue—heart, lungs, muscles, tendons and ligaments—which the show ring cannot accurately appraise. In short, we must strive to keep the breed dual-purposed—for the sheer health of it.

By and large, however, despite the divisions within the breed between the racers and the show enthusiasts, the last thirty years have been good to the Siberian. We have seen it evolve from a more or less rare breed to one of immense international status and popularity, and it is still the breed most AKC judges claim as the soundest of all breeds.

So if, over the coming decades, we can but reestablish performance capability as of primary importance, not only on the trail, but as the basis of our understanding of the Standard as applied to dogs in the show ring, then we shall truly have done the breed a valuable service.

A classic "dark faced" Siberian: Kimlan's Erica of Turick, a daughter of Am., Can. Ch. Yeso Pac's Gray Wolf.

Rix's Crackers of Bain's, CD, owned by Sue Bain, is an example of the moderate bone and body proportion that allow a Husky to run fast and far.

The kiss—a classic by any standard. Ch. Monadnock's Pando and Ch. Monadnock's Belka demonstrate the social affability that makes Siberian Huskies such a delight to their owners.

11

Owning a Siberian

SINCE THE AVERAGE DOG REMAINS WITH A
family longer than they own their car, and, in many cases, longer than
they own their house, it is ironic and not a little sad that the consideration
given to selecting a pet is often less than that given to selecting a new pair
of shoes. With the pet population increasing at an alarming rate, and with
it the number of unwanted pets as well as the amount of legislation and
sentiment levied against pets, this trend of casual acquisition imperils the
entire canine population. If the tradition of man-dog relationships is to
continue, then, it can only be hoped that acquiring a family pet will more
and more be approached with the same careful consideration one gives to
bringing a child into the world, for the commitment of time, money and
affection over a ten- to fifteen-year period is not that dissimilar.

Some of the best reasons *not* to acquire a pet are the casual "it might
be nice to have a dog about the place," or "the kids want one," or worst
of all, "it will teach the kids responsibility." In regard to the latter, although
there is nothing more appealing than a child-dog relationship, it is totally
unfair to expect a child to take the full responsibility for caring for an
animal; he will only grow up to resent it as a chore. And by the same
token, there is nothing more perverse than to bring a young puppy into
the house to have his tail pulled and eyes poked under the pretext of
teaching a child responsibility or the value of life or whatever.

The Siberian pup's insatiable desire to run. Quiquern's Commando; at eight months.

Playtime at Synordik Kennels.

234

WHAT THE SIBERIAN IS NOT

Providing one really is committed to acquiring a dog, however, one of the great advantages of purchasing a purebred dog is that one has a pretty good idea what the cuddly eight-week-old puppy will grow up to be, not only in terms of size and general appearance, but in terms of temperament. Each breed has been developed to perform certain functions. But no breed is of the proper size or disposition to suit *every* family's particular needs. Since throughout this text we have devoted ourselves to the positive aspects of the Siberian, it is only fair to note here some of the negative considerations.

First of all, the Siberian has none of the protective instincts or even the inclination to bark found in good watchdogs. He is utterly democratic in his affection and will normally greet the burglar as happily as he would his family. He has an insatiable desire to run, has no "traffic sense" and should be kept in a fenced yard or pen or on a leash at all times. He is very energetic and can be extremely destructive if left in a house alone for periods of time. This is especially true of puppies. Even outside, many love to dig holes. And last but not least, the Siberian has a very thick coat which, although normally odorless and nonallergenic, does come out once or twice a year in enormous quantities.

If, on the other hand, one is willing to put up with these drawbacks in order to own what we in the breed feel is the most affable and beautiful of all breeds, then the following chapter on the selection and care of the Siberian, by Kathleen Kanzler, should prove useful.

Short Seeley and friends.

12

Selection, Care and Maintenance of the Siberian Husky

by Kathleen Kanzler

So YOU WANT A SIBERIAN HUSKY PUPPY! THIS chapter will explain how to make the new family member more joy than trial. All puppies are appealing but the most appealing puppy is not necessarily the best one for you. First you must decide whether you want a family pet, or a dog to show in conformation shows or for Obedience. You may decide that you want a foundation bitch to start your own kennel.

If you are looking for a show or breeding animal, obtain the best available. The Siberian Husky Club of America publishes a breeders' directory that may help you locate the puppy you want. Local veterinarians and persons active in other breeds may be of help in directing you to a reputable breeder. Do not limit your search to your local area. Dogs may be shipped safely and economically from most areas of the country by air. Bargain hunting in the dog world is a mistake; one gets what one pays for, and if a top-quality show dog is required, one should obtain the best regardless of price.

After initial inquiries let you know what is available and the general price range, use common sense in deciding on a breeder to buy from. If you want a show dog the seller should have some credentials that qualify him to recognize a show puppy. How actively do they show dogs? What qualities did the sire and dam of this litter have that made the breeder feel this would be a successful litter?

CHOOSING THE RIGHT PUPPY

A dog is a responsibility that a buyer takes on for the life of the dog. Such a longtime commitment should not be entered into casually.

Siberians should be friendly and relatively tractable in a situation familiar to them. Certainly, excuses should be made for the dog just brought in from a kennel run. After he has had time to express his joy at being a "people" dog again, he should settle down and act civilized. If he runs around constantly crying and being a nuisance and a firm tone of voice does not calm him down, he may be hyperactive and a poor choice. Try and see the parents of a dog you are interested in buying and determine what kind of temperament they have. We will assume they have good dispositions or they would not have been bred. However, if one or both parents is hyperactive—always on the go, difficult to calm down—their offspring may have inherited this tendency. A hyperactive Siberian is very difficult to live with. Its tendency to "self-destruct" can take much of the joy out of living with a Siberian.

A sweet, quiet type female is often much the best choice for a family of young children, especially if the woman involved is a small, rather quiet person. The aggressive, into-everything, knock-it-over-and-eat-it puppy is the natural eye-catcher in a litter and has great appeal. This puppy is better placed with a strong no-nonsense type family that has, ideally, coped with a dog before.

When you are choosing a puppy, either for show or pet, its appearance as well as temperament should appeal to you. However, remember that eye color and coat color are superficial and are not the qualities upon which Siberian Huskies are judged. Be wary of the breeder who sets different prices simply on the basis of eye color or coat color, and when one is choosing a puppy these factors should be the last consideration.

The most reliable way to buy a Siberian is to contact a breeder in whom you have confidence and whose judgment you rely on. There are many variables that go into selecting a puppy, both for pet or show. The breeder knows his puppies and their ancestors and the character traits and physical characteristics that are apt to be produced in his line of dogs.

The uniformity of a litter gives some indication of the range of genetic variables, and the smaller that range, the greater will be the tendency of a given puppy to produce offspring similar to himself. It may be that the litter under consideration is a repeat breeding of the parents. The overall quality of the previous litter may influence your decision. Again, the breeder's selection may be the best choice. The breeder is familiar with the tendencies of his own lines. In selecting a show dog, the pedigree and

A puddle of Synordik puppies—just a few weeks old. Breeder, Dr. Cynthia Nist.

A group of serious eaters at Monadnock.

239

overall consistency of the litter are factors that should weigh as highly or higher than the appearance of a given puppy. Show dogs are breeding stock, and the chances of a single beautiful puppy in an otherwise mediocre litter producing offspring as good as himself are very slim.

Some considerations that may be successful in choosing a Siberian for quality are provided in the following paragraphs.

A puppy whose front feet turn out to the sides at seven weeks probably won't have a proper front as an adult. A puppy with a snap tail probably will always have a bad tail. Tails on Siberians may turn into snap tails as late as four to six months of age. The mouth on a Siberian puppy should show a scissors bite. In some individuals, the alignment of the teeth may change during the growth period, but if the bite was correct as a puppy, it is realistic to hope that the mouth may be proper as an adult. Ear set on a puppy should be high on the head and hopefully not too large.

GROWTH PATTERN OF THE SIBERIAN

This may be the place to attempt to explain the growth pattern of Siberians.

A newborn puppy weighs about one pound. At ten weeks the puppy may weigh fifteen pounds. Keep in mind that this young animal will go through many stages of growth. Depending on the family characteristics of the puppy he may obtain most of his height by about eight months. Very possibly this fast-growing puppy will be awkward, gangly, and may be high in the rear—in fact, may appear to have excess skin that rolls when he moves rapidly. Ears, depending again on family characteristics, may be large in this juvenile stage. Some ears that look hopeless do come around in the adult dog and appear smaller than they once did.

Some of these fast-growing puppies are loose, move sloppily with large feet, heads and ears; their bodies lack depth in the rib and brisket area. Generally it is males that go through the most difficult adolescence.

If you have one of the above types of dog, be realistic in your expectations. This is not the type of animal that should be shown as a puppy. Wait on this dog until he is about two years old before you start showing him. In actuality he may be three before he is mature.

Another common growth pattern is the puppy that grows evenly throughout most of his first year. Hopefully, this puppy has a full coat that covers some of its immaturity. He looks "all of a piece," a miniature Siberian. These pups are great fun as they usually do well at puppy matches and bring favorable comments from friends. This type of puppy may appear small at seven or eight months. Usually they will go into a growth spurt around a year of age. This type of dog will continue to grow slowly through his second year.

Both types of dogs will mature through their third year. Do not be impatient with the development of your young dogs. If a basic soundness and quality is apparent, time should produce a good Siberian. A male usually is not mature enough to pick up the points before he is two years old. A female often is ready by eighteen months.

THE RIGHT START

When you finally purchase this well-considered puppy some type of guarantee of good health should accompany the bill of sale. Once you have brought the puppy home, it is important to have him examined by a good veterinarian. His advice, along with a complete book on dog care, will prove invaluable throughout the dog's life.

If the puppy is to be a house pet, never to be shown or bred, it is highly advisable to have it either spayed or neutered. Many problems are alleviated by this simple surgery which has virtually no effect on the dog's personality. A basic obedience course is extremely helpful if the puppy is to become a well-adjusted member of the family.

Puppies love to chew; great care should be taken in removing all items from reach that might be harmful. Bones, contrary to popular opinion, are dangerous for dogs as they may break and cause damage to the stomach lining and intestines. The most suitable toys are rawhide chew toys that are digested when eaten. Rubber balls and squeak toys, if used at all, should only be brought out for supervised play.

HOUSING YOUR SIBERIAN

Ideal housing for your Siberian would involve the purchase of a portable chain link dog run. This pen, approximately six feet wide by twelve feet long by six feet high is adequate, set on concrete or concrete patio blocks, and will provide a safe, comfortable home for your active Siberian throughout his lifetime. The initial investment is offset by protection of your property from your own furry "jaws." A chewed sofa or shoes will soon add up to the price of a pen. The other rationale is the safety of this lovable Indian that knows no fear of cars.

Often people say that my dog is to be a "house dog"! A house dog needs a secure place to stay when the family members are shopping or away for the day. A pen convenient to an outside door keeps the rest of a nice backyard nice. The addition of a doghouse and a bucket of water provides a complete housing facility for the dog while giving the owner maximum mobility.

The other useful purchase for the puppy is a collapsible wire dog crate. The puppy may be fed in his crate to get him used to being in it. It is a very useful tool in housebreaking your puppy. Putting the puppy in his crate at bedtime in your bedroom will keep him from being lonesome and howling. If you are a light sleeper he will let you know when he has to go out to relieve himself. He will fuss before he dirties his cage. His instinct is not to mess where he sleeps.

The cage may be used in the car for short or long trips. The dog is safe in the car and the windows may be left open without fear of the dog escaping. Traveling to "non-doggy" friends' or relatives' homes is possible if the dog is kept in his crate, except for exercising during the visit. Babies are prepared for by the purchase of a crib and playpen. Puppies are live, lively young beings that need some facilities for their confinement.

FEEDING YOUR SIBERIAN

Modern commercial dog foods are generally well-researched and well-balanced diets. Siberians in particular utilize a low-bulk dog food more effectively than some of the high-bulk popular diets manufactured for some of the less energetic breeds. A dry, bite-sized, highly palatable feed made mostly of chicken has seemed to work very well for Siberians of all ages. However, never feed raw chicken.

One of the continuing problems in raising Siberian puppies has been loose stools. Assuming that any parasite problems are being controlled, many puppies continue to have loose, unformed stools during their early rapid growth period. This syndrome often makes housebreaking chaotic and produces near desperation in new owners. If the puppy is gaining weight steadily and has a healthy coat and lively attitude, it is probably just a feeding problem.

Whole milk and most table scraps are not recommended for growing puppies. These additions often upset the delicate balance of the puppy's digestion. A complete dry type dog food, preferably the chicken-based feed, is usually the answer in reaching a balance between large food needs in the fast-growing puppy and his digestive capabilities. The addition of vitamins or minerals is seldom necessary in a healthy, parasite-free animal. However, if a puppy is anemic, he should be fed an iron supplement.

Several methods of feeding are acceptable. A few well-organized people may find that feeding three to four measured meals a day suits them. Many people find that self-feeding or the dry ration works well for them. Free access to food works well for many Siberian puppies' digestion. Small amounts of food often keep a Siberian's digestion working efficiently. Some puppies need to be taken off self-feeding at four to six months because they overeat. If your puppy becomes too fat, change to measured meals two or three times a day depending on age.

Often a feeding problem develops when the puppy has gone through his most rapid growth period. He becomes a finicky eater. Often he appears thin and if he is lacking in coat he looks starved. Trips to the veterinarian determine that parasites are not a problem and the dog appears healthy but thin. This is a common syndrome of adolescent Siberians. There is no "cure."

Some things to try: mix dry feed with a small amount of canned meat or table scraps and water. If feeding once a day, try two feedings a day. Determine if more exercise might improve the appetite. Be aware that some dogs will become tyrannical. They know you are anxious about their eating habits and pick at their food knowing you will open more cans and keep tempting their palates with more goodies. Some success is achieved by putting down the dog's food twice a day for ten or fifteen minutes and then picking up any uneaten food and offering nothing between meals. This method may take several days or a week of willpower on the owner's part. It is a power struggle, the "Morris the Cat" syndrome.

The mature Siberian (between two and three years of age) is normally a very easy keeper and will carry the proper weight on one feeding a day. A low-bulk, high-protein diet is preferred even for the older dog.

GROOMING YOUR SIBERIAN

One of the joys of showing a Siberian is the easy transition he can make from the team or the house to the show ring. No elaborate grooming is usually necessary. Sometimes it is difficult to discover just what to do with him to make the most of his natural beauty.

A Siberian in new, tight coat usually can take a warm bath in a mild detergent or Castile shampoo. Rinse until he squeaks. After towel drying, if practical, lay or stand him on a table and brush dry using an electric hair dryer. Aim the dryer at the area that you are brushing with a pin or slicker brush. The object is not to remove hair but to dry him quickly and to end up with a coat that looks its best. If it is fashionable in your area to trim whiskers, do this with a good-quality scissors the day of, or before, the show. Trim as closely as possible for a clean-looking profile.

Grooming a Siberian that is blowing his coat or approaching a shedding period is more of a problem. A moment of silent prayer is recommended. An allover bath is not advisable. Washing the dog's legs, chest, face and tail with Castile soap and cool water usually won't accelerate shedding. Again, the dog must be rinsed properly to turn out white. Several products that are mixed with water in a pan and sponged into the white areas or the entire coat if necessary are useful for the lightly soiled or shedding Siberians. The foam from the solution is used and the soil is rubbed out by toweling the area.

Siberians shedding in their unique patchlike way look better if the worst areas are brushed out with a slicker brush, metal comb and rake.

"My, what big teeth you have."

Curious by nature.

The absence of hair on the hips and sides detracts less from the dog than the bumps and hollows that result from leaving the hair in place.

If the neck, tail and britches are fairly tight, the appearance is usually enhanced by combing out the worst of the body hair. Wash nonshedding areas that need it. Brush lightly to fluff up the coat. Spray sparingly with water or a coat dressing and towel body coat gently to remove dust and make the coat shine. If the dog is still looking patchy, pick tufts out with the fingers or the end of a comb to give the dog a tidy outline.

Stand back and examine the dog. If the middle of his back has shed, rake the shoulder area and over the hips to blend the coat areas and maintain a level topline. A dog with a shed-out midback with hair left in shoulder and rear areas appears weak in topline.

Proper grooming of a full-coated Siberian will do much to enhance the overall appearance of the dog. A rake, a wooden grooming tool with two rows of naillike teeth, is a most valuable grooming aid for the Siberian.

Raking through a new coat three times a week from the top of the head through the body and chest areas and two inches down the tail keeps the coat healthy and open. Many dogs can be kept in show coat indefinitely with this method of grooming. Dead hair is removed constantly, allowing the skin to stay clean. The undercoat replaces itself continually without "packing up" and giving the dog the signal to shed. Many dogs' coats are such that with this constant grooming they rarely go into a full shed. With this type of dog, on this type of grooming program, the dog may be shampooed before every show weekend.

A problem-coated dog with dry, harsh hair that will not shed properly, that appears rough and dry, should have hair-conditioning treatments. Rake through the coat. Wash and rinse the dog thoroughly. Towel dry and apply oil conditioner to the coat generously. Apply hot, wet towels for twenty minutes, rinse and dry. Repeat once or twice a week, raking the coat daily until the coat is improved. Use conditioner after all regular preshow baths. This is especially useful on red Siberians. Keep red dogs in covered runs out of the sun to prevent sun bleaching and coat damage.

If your Siberian's toenails are too long, cut back to, but not into, the pink quick. To eliminate the problem of a bleeding nail on show day, trim nails at least a day ahead of the show.

The question of chalking the white areas is a matter of opinion. Usually if there is time and the facilities prior to the show to wash the white areas, the results will be more satisfactory. If washing is not practical, chalk with caution. Whitening, even when used for cleaning, that remains in the dog's coat and is apparent to the judge can cause the dog to be disqualified. So brush and lightly "pound" the chalked areas until no chalk "flies."

When preparing the Siberian for showing, an image of a clean, glowing coat with a trim outline is to be maintained. A show Siberian in new coat is simply a clean, brushed dog. A Siberian shedding or preparing to shed should be groomed cautiously. Clean him as well as possible and remove hair necessary to maintain a proper outline.

BREEDING THE SIBERIAN

Much of the preceeding discussion on buying a puppy has been based upon the dubious assumption that a person knows from the outset if he is interested in a single house pet, a show dog or breeding stock. This, of course, is seldom the case. Much more common is the person who, after having a pet Siberian for a period of time, decides he is sufficiently interested in the breed to start exhibiting and breeding. And such a decision usually raises the question of whether or not to breed the dog already in one's possession or to go out and buy another.

Because Siberian breeders seem to be, by and large, somewhat less stuffy in placing their top-quality puppies than many owners of other breeds, it is very possible that, if one has purchased his dog from a top-quality kennel, the dog may be of the caliber to breed. On the other hand, one of the most difficult adjustments to make in becoming a breeder is to divorce one's sentimental attachment for a given animal from one's overall interest in the betterment of the breed. But this kind of objectivity is especially crucial in a breed that, like the Siberian Husky, has mushroomed so rapidly in popularity, for unless great care is taken in breeding only the best-available specimens, there is the ever-present danger that the breed as a whole will degenerate. But not only does one do a disservice to the breed in breeding a mediocre specimen, in the long run one does a disservice to oneself, for the money spent in trying to upgrade one's stock, if it is founded upon a mediocre specimen, will be far greater than the money that is necessary to invest in obtaining a top-quality specimen to begin with; and even after years of frustration and careful breeding, the results are not likely to be as good as could have been attained in the first generation if one were using only first-rate specimens.

So if one is considering breeding a dog, it is important to ascertain if he is of high enough quality, and the decision should be based not only upon one's own appraisal after a careful reading of the Standard and attending a number of shows, but upon the opinion of a number of qualified breeders.

Lastly, of course, one should consider whether one has the time, money, and facilities to have a litter of puppies. The time spent whelping and rearing puppies is extensive; the return on the litter will generally be far less than the amount spent; and one should have facilities to adequately accommodate five or six dogs until they are six months or so of age as buyers may be scarce.

And for all of the above reasons, under no circumstances should one consider breeding a dog for such vague reasons as "it might be interesting to have a litter," or "it would be educational for the children," or "we might make some money." Among good breeders, there is no such thing as a "casual" breeder. There are breeders who breed more frequently or less, who maintain larger or smaller numbers of dogs, but each breeding is approached with seriousness, a definite sense of the purpose of a specific breeding, and a knowledge that the frustrations will always outnumber the successes.

Once armed with the proper motivation and the bitch of quality, one must take some practical considerations when breeding dogs.

The bitch should be X-rayed and certified free of hip dysplasia. Also her eyes should be checked by a canine opthamologist and certified free of hereditary eye diseases. The stud should be selected and his owner should have had the dog's hips and eyes checked. The stud's owner should be informed when the bitch is due in season. When the bitch comes in season the stud's owner should be informed immediately. Shipping or arrival details should be arranged for the bitch to arrive, usually by the tenth day. The bitch should have been checked for parasites and wormed if necessary. Generally breedings will take place between the eleventh and fourteenth days. Two breedings are usual. One breeding may be agreed upon in the case of the older or extremely popular stud dog. The stud fee is due when the bitch is bred and ready to be returned to the owner. Delayed payment or a stud puppy (usually the choice puppy of the litter) should be agreed upon in preliminary discussions. This agreement should be in writing and signed by both parties.

The stud owner's responsibility includes safe, maximum-security housing for the bitch in his care. When a male is put up as a public stud, his owner should have educated himself in the mechanics of training and managing a stud dog. All stud services should be supervised for the safety of the dog and bitch. The bitch's owner should have confidence that his bitch will be bred. This is not accomplished in a well-ordered manner by putting the two dogs together and letting "nature take its course." Each breed has its breeding peculiarities. Siberian females may be willing partners until the male breeds and ties her. Often she will decide this is not at all what she wants. Screaming is the usual reaction. Often she will struggle, attempt to bite, throw herself on the ground and turn into a whirling dervish. This is where the stud owner needs to be aware and prepared. Two people are needed, one to hold the bitch and support her and the other to work with the stud. The bitch, if she is an unknown quantity, should be muzzled. A humane muzzle is a wire basket that fits over the muzzle. This does not cut the bitch's air supply, as a bandage type may.

It is of paramount importance to keep any breeding under control. The bitch must be held steady and on her feet. The stud is the partner most likely to be injured in a breeding. Do not let him fall or roll over.

The bitch should be watched for the rest of her season as she may be bred to another dog before she goes out of season.

WHELPING

Upon her return home it is wise to have the bitch checked for parasites about three weeks into whelp. She may maintain her usual level of exercise, generally, as long as she wishes. She will tend to slow herself down at about six weeks into whelp. Her food should be increased from four weeks in whelp.

The matter of proper housing for the bitch and puppies should be dealt with early. It is unrealistic to approach a Siberian litter without a good secure pen. A portable dog pen with a whelping box or dog house is ideal. If the puppies are to be born in the house, set up an exercise pen or some other arrangement that will confine the bitch to the spot you have chosen for her. She should be put in her whelping area at least a week before her due date as she needs this time to become acclimated and she may deliver her puppies from the fifty-eighth to the sixty-third day, or even a few days later.

The bitch probably will not settle down the morning of the sixty-third day and deliver her puppies by evening. She may be anxious, restless, whining on and off for several days. This is not labor. She is not in trouble. Bitches ordinarily do not eat the day they whelp. True labor usually sees the bitch digging her newspapers, panting heavily and having contractions. When real pushing contractions begin, a puppy should be delivered in about fifteen minutes. If the bitch is really pushing and trying to expel a puppy, do not let her go more than one hour before getting veterinary assistance. After an examination the veterinarian may be able to determine that the puppy is correctly placed in the birth canal and a pituitary shot that produces stronger contractions may deliver the puppy.

Siberian bitches as a breed are good, natural whelpers. Many of the problems that people get into at whelping time are brought on by their own anxieties. If the bitch does not have a dark, smelly discharge and is not obviously ill with an elevated temperature, she is probably all right. Some bitches make quite a production of getting down to business. One thing that helps is if the owners treat her matter-of-factly, observing her but not talking baby talk and overly sympathizing with her condition. It is fact that some very spoiled house pets simply will not start into labor. As soon as they are uncomfortable they cry and quit. Be prepared for a couple of days of prelabor. This activity gets everyone into a fever pitch and one must resist the impulse to take her to the veterinarian and tell him to do something.

Siberians are as prone to whelping after the sixty-third day as they

248

are before that time. It is not the moment for panic if the due date arrives and she is showing no signs of labor. Larger litters may come earlier. Small litters may be very comfortable where they are and if the bitch is showing no signs of discomfort, be patient. Most textbooks say the sixty-sixth day is a cutoff date for waiting. Certainly have her checked by the veterinarian, and if he sees no problem, you may decide to wait a couple more days. Many caesarian sections can be avoided if the breeder has patience.

Note that if a section is done, the puppies must be with the mother when she wakes up. Owners tend to feel so sorry for the bitch that the pups are kept away and introduced to her when she is fully awake. Since she did not go through the birth process she may not have the natural maternal instincts she would have had if she had delivered normally. It is preferable to put the pups on to nurse while she is still groggy although supervision is a must in case the bitch should try to bite one of the puppies. But this way any initial discomfort is out of the way before she is fully conscious.

A temperature check is a useful tool for determining approximate whelping time. A temperature check several times a day when you think she is close to whelping may give you an indication of progress. A dog's normal temperature is 101 degrees. This usually drops a degree or more as whelping time approaches. This check may be useful if you must be away for the day and are uncertain whether she should be left alone. In this chapter we are talking about Siberians in particular of course, but the basis of the chapter is simply good animal management.

Supervised whelping is a necessary part of dog breeding. The bitch may not attend to her first puppy, particularly in a first litter, with the needed speed. She may nose it and seem confused about her role. This is the time to get involved. Remove the membrane from the face of the puppy with speed. Your fingernails will do. Wipe his face and the inside of his mouth. Remove the rest of the membrane from the puppy. Often the afterbirth is still inside the bitch so the cord is holding the puppy closely to the mother. Gently pull the cord until one or two inches are outside the bitch and cut the cord, leaving at least one inch or one and one-half inches attached to the puppy. Time is critical when you are delivering a puppy. Pick it up with its head down to let any fluids drain from the mouth and lungs. Rub vigorously with a towel, wiping out its mouth often. The puppy should be crying and squirming. Do not be afraid to handle it. You probably will not be too rough. Pats and soft rubbing are out of order when you are trying to get a puppy introduced to life. If the puppy's nose is blue and he is not breathing properly, give artificial respiration or mouth-to-mouth. The pup may have fluid in his lungs. Rough him up, stick your finger down his throat, any action that will force him to rid himself of excess fluid and begin breathing. When the puppy is separated from the umbilical cord he must begin breathing on his own.

During a normal whelping the puppies may follow each other by fifteen minutes to one hour. An interval of two hours is not cause for alarm if the bitch seems free of distress. In large litters a bitch may settle down with several puppies, cleaning and nursing them, and rest for as long as three to four hours before she gets on with the business of producing the rest of the litter.

Some bitches have their entire litter in two hours; some take all day. As each puppy is born, wait and see if the bitch is willing to take care of the puppy herself. If it is crying and moving and she seems to have the situation under control, observe, do not interfere. If the bitch thrashes around the pen a great deal as she prepares to deliver another puppy, remove the first pups, dry them off and place them in a box with a towel and a heating pad set on low.

Many bitches will be happy with one puppy with them and allow you to keep the rest warm and dry until all the puppies are delivered. Keep dry newspapers in the whelping box so the puppies do not become chilled. Puppies at this time need to be kept at a temperature of ninety degrees, so it is important not to let them stay wet and cold.

As the bitch's stomach flattens, try and guess how many more puppies are to come. The bitch that is finished whelping will tend to look for a comfortable place to settle and encourage however many puppies she has with her to nurse. She then tends to lick and clean them. This is a sign that she may indeed be finished. Take her outside to exercise on a leash. She may be reluctant to leave her new family. The reason for exercising her on a leash is that she may very well have another puppy while she is outside.

Take this opportunity to clean her whelping area and put a thick layer of clean newspaper down in her pen. When the bitch is installed in her clean quarters with her litter of puppies, offer her water and food. Within twelve hours, it is a good idea to take her to the veterinarian for a checkup. He may want to give her a pituitary shot to clean out any retained afterbirths and to stimulate milk production.

13

Breeding as an Art

DEVELOPING AN EYE

In his book *The Art of Breeding Better Dogs*, Kyle Onstott claims that breeding is an art, not a science. By which I think he means not only is the manipulation of seventy-eight chromosomes too vast and unpredictable an undertaking to manage on a purely scientific basis, but even more important, breeding is first and foremost about "seeing."

A Siberian breeder is an artist who creates living artworks according to his or her observations of two dogs (and their pedigrees) and their relative relationship to an idealized animal running around somewhere inside his or her head. So the first job of would-be breeders is to train their eyes to find their ideal, an ideal that should be based on historical, functional and aesthetic perspectives.

HISTORICAL VIEWPOINT

As we've tried to stress throughout this book, the breed we know as the Siberian Husky came to this continent as an extremely sweet-tempered, foxy-looking (if somewhat varied), not very large working dog who could simply outrun anything on four legs that would pull a sled for long miles in arctic conditions.

Ch. Highpoint Veleah Quiksilver, owned by Vel Leahy, won the SHCA Brood Bitch of the Year award. The dam of a BIS winner, "Silver" exemplifies the tremendous importance of quality bitches to any breeding program. *Fleshman*

Ch. Toko's Twenty-Four Karat Gold, CD, bred by Jean Fournier and co-owned with her by Jackee Fournier. A descendant of Ch. Marlytuk's Red Sun of Kiska out of Ch. Fournier's Tiffany of Toko, this dog inherited the family trait for longevity and lived to the wonderful age of seventeen.

Ch. Demavand's Shiva, displaying the characteristic expression—keen yet friendly, interested, and even mischievous—the hallmark of the Husky. Note, too, the relatively high earset (though not quite at full attention here) and how thick and well-furred the leathers are. *Silja Mikkelsen*

FUNCTIONAL VIEWPOINT

In order to do this, we know—both from pictorial evidence, observer testimony and what contemporary research on the working dog has shown to be necessarily true—that he had to have good feet, longer leg than depth of chest, a long upper arm, good tuck-up, a double coat, a body only slightly longer than tall, intelligence and heart (something which the great dog driver "Doc" Lombard says is spelled GUTS).

AESTHETIC VIEWPOINT

If dog shows are not merely fashion shows, where the overall look of a breed is allowed to change according to the whim of the day, then aesthetic ideals must be based historically and functionally. The early Siberians were certainly a varied lot, and perhaps their paint jobs (markings) were not so fancy as those of contemporary show dogs, but they mostly exhibited an obvious spitz heritage, and from them were gleaned the principles of type that we, as breeders, try to maintain and make more consistent. The head of the import Kreevanka, for instance, is as ideal today as the day he set foot on this continent in 1929. His moderate frame and fairly short back are also worthy of notice. Bitch head type might be said to exist on a range between Ch. Kenai Kittee of Beauchien, CDX, on the more refined end of the spectrum, and Ch. Belka of Monadnock, representing the more substantial end. (Both pictured elsewhere.)

There is always going to be a range of what is acceptable, in terms of the Standard, and a narrower range of what is excellent, but unless a breeder can appraise a Siberian from these various viewpoints, only dumb luck will let him or her produce a truly good one.

BE WILLING TO LEARN, SLOWLY

Of course, every Siberian is a little different, none is perfect, and even more problematical, every judge and every breeder sees every dog just a little differently. So learning to see requires a great deal of looking and listening. It takes years, and usually involves numerous revisions and corrections of one's original impressions and ideals. It should also involve learning from a number of different mentors—show breeders, racers, judges, authors, and even sometimes people far outside the Siberian fold—sight-hound people, for instance, or field trial enthusiasts.

It is important, therefore, not to be too hasty. A sad fact of the dog game is that most fanciers participate only about five years—because they make mistakes, or have bad luck and get discouraged. And the most frequent mistake is simply acquiring too many animals too quickly, overbur-

Ch. Bobkat's R.U. Aunt Nora Too, owned by Bob and Katie Gardner, exhibiting just about ideal Siberian movement. Note the extended head carriage as the dog moves.

dening their resources of time, money and space, as well as making future developments too dependent on selecting animals before developing a truly educated, judicious "eye."

In short, if every would-be breeder spent several years acquiring both a hands-on "feel" and more abstract knowledge of its history, function and aesthetic ideals, we'd have many fewer mediocre specimens of the Siberian and many fewer frustrated people.

AIM FOR GOOD DOGS, NOT JUST WINNERS

The goal of every wise breeder is to produce a consistent level of good, sound, happy, healthy, typey puppies, most of whom will be sold as pets. Temperament, then, must remain at all times a primary issue, along with type and basic athleticism. Compromising temperament is the most dangerous thing a breeder can do because it produces unwanted animals, perhaps hurting the breeder's reputation and certainly hurting the breed's.

This is not to say, however, that all Siberian puppies should exhibit a gundog unflappability in the face of every strange and/or noisy circumstance. A certain skittishness is quite common among younger animals at various stages of development, particularly among bitches in adolescence. Usually they outgrow it, but if you wish, for example, to show a given puppy, it should be socialized with a certain caution in the full recognition of what weird places dog shows really are from a dog's point of view: hundreds of dog noises and smells, loudspeakers and, particularly indoors, a noise level that can only be described as an unholy din amid lurid, noxious clouds of chalk dust and hairspray, swirled this way and that by dragon-necked, roaring hair dryers.

So the wise breeder does not aim for the quickest way into the ribbons if it means compromising on temperament, type or health. He or she knows that so-called great dogs simply happen (one in four hundred says Earl Norris), and sometimes they happen after years of hard work, and sometimes they happen out of dumb luck.

But a top winning animal that comes from a long line of happy, healthy, typey, athletic animals is much more likely to be of service to the breed than the big winner whose mother lacked type, whose father was epileptic, and whose grandmother cowered under her dog house for most of her life. The former may be truly a great dog, the latter simply a big winner who is liable to do more harm than good to the breed.

On these two pages there appear six generations of the author's Demavand Siberians. It is interesting to note the gradual, if not entirely constant, increase in length of leg and angulation while type and balance are both maintained. The dogs on this page are Ch. Goldspur's Ahzrahk Bannu (top), Ch. Demavand's Ahtesh (center), and Ch. Demavand's Czar of Adaconda (bottom).

Continuing this Demavand photo genealogy is Laika's Kira of Cedarwood (top) with what is probably the best front assembly of the dogs shown here, Demavand's Akela (center) and Ch. Demavand's Liyaza Cassandra (bottom).

SELECTING STOCK

Once you've started developing an ideal, an eye, select breeding stock on the basis of their approximation to this ideal. Get lots of advice, sift it, and adopt what makes sense. It usually pays, for instance, to bring along two family strains simultaneously, along with some sort of outcross potential. Study pedigrees but don't become obsessed with them. Too many inferior animals are bred by people in love with what the pedigree looks like, and not enough on what the actual animals look like. Know what lines tend to produce what characteristics (both good and bad) on a fairly regular basis. Realize every individual varies enough that the issue on any given breeding should be the actual dogs themselves, their phenotypes, and only secondarily their pedigrees. As much as possible, breed like to like in terms of the strengths of the pair, and unlike to unlike in terms of faults. That is to say, double up on strengths, and don't double up on weaknesses.

TYPES OF BREEDING

Generally speaking, there are three kinds of breeding: linebreeding (though purists in the field of genetics dislike the term), inbreeding and outcrossing.

So-called linebreeding—that is, dogs that are loosely related within three or four generations—has long been the staple of consistent, fairly safe breeding practices in both contemporary and primitive cultures. Inbreeding—the breeding of cousins and closer relatives—can yield dramatic, sometimes lovely, sometimes disastrous results, and should only be undertaken with great caution and probably some years of experience. Outcrossing, the breeding of unrelated animals, is only partially possible in a breed as generally related as the Siberian, but should be used as a way to keep from painting yourself into a corner—to bring in new and (it is to be hoped) desirable characteristics and to shake up the gene pool from time to time. It's less predictable than either linebreeding or inbreeding, but an integral part of any long-range breeding program. It should be understood that, in fact, we are always reinventing the breed with each generation, and that genetic variety is important for maintaining both vigor and type.

ASSESSING AND APPRAISING, AN ONGOING PRACTICE

Once you've acquired a promising animal or two, start assessing them and your early breeding results. Some lines may work for you better than others, but remember—just as there are no perfect specimens, there are no perfect lines. Every breeding is a gambling game played with seventy-eight chromosomes and is, therefore, something of a crapshoot. So don't blame everything on the original breeder when things go wrong. If it were easy, we'd all have perfect dogs and there'd be no reasons for dog shows, dog races, etc.

Study the growth patterns in your puppies and the ongoing development in your adults. Different lines develop at very different rates, and understanding the differences will affect your selection of "keepers." Many breeders assess overall balance sometime in the first few days of the puppies' lives, before they've got much body fat obscuring the outline of the skeleton. Type manifests itself in puppies at four or five weeks when the ears come up (if they come up at that age) and are still relatively small. But movement is still very clumsy and cannot be assessed much until seven or eight weeks. Sometime between six and nine weeks puppies theoretically pass through phases of miniature adulthood before getting down to the serious job of growing.

As they grow, many go through awkward stages in which they look narrow in head or small in head, narrow in front or high in the rear, long tailed or just plain gawky. Some look gawky by ten or eleven weeks and don't look good again until they're two or three years old. Most have periodic foreshadowings of promising adulthood—often six to nine months is particularly appealing. But even those puppies who seem always to grow in proportion to themselves often go through a gawky adolescence as the beautiful puppy seems to vanish with the first shed of coat, leaving something behind that's suddenly unrecognizable—scrawny, hairless, big eared and narrow headed. Most, however, do make the return from the land of the uglies.

In looking at puppies, don't fall in love with the biggest male in every litter, or the blackest coat, or the blue-eyed ones. Look deeper. Look for balance, agility, type and temperament. Think first in terms of the whelping box, second in terms of the show ring.

Select animals on the basis of their positive characteristics, not just the absence of obvious faults. The slightly narrow-in-the-rear animal with the great front may be more valuable to you than the better-in-the-rear but not-so-good-in-front, flashier animal. Peggy Koehler of Alakazan Kennels once remarked that the art of picking puppies involved the ability to pick the *best puppy in a litter, not the best puppy in the world.* Moreover, different sorts of puppies may be valuable to you at different points in a breeding program—depending on which battles have been won and lost.

Don't fall into the "teddy bear" or "big bear" syndromes of either selecting only the cute, stubby animals or the big-chested, heavy-boned monsters. Look for the moderate, the athletic and where possible, the slow-maturing. Broad heads usually prefigure broad chests; long heads long backs and loss of type; short necks often mean steep shoulders; while loose skin usually indicates loose tendons and muscles. As important as

259

Consistency of type is one of the most important ways a breeder has of testing the effectiveness of a breeding program. Here, four generations of Tawny Hill champions demonstrate they have much in common! They are (from left), Ch. Tawny Hill Tanja of Monadnock, Molina, Gamyn and Melaphyre. All are owned by Adele M. Gray.   *John Ashbey*

Another way to gauge consistency of a breeding program is through brace and team classes at dog shows. Although offered infrequently, brace (two matched dogs) and team (four matched dogs) competitions show how well the breeder is developing a uniform strain. Shown here is Sue Bain's superb team including Chs. Bain's Northern Ryan, Rebel, Boika's Kyo and Bain's Northern Robler.

the proper length and angle of each bone in the skeleton is, it is not nearly so crucial to the health and performance of an animal as the soft tissue—heart, lungs, muscles, tendons, ligaments.

It's generally best to avoid breeding extremes, a very large dog to a very small bitch, for instance, because often the resulting litter will simply split into big ones and little ones, rather than providing a blend.

In most litters you can generally identify at least one puppy that resembles each parent, and often individuals that resemble each grandparent; so grandparents are extremely important in the consideration of any breeding. Furthermore, if the imagined blend of two animals does not actually turn up in a given breeding, be patient; it may well turn up in the next generation.

RATING YOUR DOGS

Once you've got a few dogs and an ideal in mind, it's a great help to establish some sort of rating system—a scale of 1 to 10, for instance, with 10 being perfect (and therefore impossible), with the minimum for a championship-caliber animal being perhaps a 6. Each factor you'd like to change in your animal gets a unit of 1 subtracted from the ideal 10. (Some factors, of course, might get more heavily weighted, as in the case of temperament problems or entirely faulty portions of the assembly, or bad coat or poor type.) Animals critically appraised at, say, 7s and 8s are really very good dogs and, if bred judiciously, with few common fault-tendencies (both phenotypically and genotypically) and many common strengths and similarities, the resulting puppies have a truly good shot at excellence.

An even more thorough rating system can be established by instituting the 1 to 10 scale in several categories: type, temperament, athleticism and overall balance and movement. In such a system, of course, 10s *are* possible, and ratings where the sum totals of parents are 16 or better in each category are certainly breedings worth trying—unless their pedigrees indicate a doubling up on potential health problems.

Thus, a dog rated a 7 for type (a bit short coated and plain in head), a 10 for temperament, an 8 for athleticism (quick and well muscled but a little steep in shoulder), and a 6 for overall balance and movement (a little short on extension) might be an excellent matchup for a bitch rated a 9 for type (ears well-set but a bit tall, wonderful head and coat), a 7 for temperament (friendly, workable but a little wary of strange circumstances), and a 9 for balance and movement.

The method is really not that important. The point is to keep the quality of your animals high in as many categories as possible, and your litters as consistent as possible, while avoiding all the hidden health problems that inevitably plague any breed, especially one as popular and numerous as ours.

Am., Can., Japanese Ch. Blueridge Soma's Judy Garland, bred, owned and handled by Bart and Patti Miller, has won six BIS awards and was Canada's top bitch in 1988. *MikRon*

Ch. Saroja's September Scheravari (Ch. Demavand's Sa Shunka of Sno Den ex Ch. Saroja's Scheherezade, owned by Sandra James. *Cott/Daigle*

Ch. Alchemy's The Iceburg Cometh, owned by Sarah Meizlik, shows a beautiful front assembly, overall body proportions and moderation throughout. She was Winners Bitch and the recipient of the Short Seeley Memorial Trophy at the 1988 SHCA Specialty. *Janet Seltzer*

Wise breeders breed for themselves, not for what judges want (though it's nice to have what a judge is looking for), and certainly not simply for what most of the buying public wants (big, hairy, black and white, blue-eyed ones—no one seems to know quite why). In the show ring there are inevitably swings of the pendulum of fashion and focus—large to small, red to gray, one marking pattern to another, one handler to another, and so on. And in the pet world at large, there's simply the ignorant desire for size and bulk as a first aesthetic principle. Anyone who's ever walked a Siberian through populated places, for instance, knows that there are incredible numbers of people who have a brother or friend or cousin who has "one of those huskies who's *this* tall," his outstretched hand floating somewhere between waist and chest, his eyes growing larger as he describes this veritable mountain of canine splendor.

Last, but certainly not least, wise breeders progress only at the rate their resources of time, money and energy allow. They know the most valuable kennel in their yard is the empty one that can house the next promising puppy. They know that over time the small kennel can contribute as much to the breed as the large kennel, that in fact the well-managed small kennel is more efficient than its larger counterpart, and a lot more fun. And they always remember that their particular art form lives, breathes, and is meant to have fun with, that every dog in their yard deserves their love, respect and attention.

For a breed that has always been able to relate to people, therapy work comes easily for a Siberian Husky. Shown here is Mary and Bob Gadbois's Tiffany, one of three Siberians—registered therapy dogs—they own. Tiffany shares a quiet moment with Annetta Marlowe during a regular nursing home visit where she, Sabrina and Clover dispense their own brand of Siberian love.

Ch. Kodiikuska de Sforza, CDX, and owner Antonio Zarlenga. "Kodii" saved his master's life by rousing him to the danger of escaping gas.

264

14

Heroes, Mascots and Something Called Character

IT IS TRADITIONAL IN BREED BOOKS AT ONE point to recount some of the unusual or heroic acts performed by dogs of the breed. But since for countless centuries, the Siberian has played such an integral part in the human struggle for survival, it seems almost pointless to single out individual acts of canine heroism.

Nevertheless, the incredible rise in popularity of the Siberian over recent decades has been largely attributable to his ability to adapt to the role of house pet—a role that requires somewhat different behavior patterns from those of the sled dog, yet which, from time to time, elicits responses that can be as heroic, in their own way, as those of a working sled dog.

Such was the case when Kodiikuska de Sforza, CDX, smelled gas escaping in his owner's house on a fall night in 1966 and managed to rouse his master, Tony Zarlenga, and, by continual yipping and prodding, was able to get the almost unconscious man out of the house in time to save his life. Such was also the case with Czar of Monadnock who, seeing his owner, Charles Rizzo, held at gunpoint by an intruder, leaped at the man's throat and was shot. Although the bullet was lodged too close to the spinal column to risk removal, Czar survived and was nominated for an ASPCA award.

Perhaps less spectacular, but certainly no less noteworthy, have been the number of Siberians trained as Seeing Eye dogs. Among these is a bitch named Mischa living in the Midwest who, like clockwork, awakens her mistress at 6 A.M. every morning and accompanies her to the factory where she works. There she lies patiently until quitting time and the journey home. Her only failing, it is reported, is that, like many humans, it takes her three days to adjust to the time change when daylight saving begins in April and ends in October.

Like many breeds, in its rise to popularity the Siberian has enjoyed a certain vogue with celebrities. President Herbert Hoover was the proud owner of one of the earliest Siberian Huskies, a dog named Yukon bred by Julian Hurley in Alaska in 1929.* A decade later, Petya of Monadnock, owned by correspondent Bertram Hulen and his wife (longtime Siberian Husky Club *Newsletter* editor), enjoyed great popularity in Washington, DC, and was even the subject of an on-the-street interview by a young newspaperwoman named Jacqueline Bouvier. Carole Lombard also owned a Siberian, as did Clara Bow—who spent her last reclusive years with the dog as her constant companion.

And from the time that the schoolchildren of New York City contributed their pennies for the statue of Balto erected in Central Park after the famed Serum Run, the Siberian has enjoyed a special popularity with the young. Pando, of course, was the longtime mascot of the Monadnock Regional High School whose yearbook is still called the *Pandorian*. Nalegaksoa II of Peary, call-name King, bred by Yeso Pac Kennels, served for many years as the mascot of the Robert E. Peary High School in Rockville, Maryland, and not only attended athletic events but was even handled in the show ring by members of the student body, winning numerous ribbons and trophies, all of which were proudly displayed at the school. When a handsome black and white Siberian appeared in a family group one year in the National Geographic Society's Christmas brochure, it created a mild flutter in the Siberian Husky world until the identity of the "borrowed dog" was established as that of King.

It is an established tradition for the University of Connecticut at Storrs to have its Siberian Husky mascot present at athletic contests. This mascot is unique in that he must be white and his name is always Jonathan. At this writing, it is Jonathan IV who holds this esteemed position.

Northeastern University in Boston has also had a series of Siberian mascots, all named Yukon. The student body is strongly devoted to these mascots, and one year a bronze statue was commissioned of the reigning Yukon. A tradition quickly arose of rubbing the statue's nose for luck before examinations, and Yukon's nose brightens with each passing year.

More recently the Siberian has also been used extensively as a Ther-

*Yukon by Northern Light Star ex Alaska Silver Moon was listed in the AKC Stud Register of February 1931 as being owned by Lou Henry Hoover, the president's wife.

"Yukon", mascot of Northeastern University, Boston.

Ch. Monadnock's Belka being trained as a guide dog for the blind.

apy Dog. It has been known for quite some time that so-called pet therapy works miracles with the convalescing, the depressed and the elderly. Patients with Alzheimer's disease, for instance, are particularly helped since pets seem to stimulate childhood memories, and memory stimulation is the key to treating the disease. But the nonjudgmental nature of pets and their simply proffered love seems to help patients of all ages; so much so that an organization based in New Jersey and founded in 1980, Therapy Dogs International, offers degrees for therapy work, and many Siberians now rank among those animals providing this unique humanitarian service to hospitals and nursing homes across the country.

It is easy to see, then, that in somewhat over half a century, the breed we call the Siberian Husky has come a long way: it is many miles and many life-styles away from the ice packs of the Arctic Ocean to the football fields of Massachusetts, or from the Chukchi village to a living room in Florida. And with the popularity of the breed soaring dangerously high, it can only be hoped that it has not come too far too fast, for it would be a terrible irony if the very adaptability of the Siberian should be his downfall.

It is undeniable that the Siberian of today is not the same dog that arrived scruffy and half starved in the villages of Alaska. Yet it is the pride of the Fancy that he is not far removed. Beyond the greater consistency of markings and refinement of features and furnishings, there lies the same affable clownishness, the same insolence, the same rakish nobility and the same indomitable exuberance that allowed his forebears to survive the harshest of all possible environments. Today, although he lives in what is perhaps the softest of all environments in human history, it is this same combination of qualities—which for want of a better word we call character—that constitutes the heritage and tradition of the Siberian Husky, a tradition which has allowed him to outlive at least one human tradition and enter another.

The following essay by Betsy Korbonski, reprinted from the April 1972 issue of the Siberian Husky Club of America's *Newsletter*, is about tradition, about the powers of rejuvenation found in tradition, and, most of all, it is about character.

Call It Character
by Betsy Korbonski

A gentle wind ruffles the fur on the old dog's shoulder. His magnificent coat is dense, seemingly depthless—no sign of shedding yet, though the Santa Ana winds have blown through most of March. My fingers touch it lightly, letting the early morning sun filter through its varied shadings of gray, black and white. Age has frosted over the old dog's once velvet-black ears, but his fur is vibrant, indestructible. He is still the most beautiful of all my dogs. Even in death.

A truck has pulled off Sunset Boulevard onto the empty service station lot.

It is Easter Sunday, and the service station is closed. A metal door slams, I hear muffled steps, and someone is standing beside me.

"How did it happen?"

I look toward the questioner, and through him. He is all darkness; his face, his clothes, his boots and hat, all one color, a sooty brown. He reminds me of the chimney sweeps of Europe; they too stopped to admire the old dog, an eyecatcher wherever he went.

In Europe they say a chimney sweep so early brings good luck all day. But this dark apparition brings no such omen. Finally I manage an answer: "He was old. I don't know how. It doesn't matter."

"I'm sorry," he says gently. "Somebody already reported it."

Only now I place him. "You're from Animal Rescue."

"You'll want the collar," he says, searching for it in the depths of the dog's mane.

"If I hadn't found him first"—I am crying now—"would I have known?"

"Yes, we always call if there's a tag on."

So I help with the loading and start to leave. Some reflex halts me, and I reach in my pocketbook for a dollar bill. "Here, take this"—I hand it to him—"after all, you did have to come out Easter morning."

"Thanks, thanks a lot." And he is gone. Did he have a face, that soft-spoken phantom? I can remember only the darkness of that first impression.

My two young daughters are in the backyard planning our Easter egg hunt. They know I have been out looking for the dog, so I call them with a deliberate edge to my voice. "Holly and Ellen, I have something to tell you."

Ellen is six. She stops in midstride and faces me directly. "Tavi's dead," she says tensely.

"Yes."

She squares her jaw, expressionless, and continues her passage across the yard, where she squats to stroke the puppy.

Holly, who is eight, has heard us and now she is sobbing. Her tears flow splendidly—she really looks beautiful when she weeps, not blotchy like most of us. Suddenly, she stops and points at me accusingly: "Mommie, you're not crying!"

"I did," I say shakily. "But all alone, and now I'm finished. He had a good life. He lived the way he wanted to live, and he died the way he wanted to die. What more can you do for a dog?"

"Ellen!" She is merciless. "Why aren't *you* crying?"

"I don't know," Ellen moans helplessly.

"That's all right, Ellen," I sympathize. "I could always cry over my dogs. But when my mother died, I couldn't cry."

She looks at me doubtfully. "Not at all?"

"Not for a long time. And then only because some stupid salesgirl was rude to me. Then I thought I'd never stop."

Holly looks at the two of us in despair and retreats into a long, low lament.

But we must be done with this for now, I tell them firmly. The neighbor children will come soon for the Easter egg hunt. The show must go on.

The puppy is chewing a daffodil, but I walk past him to Baika, his dam and the old dog's granddaughter. She looks like a scrawny coyote just now, having lost

"Paws across the water." Ch. Foxhaunt's Tovarisch, the first AKC-registered Siberian Husky to travel behind the Iron Curtain, is seen in front of the Stalin Palace of Culture (above) in Warsaw in 1966. Below, making friends with a Pole.

her coat once the puppies were weaned. I grasp what is left of her ruff and look deep into her gentle brown eyes. "Tavi's dead, Baika." But she is only a dog, she does not understand. And tonight, as we take our bedtime walk she will be looking for him; she will get excited when she thinks she sees him nosing about a garbage can; then when it turns out to be a strange dog, she will walk past aloof and unseeing. And probably, as long as the puppy remains with us, she will not miss him at all. She will sleep on his rug by my bed and be queen.

Queen? She was supposed to be his consort, too. But by the time she was old enough, he was too old. He never fully recovered from the shock of his failure. His placid nature disappeared, he became so nervous and destructive that for two months I had to keep him on tranquilizers. My husband, otherwise less in tune with the vagaries of canine mentality, had shuddered in sympathy.

My husband comes up to retrieve the puppy who is rooting out the Easter eggs as fast as I hide them, "Well," he grumbles, "*now* I suppose you'll want to keep Archie."

Keep Archie? It hadn't occurred to me. He is the last of the litter, the only puppy I haven't been able to pronounce a possible show prospect. "Some people may be coming over later today to look at him," I say, wondering privately if indeed they actually will, since the past weeks of advertising have taught me that most of those who promise to come seldom do. If they do, they will buy him, and at *my* price. Of this much I am confident. They only want a "pet" and now that the puppy, the only one left unsold, has been brought into the house, he is made to their order, the epitome of the bouncy, friendly puppy.

Archie wriggles free of my husband's grasp and dashes off with an Easter egg. Ah, yes, he's cute all right. Well built, lovely coat, nice strong high-set ears. But really he *is* small. And that little pink spot above his nose does detract from the overall symmetry. Yet I cannot bring myself to sell him at "pet" prices. He does have something, quality, I guess I'd call it. Of course, nothing to compare with the old dog.

Tavi. Say it broadly, Tah-vi, a soft sound, a sweet dog, so stubborn but so sweet.

Tavi with the laughing eyes.

Tavi with the ice-blue laughing eyes.

Tavi with the mask of Marcel Marceau, the grin of Mephistopheles, and, on cue, the voice of chanticleer.

Tavi, now the elegant New Yorker, browsing through the litter in Riverside Park, captivating our landlord, and crowing for our fellow apartment dwellers as the elevator made its laborious way up to the eighth floor.

Tavi, now the leisured Californian, lying beneath our jacaranda tree, bestrewn and bedecked with daisies and geraniums offered to him lovingly by our once-toddling two-year-old as to some benign far-northern deity. Yelping to come indoors when the long-awaited rains began. And creeping from my side during our Sunday-night bedtime walk with the stealth of a cat, lest the chinkle of his collar warn me of his intent to hide among the neighborhood garbage cans placed along the curb for the Monday-morning trash collection.

Tavi, Mr. Continental, charming *our* way across Czechoslovakia and Poland, where he joined us during my professor-husband's sabbatical year abroad, and where his insouciant disregard for international boundaries could have landed us all in jail in East Germany had he not somehow touched the chord that made potential one-worlders out of the most calloused border guards.

Tavi. Answered also to his real name, Tovarisch. In Russian it means "comrade," but in the lands lying near modern Russia it means fellow Communist, so it was politic to stick to the diminutive, which in time acquired a wealth of Slavic suffixes; Tavchik, Tavichku, Tovarish-chik. A free spirit, a true communist; what was thine was his, especially if you were eating it.

A show dog, too, ranking among the best. When wind and weather were right, he bore himself like a champion and in time became one; oh yes, he beat them all—once or twice. But never often enough to be taken for granted. He could acquire the stance of a dairyman's dog and the gait of a plow horse if the day was hot, or the wind brought the scent of snow—from the *other* side of the mountains.

And in Obedience competition, too, his performance fetched many a trophy and the best scores of any dog I have trained. Also the worst. For it was never more than a "performance"—a roll of the eye as we entered the ring to suggest, "Shall we show 'em today?" Or that malicious gleam which I learned to dread: "Thought you had me figured, didn't you?" as, with the finesse that only a fully trained dog could muster, he executed a perfect retrieve-and-finish—in front of the *judge!*

And as if dedicated to the task of proving that Obedience training does not break a dog's spirit, he remained steadfastly disobedient to the end, when, chafing perhaps under the regimentation of the nephritic's diet, which could never satiate his appetite for garbage—or lusting after the scent of some faraway female, which his arthritic spine would never have allowed him to mount—he barged past me through the half-open door and vanished into the night. Well, he has done his thing.

Archie lies curled in a tight, miserable little ball. He has just vomited up a collection of brightly tinted Easter egg shells. My husband, commiserating with him, says grudgingly, "Well, if you want to keep Archie, you have my permission."

But my husband had been counting the days till we were back to only one dog! He chuckles sheepishly. "I guess I've gotten used to having two dogs."

I glower over toward the puppy. "Archie." Even the nickname taunts me. It was meant as a joke, short for Anarchist, in tribute to the jolly irreverence of his breed. But "Archie"? You whippersnapper, you. You cull. You *runt!*

("But he's *not* a runt," my veterinarian told me indignantly, "A runt is deficient in some way. But *look* at him! And the pink spot will go away.")

Archie rouses himself, his beady dark eyes intent upon an errant jelly bean.

You do not have those ice-blue laughing eyes, little one. You do not grin like Mephistopheles, nor crow like chanticleer. You do not have that look of majestic insolence that was the hallmark of your magnificent forebear. There may be things about you I like as well, even better, but you will never be as utterly ingratiating, nor yet as infuriating. For you are not he. You will not take his place.

The people who have promised to look at Archie that afternoon do not come.

At night I lock him up in the pantry, newspapers spread near the door. Probably he will howl all night, his first quite alone. Probably he will chew up the wires of the washing machine, and mess all over the floor. Then my husband will change his mind anyway.

272

He whines twice and is silent. Next morning I find him standing in sleepy dignity upon the newspapers, a puddle of gargantuan proportions slowly forming about his feet.

I go out with him into the early morning sunshine. He spots a mockingbird and his sturdy nine-week-old frame goes taut. In his stance, and in the arch of his neck he is all male. His shoulder slopes strongly; his chest is deep. His feet have grown during the night.

So something has rubbed off onto him, it seems.

A gentle wind ruffles his fur, and off he frisks, heedless of the mantle which has fallen about his shoulders.

The king is dead.
Long live the king!

Long live the King! "Archie" (Ch. Tovarin's Merry Anarchist) handled by owner, Betsy Korbonski, winning the National Specialty, 1974, under judge Donald Booxbaum.

Acknowledgments

In a book of this sort, it is not always possible to thank all the people who have helped in one way or another. For this we are sorry. However, we would like to especially thank the following people and organizations:

Jean Fournier, for her flattering Foreword.

Jane Burrell for help in compiling Canadian Kennel chapter.

Betsy Korbonski for the use of her article.

Robert Crane, for providing all of the information contained in Chapter 2.

Elizabeth Nansen, for clarifying details in Chapter 3.

Ann Cook, for writing the "Racing" chapter.

Wes Meador, for permission to use his article in Chapter 7.

Rachel Page Eliot, for advice on the presentation of Chapter 9.

Kathleen Kanzler, for writing Chapter 11.

Anna Mae Forsberg, for providing various historical information.

And *Peggy Koehler*, for advice and encouragement beyond the call of duty.